Entanglements of Life with the Law

Entanglements of Life with the Law:

Precarity and Justice in London's Magistrates' Courts

By

John R. Campbell

Cambridge Scholars Publishing

Entanglements of Life with the Law:
Precarity and Justice in London's Magistrates' Courts

By John R. Campbell

This book first published 2020

Cambridge Scholars Publishing

Lady Stephenson Library, Newcastle upon Tyne, NE6 2PA, UK

British Library Cataloguing in Publication Data
A catalogue record for this book is available from the British Library

ISBN (10): 1-5275-5977-7
ISBN (13): 978-1-5275-5977-6

TABLE OF CONTENTS

List of Boxes, Tables, and Figures

Boxes

Tables

Figures

LIST OF CASES

Remand hearings

Extradition Bail Hearings (EB)

Extradition Hearings

Trials

CASE LAW, LEGISLATION, AND LEGAL DOCUMENTS

Bail Act 1976
Brutus v Cousins [1973] AC 854
Communications Act 2003
Computer Misuse Act 1990
Criminal Damage Act 1971
Criminal Justice Act 1967
Criminal Justice Act 1973
Criminal Justice Act 1988
Criminal Justice Act 2003
Criminal Procedural Rules
CPS Violence against Women and Girls (VAWG) Strategy
DPP v Orum [1988] 3 A11 ER 449
DPP v Smith [1960] 3 W.L.R. 546
Domestic Violence, Crime, and Criminal Act 2004
[2015] EWCA Crim 1568
Extradition Act 2003
Family Law Act 1996
Firearms Act 1968
Forced Marriage (Civil Protection) Act 2007
Harvey v DPP [2011] EWHC 3993 Adm
Leke Prendi aka Aleks Kola v Government of Albania [2015] EWHC 1809 (Admin)
Malicious Communications Act 1988
Mental Health Act 1983
Metropolitan Police Act 1839
JJC (A Minor) v Eisenhower [1983] 3 W.L.R. 537
Misuse of Drugs Act 1971
Offences against the Person Act 1861
Prevention of Crime Act 1953
Prevention of Terrorism Act 2005
Powers of Criminal Courts, Sentencing Act 2000
Protection from Harassment Act 1997
Race and Religious Hatred Bill (Part 3A) 2005
R v Batt (1994) Crim. LR 592

R v Donovan 25 Cr. App. Rep. 1, CCA
R v Golding [2014] EWCA Crim 889
R-v-Liam Stacey
R v Morris (1995) 2 Cr. App. R. 69
R v Povey [2008] EWCA Crim 1261
Rahmdezfouli v Wood Green Crown Court [2014] 1 All ER 567
Rance v Mid-Downs Health Authority (1991) 1 All ER 801
Serious Crime Act 2015
Southard v DPP [2006] EWCH 3449 Adm
The Access to Justice Act 1999
The Coroners and Justice Act 2009
The Criminal Justice Act 2003
The Criminal Justice and Courts Act 2015
The Criminal Justice and Public Order Act 1994
The Criminal Justice and Immigration Act 2008
The Criminal Procedure and Investigations Act 1996
The Fraud Act 2006
The Legal Aid, Sentencing, and Punishment of Offenders Act 2012
The Magistrates' Courts Act 1980
The Misuse of Drugs Act 1971
The Offences against the Person Act 1861
The Offensive Weapons Bill 2018
The Police Act 1996
The Police and Criminal Evidence Act 1984
The Public Order Act 1936
The Public Order Act 1986
The Prosecution of Offences Act 1985
The Protection of Children Act 1978
The Protection of Harassment Act 1997
The Prosecution of Offences Act 1985
The Sexual Offences Act 2003
The Terrorism Prevention and Investigation Measures (TPIM) Act (2011)
Theft Act 1968
Vagrancy Act of 1824
Voyeurism (Offences) Act 2019: Implementation of the Voyeurism (Offences) Act 2019

International Conventions

European Convention on Human Rights
UN Convention against Illicit Traffic in Narcotic Drugs and Psychotropic Substances, 1988
UN Convention against Transnational Organized Crime

Glossary

Allocation of case
A decision by magistrates and District Judges regarding the seriousness of the crime; serious and "either-way" offences are referred to a Crown court to be tried. It was formerly referred to as "mode of trial" decisions.

Bail
The temporary release of an accused person awaiting trial, sometimes on condition that a sum of money is lodged to guarantee their appearance in court.

Bench
Term used to describe two or more magistrates or a magistrate sitting with a District Judge who preside over a hearing/trial.

BME
Term used to describe individuals from black and ethnic minority communities.

Breach of bail
When a defendant does not comply with their bail conditions, they can be arrested and charged with failing to comply with bail.

Case management review
A pre-hearing of a case by a magistrate or a District Judge held to ensure that all the evidence will be available at the hearing.

Claimant
The victim. This person may also be a Crown Prosecution Witness called to give evidence at a contested trial.

Colloquial language
Ordinary spoken English as used by defendants.

Committal path
Ministry of Justice guidance outlining how individual police stations should refer criminal cases to specific magistrates' courts to be heard, and for magistrates to refer serious or either-way offences to specific crown courts for trial.

Contested trial
Convened to prosecute an individual who contests the evidence against him/her by pleading "not guilty"; in magistrates' courts these cases are decided by magistrates or District Judges, not by a jury.

Control order
Under the *Prevention of Terrorism Act (2005)* the SSHD could impose an order on a suspected terrorist to restrict his or her movement, activities, place of residence, ability to meet/converse with others, or any other activity deemed to be in the interest of protecting members of the public.

Court list
Lists—displayed at the entrance of each court and outside each courtroom—that state the names and case numbers of the defendants who are to be prosecuted.

Criminal Behaviour Order
A CBO can be issued by a court against an individual convicted for a criminal offence. An order is aimed at tackling the most serious and persistent offenders. CBOs include prohibitions to stop anti-social behaviour and may also include requirements imposed on the person that aim to address the underlying causes of the offender's behaviour.

Criminal Justice System (CJS)
Composed of the police, the CPS, magistrates' and Crown courts, and Her Majesty's Prison Service.

Criminal procedure rules
Rules set out by the Ministry of Justice that define the objectives of the criminal justice system, which is to ensure that cases/prosecutions are dealt with fairly and expeditiously.

Crown Prosecution Service
Created in 1985 to improve public confidence in the CJS by counter-balancing the power of the police; they are lawyers responsible for prosecuting cases in the courts.

Culpability
Magistrates and District Judges determine whether the alleged behaviour of a defendant was wrong.

District Judge (DJ)
A qualified lawyer who is appointed to decide cases in magistrates' courts in urban areas with large criminal case loads.

Dock
A specific place in the court where defendants are placed during their hearing or trial; the vast majority of docks are lockable, enclosed Perspex boxes.

Drug Rehabilitation Requirement
A court order requiring a convicted person to undergo a specified treatment for substance abuse.

Duty solicitors
Solicitors attached to a court who are paid on a pro-rata basis through legal aid to defend defendants who cannot afford to hire a legal representative

Either-way offence
An offence that may be tried either as an indictable offence in a crown court or as a summary offence by magistrates.

European Arrest Warrant
An arrest warrant valid throughout all member states of the European Union (EU). Once issued it requires another member state to arrest and transfer a criminal suspect or sentenced person to the issuing state so that the person can be put on trial or complete a detention period.

Extradition
Treaties linking countries that require them to arrest and handover/ extradite individuals for trial in the country where the crime was committed or to serve the remainder of their sentence in that country.

Her Majesty's Courts & Tribunal Service (HMCS)
An executive branch of the Ministry of Justice that manages the courts; staff include legal advisers, ushers, IT personnel, administrators, and security.

Indictable crime
A serious offence that can only be tried on indictment in a crown court.

Insurance Fraud Enforcement Department
Funded by large insurance companies and hosted by the City of London Police, it investigates large-scale insurance fraud; cases are referred to the CPS to be prosecuted.

Language of the law
As found in legislation, statute, and legal documents. See *legal discourse*.

Legal adviser
Formerly known as court clerks, these legally qualified barristers advise magistrates about the law and make a record of proceedings.

Legal Aid Agency
An executive agency of the Ministry of Justice that decides and allocates legal aid funds to counsel who represent defendants in civil and criminal hearings; it also runs the Public Defenders Service that prosecutes serious and complex cases in Crown courts.

Legal applications
A declaration made to the court to initiate legal action; these include statutory declarations, interest of justice applications, applications for a bad character reference and arrest warrants.

Legal discourse
Stylised, ritual language used by lawyers and judges characterised by a highly technical vocabulary which uses colloquial terms in specialised ways; it is replete with lengthy noun phrases, the use of the passive voice, multiple negatives, complex grammatical structures, and multiple, embedded clauses.

Legal procedure
The stages through which a remand hearing, trial, bail hearing, and extradition hearing proceed; each stage has a different purpose. The purpose of the procedure is to allow magistrates and District Judges to decide a case.

Magistrates
Unpaid laymen and women who decide cases in magistrates' courts.

Metropolitan Police
The police force responsible for policing Greater London.

Mitigation
An attempt, usually by solicitors representing a defendant, to make the offence appear less serious and reduce the sentence.

National Crime Agency
A national police agency that investigates serious and high-level crime.

Neoliberalism
Policies aimed at market-oriented reforms that are intended to shift responsibility, and the costs of the policies, on to citizens and away from the state.

OCGs
Organised criminal gangs.

Pleading bar
A designated place in a courtroom where the defendant stands to "plead" his/her case; this space was removed from the majority of courts in the 1970s and replaced by an encased, lockable, Plexiglas dock.

Public order offences
Offences defined in the *Public Order Act (1984)* that include riot, violent disorder, racial hatred, affray, harassment, and "threatening or abusive or insulting words or behaviour," that is, illegal speech acts. Many of these offences can be prosecuted on the word of a police officer.

Practice directions
Procedures issued by the Ministry of Justice setting out how District Judges and magistrates' should manage legal proceedings, hear evidence, pronounce sentence, and so on.

Practice Rules
Rules issued by the Ministry of Justice that are supposed to be used by magistrates and District Judges to ensure that hearings and trials progress to a just and fair conclusion.

Precariat
A social class formed by people suffering from precarity, which is a condition of existence without predictability or security, affecting material or psychological welfare.

Probation Service
Formerly a government department, most of which was privatised. Officers are responsible for identifying a defendant's criminal record and assessing his/her mental health and problems with substance abuse. They also make sentencing recommendations.

Remand
Defendants who have committed a serious offence or who are awaiting their hearing and who are unlikely to abide by his/her bail conditions are remanded into custody/prison to await their hearing/trial.

Remand hearing
The initial hearing of a criminal offence heard by a magistrate or District Judge

Sanction detection rates
A sanctioned detection occurs when (1) a notifiable offence has been committed and recorded; (2) a suspect has been identified and is aware of the detection; (3) the CPS evidential test is satisfied; (4) the victim has been informed that the offence has been detected; and (5) the suspect has been charged, reported for summons, or cautioned.

SSHD
The Secretary of State of the Home Department.

Sentencing hearing
A separate hearing at which magistrates or District Judges hear recommendations from the Probation Service and sentence a guilty defendant.

Sentencing guidelines
A requirement of the Ministry of Justice, formulated by the Sentencing Council, to ensure uniformity of judicial decisions for different crimes; magistrates and District Judges are required to follow the guidelines unless there is a substantial reason not to.

Serious Fraud Office
A national agency that prosecutes serious or complex fraud, bribery, and corruption.

Solicitors
Solicitors trained in criminal law who work for private law firms.

Statutory Declaration
A formal statement made affirming that something is true to the best knowledge of the person making the declaration. It must be signed in the presence of a magistrate. Statutory Declarations are generally used to satisfy a legal requirement or regulation when no other evidence is available. This means that if the declaration is granted by the court, the defendant will have the original decision set aside and a new trial for the offence will be scheduled.

Stop and search
A police officer has the power to stop individuals and ask their names, what they are doing in the area, and where they are going to. Officers can search a person if they have "reasonable grounds" to suspect that he/she is carrying illegal drugs, a weapon, stolen property, or something that could be used to commit a crime, such as a crowbar.

Summary offences
"Minor" offences that are prosecuted in magistrates' courts (see Box I.1).

Summary justice
Proceedings in a court of law carried out rapidly by the omission of certain formalities required by the common law. In the eighteenth century, it meant "performed or effected by a short method, done without delay."

Summons
An order issued by a magistrate or District Judge authorising the CPS/police to arrest an individual and/or to require a witness to attend a hearing to give evidence. It is sometimes referred to as a requisition.

TPIM
The Terrorism Prevention and Investigation Measures (TPIM) Act (2011) repealed earlier control orders and replaced them with new powers that allow the SSHD to impose more flexible overnight residence requirements, more limited power to impose tightly-defined exclusions from particular

areas; individuals subject to the measures must be permitted a landline and a mobile telephone, and a computer with internet connection.

Trial

Trials are convened in a crown court and decisions are decided by a jury.

PROLOGUE AND ACKNOWLEDGEMENTS

The initial purpose of the research that underpins this book was to understand the quality and nature of justice dispensed in London's magistrates' courts, and the impact that these courts have on Londoners. In the course of my research I came to see that the principle role of these courts—as in the past—is to discipline London's "dangerous classes." Indeed, a very large proportion of defendants appearing in London's magistrates' courts are young, if not destitute then poor, (educationally and legally) illiterate, and from black and ethnic minority communities who work in unstable occupations or are unemployed. Furthermore, a very large percentage of defendants have a long history of involvement with the Criminal Justice System (CJS) that "recycles" them through our jails, courts, and prisons. In short, many defendants live precariously.

The Shorter Oxford English Dictionary (1933) defines "precarious" as follows:

> 1. Held by the favour and at the pleasure of another; hence uncertain. 2. Question-begging; taken for granted; unfounded, doubtful 1659; 3. Dependent on circumstances or chance; unstable 1687; 4. Perilous 1727. +5. Suppliant; importunate 1697. 1. *tenure*, a tenure held during the pleasure of the superior. 3. A scanty and p. support 1794. 4. The p. track through the morass, Scott. Precariously adv.

There are two senses in which the term "precarious" is employed in this book. First, I use the term to identify a large class of defendants who are arrested and tried in magistrates' courts. In this sense, I adopt a modern version of the precariat. Standing (2011; 2018, 2) argues that the precariat is a growing class of people who are affected by the globalisation of the labour force and the growth of "big finance" and who are "characterized by unstable labour, low and instable incomes and loss of citizenship rights." He argues that the precariat is the new "dangerous class" that has arisen since the 1980s, which has been created by neo-liberal economics, rapid de-industrialisation, and the integration of China into the global economy. The precariat depend upon unpaid, non-wage work, they live in debt, have been gradually losing their cultural, civil, social, economic, and political rights and are supplicants to the state from which they must negotiate access to housing, welfare support, and health care (Grenier et al. 2017; Jivraj 2020).

According to McKeever, Simpson, and Fitzpatrick (2018, 3), in law "a person will only be considered destitute if [they are] unable to secure access through charitable or family donations . . . a person is destitute if unable to access two or more essential needs or if unable to afford all of his or her own resources." For citizens the income support provided by the government is £70 per week for a single adult, £100 per week for a couple, and £20 a week per child. It is important to note that the British state is not subject to a duty to prevent/relieve destitution as the cases discussed in this book amply illustrate. The lives of destitute individuals are truly precarious and uncertain and are made more so by their encounters with the law.

Alongside other, better-off citizens charged with an offence, the precariat appear in magistrates' courts as defendants who are characterised by their poverty, race, history of drug/substance abuse, high levels of criminal recidivism (i.e., as repeat offenders), and relative youth. Regardless of their conspicuous presence in court—and undoubtedly in prison—there is little research that looks at the intersection between justice and the precariat, and in particular how the police and the courts reinforce the insecurity and problems they face. As will become clear, a very high proportion of the precariat are arrested and convicted for loitering, begging, and sleeping rough, for committing public order offences, drug offences, assault, and fraud (cf., Pratt and Miao 2019). The full extent to which the courts discipline the precariat and others becomes clear in the cases examined in chapters 2–6.

The term "precarious" can also be applied to the quality of justice available to defendants being tried in a magistrates' court. In this sense, the term "precarious justice" has been used by Human Rights Watch (2008, 8) to describe the absence of due process rights in countries such as Saudi Arabia. As we shall see, summary justice in England and Wales is also notable for the absence of due process rights. Rather than drawing an invidious comparison between the UK and other societies, and to avoid arguments over legal ideology or ideal constructs such as the "rule of law," I address questions about the quality of justice through careful empirical research.

Research for the book is based largely on the observation and analysis of remand hearings and contested trials in London's magistrates' courts between 2016 and 2017. However, to understand the context in which these courts operate, I briefly outline the evolution of criminal policy and the work of the police. I draw upon David Garland's *The Culture of Control* (2002) in which he argued that a "punitive turn" towards a culture of crime control and criminal justice occurred in the United Kingdom and elsewhere. Magistrates' courts are situated between the Metropolitan Police and Her

Majesty's Prison Service, both of which are relatively well studied, whereas there is little contemporary ethnographic research on first-instance courts.

Garland's (2002) analysis of the dynamic driving penal reform in England and Wales from the late 1970s forward sets the scene for this study because he outlines the rise of a "new culture of crime control" that typifies penal policy in the United Kingdom. He provided

> . . . a series of detailed analyses that show how political actors and government agencies—police forces, prosecution agencies, courts, prisons, government departments, elected officials—were confronted by a new set of practical problems in their daily operations. These problems chiefly flowed from the prevalence of high rates of crime and disorder in late modern society and the growing realization that modern criminal justice is limited in its capacity to control crime and deliver security. (Garland 2002, x–ix)

Garland examined key "indices of change" which contributed to a pervasive sense of crisis about crime and crime prevention including: the decline of the rehabilitative ideal; the re-emergence of punitive sanctions and a desire for expressive justice; the return of the victim to the centre stage of criminal justice; a concern with protecting the public (largely by imprisoning criminals); the emergence of a politicised and populist political discourse on crime control; rising rates of incarceration (even as crime rates have declined); and a widespread shift in criminological thinking away from a concern about the links between crime and deprivation to an acceptance that there are insufficient ways to control crime. The net effect of these shifts led to the creation of a hugely expanded infrastructure of imprisonment, the commercialisation of certain aspects of crime control and new management styles and working practices that, for instance, portray the police as a "responsive public service" rather than a "crime-fighting force."

Garland (2002) also identified the political and structural processes driving changes in penal policy. First there are the ideological beliefs—sometimes referred to as neoliberalism or "zombie neo-liberalism" (Peck 2010; Wacquant 2014)—that have given rise to a crack-down on crime and the restructuring of the Criminal Justice System through a combination of extensive budget cuts and contracting out the management of prisons, probation, and other professional services to the private sector. Second, equally pervasive changes affecting the work of the courts has arisen from myriad changes in legal rules, the adoption of sentencing guidelines, the adoption of "retrospective"/hybrid legislation jettisoning due process safeguards, including reducing or reversing the burden of proof and so on as well as changes in the volume of prosecutions and sharp reductions in the number of court staff, judges, and court houses.

Regardless of changes in penal policy, the focus of "state-illegality" relations has not changed: politicians continue to criminalise "the dangerous classes" which is to say socially marginal groups whose presence is deemed to threaten social order, that is, hooligans, protestors, unemployed youth, rioters, "deviant" (black) males, drug dealers, addicts, and so on (Schneider and Schneider 2008, 352). In short, while claiming to act in defence of local communities, politicians selectively ignore[1] certain illegal activities while vigorously legislating against and prosecuting other actions. The process of labelling certain actions or behaviours "criminal" creates an arbitrary, ideological distinction between law and disorder and between law-abiding citizens and criminals.

Given my focus on magistrates' courts, it is important to briefly sketch out the work of the police who arrest and charge offenders and bring cases to court to be prosecuted. The police are predominately involved in public order policing and stop-and search operations (which are among their most widely used powers). The effect of deep cuts to police budgets has seen a sharp fall in the number of officers and a consequent reduction in the number of arrests and prosecutions.

As Sharp (2005) has argued, while policing has been subject to extensive public reviews and reforms and to growing central control by the Home Office, at no point has the effect of these reforms been properly evaluated nor has the primary purpose of policing been clearly articulated. While new forms of managerialism have introduced greater central control and financial discipline over the police, the police have failed to reduce crime.

The reason for this situation stems from the nature of police operations that focus on crime control, modified slightly by due process protections (Sanders, Young, and Burton 2010). Political protest occurs in public spaces and confronts established political order that deploys the police to restore order. Habermas (1991) has traced the genealogy of class protest from the early nineteenth century forward to the struggles of the bourgeoisie who claim the right to participate in political affairs on the basis that they constitute the "public sphere." However, access to political rights historically reflects differences of class, race, gender, sexuality, and age (Collier et al. 1995). Rights that are won can be set aside by the state in the name of protecting "the public" from unruly and undesirable social groups who are said to be intent on disrupting "public order."

[1] For example, white-collar crime, political/official corruption, and certain types of fraud.

As a result of earlier political struggles, ideas about the public sphere and indeed about who constitutes the "public" are, in part, ideological. Today "the notion of the public [is] understood as a sphere in which *everyone* is included, no matter what their position within existing power relations" (Belina 2011, 18, my emphasis). Indeed, as Belina (2011, 19) has argued, the idea of a "public/private distinction" is a normative categorisation that portrays social groups and their attempts to use public space as either good or bad, justified or unjustified. Ultimately this categorisation fails to explain why a group, at a particular time, has an entitlement to use/occupy public space whereas other groups do not have such an entitlement. The state responds to struggles over the use of public space by using the law to define the activities of particular groups as a threat to public disorder—as a social harm that justifies their exclusion from public spaces—and it authorises the police to contain disorder.

Conflict arises in part, as Jeffrey et al. (2015) have argued, because the police exercise a "dual function" as "a neutral arbiter of justice" *and* as a defender of "the propertied classes" through their efforts to "reproduce a particular kind of social order inflected by histories of imperialism and racism." Their examination of forty years of policing in Manchester concluded that the police do not spend a majority of their time on crime prevention. Rather they spend their time maintaining "a benign general order," a process in which the "dirty work" of "real policing" relies upon routine stop and search operations. The police manage public unrest in response to public policy decisions and changing socio-political conditions.

Stop and search operations[2] have a long history in England and Wales and are rooted in a differential policing of certain "publics" that the authorities believe require special attention, notably ethnic minorities and the poor. Stop and search is a form of ritual humiliation intended to remind members of these social groups of their place in society. "Stop and search" operations ensure that certain social groups are routinely searched and charged with criminal offences, whereas others are not.

Detailed studies of stop and search operations have arrived at two important conclusions. First, Bradford and Loader (2016, 242) found that,

> The evidence, in our view, invites the following conceptualisation: namely, that "stop and search" is not just about crime, nor simply about targeting

[2] The "SUS law" on stop and search is authorised in section 5 of the *Vagrancy Act of 1824*. However, general stop and search powers are also authorised in s.1 of *The Police and Criminal Evidence Act (1984)*, s.60 of *The Criminal Justice and Public Order Act (1994)*, s.23 of the *Misuse of Drugs Act (1971)*, and s.47 of the *Firearms Act (1968)*.

ethnic minorities. Rather, it is about control and the assertion of order, and the effort to do this implicates not only "fighting crime" but also regulating and disciplining marginal populations defined not simply by ethnicity but also by other key socio-demographic characteristics.

Second, in their analysis of London-wide data for the period 2004 to 2014, Tiratelli, Quinton, and Bradford (2018, 2) concluded that "stop and search has only a very weak and inconsistent association with crime. While there is some correlation, most notably in relation to drug offences, we conclude that the deterrent effect of stop and search is likely to be small." Their conclusion is reinforced by Home Office (2016) statistics that provide clear evidence regarding the ongoing and discriminatory use of stop and search powers: many more black and Asian persons are disproportionally searched, prosecuted, and given custodial sentences compared with white persons.[3] The Lammy Review (2017) and the Race Disparity Audit (UK 2017) make it clear that a disproportionate number of defendants are poor, uneducated, and from black and ethnic minorities. It is also clear that many defendants suffer from serious mental health issues as well as from substance abuse (problems that the CJS does not address).

Public order policing requires the police to negotiate a minimal degree of "accommodation" with diverse social groups to ensure their ability to manage demonstrations; however, accommodation may also be "political." A good example comes from "reclaim the night" marches by women in English cities, which began in the late 1970s and which continue today as women respond to police efforts to get them off the street rather than to address the violence directed at women, that is, rape, domestic violence, robbery, and murder (Mackay 2014). "Reclaim the night" marches challenge the selective policing of communities and gendered assumptions about the subordinate position of women in society.

The contingent nature of policing in London is demonstrated by Waddington's (1994) analysis of Metropolitan Police efforts to contain, control, and accommodate the anti-poll tax marches of the early 1990s using the Public Order Act. Waddington demonstrates the very fine line between

---

[3] Black persons are eight times, mixed-race individuals are two to three times, and Asian persons are two times more likely to be stopped and searched than white persons. Black persons are three-and-a-half times, and mixed groups are twice as likely to be arrested as white persons. Relative to the population, black persons are four times and mixed groups are two times more likely to be prosecuted in court. Though white defendants are consistently convicted at a much higher rate than other groups, black and Asian offenders are consistently given longer sentences than white offenders (UK 2017).

police attempts to accommodate protest and their use of coercion. As the policing of the G20 and other recent protests indicates, this line is constantly blurred by police "assaults" on protesters and efforts to secure intelligence to permit greater control over public events (Home Affairs Committee 2008–9; House of Lords 2010–11; Gilmore et al. 2017). In these protests police tactics, which included "kettling," and violence directed against protesters was justified as "responsible" policing. In effect standard police operations result in the arrest and/or charge of individuals who are poor and/or who are from ethnic minorities or groups who publicly object to the police and who demonstrate against state policies.

It is also important to note that the police exercise considerable discretion in the way they deal with offenders (Sanders, Young, and Burton 2010, chaps. 2–6; Stuart 2015), which is evident in their decisions to arrest, detain, release, warn, fine, charge, or prosecute individuals for a variety of offences including, but not limited to, the Public Order Act (Chapter 3), domestic violence (chapter 4), and drug offences (chapter 5). As the cases examined in this book make clear, the police fail to investigate the vast majority of summary offences, a fact that is reflected in low crime "clear up" and police "sanction rates" for recorded offences. Regardless of discretionary decisions by the police, the number of individuals arrested and prosecuted in magistrates' courts has remained constant: in 1996/97 approximately 1.3 million persons were prosecuted, in 2005/6 the number of prosecutions rose to 1.36 million, and in 2016/17 the number of prosecutions was 1.38 million (NAO 1997, 52, fig. 20; MoJ 2015b, 2018).

Controversy over policing is not new. As the remit given the police by Parliament and the Home Office has grown, it has become apparent that there is no consensus about the primary purpose/responsibilities of the police. This problem was identified in 1996 by the Independent Committee of Inquiry (Police Federation 1996, xi–xii), which found that there was no consensus about the role and responsibilities of the police. Similarly, in 2008, the House of Commons Home Affairs Committee (2007–8, ¶17) found that:

> To ensure the police can fulfil their core roles effectively, there is a need for greater clarity as to their mission and the extent of their responsibilities. Recent reviews of different aspects of policing have not gone far enough. We recommend that an independent review, such as a Royal Commission, or similarly independent review, is established to review what the police do and how they are organised to do it. This review should be focussed and time-limited, in order to provide the police with the clarity about their role that they urgently need. The Government should exercise caution in future when classifying undesirable behaviour as criminal offences.

Despite the call to rethink the role, responsibility, and primary purpose of the police, no Royal Commission or review has been established. Instead the police continue to rely on the core principles set out by Robert Peel in 1829, which legitimated the creation of the Metropolitan Police specifically, and for a public police force generally.[4] Those principles are:

> 1. *The basic mission for which police exist is to prevent crime and disorder* as an alternative to the repression of crime and disorder by military force and severity of legal punishment. 2. *The ability of the police to perform their duties is dependent upon public approval* of police existence, actions, behaviours and the ability of the police to secure and maintain public respect. . . . 4. The degree of co-operation of the public that can be secured diminishes, proportionately, to the necessity for the use of physical force and compulsion in achieving police objectives. 5. *The police seek and preserve public favour,* not by catering to public opinion, but *by constantly demonstrating absolutely impartial service to the law*, in complete independence of policy, and without regard to the justice or injustice of the substance of individual laws; by ready offering of individual service and friendship to all members of society without regard to their race or social standing. . . . 6. The police should use physical force to the extent necessary to secure observance of the law or to restore order only when the exercise of persuasion, advice and warning is found to be insufficient to achieve police objectives; and *police should use only the minimum degree of physical force* which is necessary. . . . 8. The police should always direct their actions toward their functions and *never appear to usurp the powers of the judiciary* by avenging individuals or the state, or authoritatively judging guilt or punishing the guilty. 9. *The test of police efficiency is the absence of crime and disorder*, not the visible evidence of police action in dealing with them. (My emphases)

While the "Peel principles" supposedly inform policing today (College of Policing 2013), the police do not follow them. As recent research including this book demonstrates, the police no longer respect these principles and the conditions under which they operate have radically changed. As many have argued, the Government urgently needs to rethink and rearticulate new roles for the police fit for the twenty-first century.

Magistrates' courts are the lowest level of the CJS; they hear and decide about 94 per cent of all criminal offences in England and Wales. Curiously, the vast majority of defendants in magistrates' courts either plead guilty or are tried and convicted. As I hope to show, it would be incorrect to

---

[4] Source: Sir Robert Peel's "Principles of Law Enforcement, 1829," accessed 12 December 2019, https://www.durham.police.uk/About-Us/Documents/Peels_Principles_Of_Law_Enforcement.pdf.

assume that high numbers of guilty pleas and high conviction rates arise from good policing or incontrovertible evidence of wrongdoing. Rather this situation arises from the incomprehensible "language of the law" contained in statutes and legislation, from the fact that legislation provides few legal defences, and because pressure by the police and the poor quality of independent legal counsel lead many defendants to plead guilty to an offence without going to trial.

High conviction rates are also the product of a magistracy that relies heavily on the CPS for advice and that, as I hope to demonstrate, possesses a limited "judicial vision" of its role and responsibilities. By "judicial vision" I refer to the way that Magistrates (and to a lesser extent, District Judges) are trained, their dependence on the Criminal Practice Directions and the requirement placed on them to case-manage hearings, their unquestioned reliance on police evidence and on legal argument by the Crown, and the discursive practices they use to decide cases. Taken together and reinforced by the speed with which cases are heard, these factors decisively shape their professional vision (Goodwin 1994) and their view of criminality, the legitimacy of the police, and the prosecutor who transforms "evidence" into an argument that portrays defendants as criminals. Their training imbues magistrates with a perspective that focuses on individual culpability without seeing the wider social or cultural context in which an alleged crime takes place. As Good (2004, 129) has argued in respect of immigration law, lawyers and judges are "trained to think in radically different ways" than social scientists because the cases they deal with are "divested of contextual detail" and because they see the law as being primarily about the application of "purportedly neutral principles."

Furthermore, as Danet (1980, 540f) and others have argued, the "fact-oriented" genre of legal language—which is characterised by esoteric vocabulary, syntactic complexity, violations of rules of ordinary discourse, and reliance on elaborate legal rules—claims to determine the "truth" and relevant "facts." Quite the opposite is the case because the courts are preoccupied with "legal language" at the expense of considering the relation between "language and the world." A different way of putting this important point is that the language of law involves "a construal of the world"—a binary view between criminal and non-criminal behaviours—which is radically different to the view of non-lawyers, defendants, litigants, and the public (Gibbons 1999). As I will show, the law provides a problematic lens through which to assess "facts" and determine guilt.

Following on from this point, while the law requires magistrates to assess culpability, an effective and just decision also needs to consider the social and cultural context in each case. This task is necessary to account for wrongdoing *if* the court wishes to arrive at a just decision that deals fairly with a specific offender, and *if* the court seeks to reduce repeat offending rather than merely recycle offenders in and out of the CJS. The requirement that individuals have a right to a fair trial is complicated by two further factors. First, case preparation and management depend upon the ability of the police, the CPS, and defence counsel to adequately prepare a case in advance of a hearing. Their ability to carry out this task includes assessing the evidence and deciding whether a defendant is "vulnerable" and in need of special measures to give their evidence or if the court should make "procedural adjustments" to accommodate vulnerable defendants (Gerry and Cooper 2017). Second, the pressure placed on magistrates/DJs to "case-manage" hearings to ensure that they are conducted "efficiently and expeditiously"[5] results in hearings/trials that can be very brief and that do not involve adequate oversight of the police and CPS. My observations of hearings and trials reveal that many cases are not adequately prepared in advance and that vulnerable defendants are not assessed and diverted from court. In short, there are serious questions regarding the safety of some convictions.

In 2016–17 magistrates sentenced 32 per cent of defendants to custody, 20 per cent were given a community sentence, 16 per cent were given a suspended sentence, 18 per cent were fined, and 14 per cent were dealt with by "other means" (probably a combination of fines, community orders, etc.; MoJ 2018). The fact that a relatively small but stable percentage of defendants are sent to prison for, comparatively speaking, relatively short sentences (which have increased from 12.4 months in 2007 to an average of 15.2 months in 2018) speaks to a belief among magistrates that non-custodial sentences are an effective deterrent (repeat offenders and individuals found guilty of robbery, sexual offences, violence, and possession of weapons are far more likely to be imprisoned [Cuthbertson 2017]). While the relatively small number of offenders who are imprisoned in the UK contrasts sharply with the situation in France and the USA, it is clear that once offenders are placed in custody they do not have access to adequate medical or other assistance to deal with problems responsible for their offending, such as addiction/substance abuse.

I was attracted to these courts to try to understand what they do—which partly reflected my ignorance about the CJS as a white, middle-class male—and was intrigued by what I found. This study seeks to show how the courts operate and how cases are tried, and to understand the "work" of

---

[5] See: Criminal Practice Directions 2015, Part 3A1 at: http://www.justice.gov.uk/courts/procedure-rules/criminal/rulesmenu-2015.

legal actors whose actions are assessed against the basic principles of procedural "justice" (Rawls 1971). This is an empirical study, an example of research into middle-range social phenomena (Garland 2018) that analyses how the courts operate as one form of social control alongside policing, imprisonment, and reducing/eliminating welfare benefits, and so on. By analysing criminal proceedings, I examine the normative foundations of state punishment, the nature of the police and judicial power, and the impact of judicial power on citizens.

The picture of magistrates' courts that emerges is complex because the situation in England and Wales conforms with, but also differs from, judicial/penal policy and practice in other countries that are characterised by high rates of incarceration. Magistrates' courts in England and Wales operate semi-autonomously from other institutions in the CJS. Thus, on the one hand, sentencing illustrates continued support for rehabilitation and community sentences as well as the use of longer sentences (Jacobson and Hough 2018). On the other hand, magistrates remand a high proportion of offenders into custody to wait for their hearing—more female offenders are remanded than men—even though only about one-third of remand prisoners are subsequently sentenced to custody (Player et al. 2010).

This study is based on ethnographic fieldwork in six of the eight Local Justice Areas in Metropolitan London, that is, in thirteen magistrates' courts (see Box I.3). Research took the form of sitting in courtrooms, observing legal proceedings, drawing diagrams of each courtroom to understand how court architecture influenced/constrained legal proceedings, taking verbatim notes of everything that was said, and, where possible, speaking to police officers, Crown prosecutors, defendants, and witnesses. In this way the fieldwork built upon the foundations of my earlier research on the United Kingdom's Immigration and Asylum Tribunal and the Royal Courts of Justice (Campbell 2017).

As Paul Rock (1993) noted in his study of English Crown courts, the fact that there are relatively few studies of courts is not because they are inaccessible or incomprehensible; on the contrary, court business is conducted publicly via oral argument between the prosecutor, judges, defence lawyers, and other professionals. Oral argument provided me with detailed information about judicial proceedings and individual criminal cases and has enabled me to show the variable way that these courts and legal actors work. It will become clear that just as ethnographic research into policing and prisons[6] illustrates a high degree of institutional autonomy

[6] Fassin (2017, xiv) remarks: "As one becomes progressively immersed in the correctional system, whether as a new inmate, a novice officer or a social scientist, one becomes aware of much more complex relationships and arrangements between

or "loose coupling" from penal policy, ethnographic research shows that magistrates' courts are also partially autonomous from the rest of the Criminal Justice System and it reveals the quality of justice available to Londoner's in these courts.

* * *

My interest in law began with an MA course on Anthropology and Law that I took in the Department of Anthropology at New York University taught by Professor Owen Lynch and deepened as a result of my interest in the work of Professor A. L. Epstein at the University of Sussex who supervised my doctoral thesis. It was not until 2007, however, that I was able to actively pursue this interest when I secured a research grant from the United Kingdom's Economic and Social Science Research Council to undertake two years of fieldwork on the UK's asylum system. That period of fieldwork resulted in the publication of two books (Campbell 2014, 2017, and numerous papers). My interest in courts, justice, and the law has continued apace with the fieldwork for this book.

The fieldwork on which this book is based is partly a product of teaching an MA course entitled "The Anthropology of Law" at the School of Oriental and African Studies that required students to observe and undertake basic fieldwork at Westminster Magistrate's Court and at Taylor House (where asylum and immigration cases are heard by the First Tier Immigration and Asylum Tribunal). Their observations on the court/tribunal and the essays they wrote stimulated me to rethink my understanding of the law; I am grateful to them. I also enjoyed a term's sabbatical leave in 2017 which I used to extend my fieldwork in magistrates' courts across London.

I am indebted to a District Judge at Westminster Magistrates' Court who took an interest in my work and invited me into his chambers to discuss some of the cases he presided over as well as to discuss the work of the court. I would also like to thank a small number of magistrates, Crown prosecutors, legal advisers, and duty solicitors who took time to informally discuss their work. It is regrettable that the Magistrates Association, the Metropolitan Police, and the CPS refused my requests to meet with their staff to enable me to better understand how they organise and deliver their services. My request to be allowed to photograph two courtrooms was effectively refused by Her Majesty's Courts & Tribunal Service who

the multiple agents and within the various contexts than what one expected. The imagined total institution appears as a field of forces where the rules are permanently tested, negotiated, and diverted by guards as well as inmates."

required me to pay £200.00 per hour plus VAT and to possess liability insurance for at least £10 million.

This book has gone through many iterations. I am particularly grateful to Thomas Richardson, a barrister at the Lambs Building, and to Emeritus Professor Paul Rock at the London School of Economics and Political Studies for reading and commenting on various chapter drafts. Their comments greatly improved the text, though I take responsibility for all errors or omissions. I am also grateful to Professor Michael Palmer (School of Law, SOAS, and Visiting Fellow at Hong Kong University of Law) for inviting me to participate in his network of legal researchers which led to the publication of an earlier version of chapter four on domestic violence, which appeared as "'Can law achieve happiness?' Critical reflections on Criminal Justice" in the *Journal of Comparative Law*, volume 13, number 2 (2018). A version of chapter three was presented at the Association for Social Anthropology annual conference at Oxford University in 2017. I wish to thank Dr Livia Holden, Senior Research Fellow at the Oxford Centre of Socio-Legal Studies, for inviting me to be an associate researcher on her ERC-funded project "Cultural Expertise in Europe: What Is It Useful For—Euro-Expert." The various conferences and seminars at the Centre have stimulated my interest in law further, and access to the law libraries at Oxford has been useful in writing this book.

Finally, I want to thank my partner, Sarah, and my children for their patience while I have continued to pursue my interest in researching and writing about law. Finally, the figures in this book, which were based on my sketches, were drawn by my son Alex. I would also like to thank Amanda Millar of Cambridge Scholars Publishing for all her work in putting the final manuscript together. I dedicate this book to all those who seek to understand how the law really works, and to my children Alex, Ellie, and Nina.

INTRODUCTION

This book addresses a paradox at the heart of the Criminal Justice System (CJS) raised by Dorine McBarnet (1981, 1982) and Andrew Sanders (1994, 103): how is it that the courts "are able to reach a verdict (usually guilty) without any apparent reasonable doubt, despite the elusiveness and complexity of 'truth' and 'reality'"? McBarnet argued that the answer to this paradox lies in criminal legal procedure. Sanders, however, believes that the problem stems from the court where "it is not the truth that is at issue . . . it is the veracity of competing stories." In this book I argue that while both factors shape the quality of justice in magistrates' courts, both factors are reinforced by the language of the law and the power exercised by the police, prosecutors, magistrates, and District Judges (DJs).

In writing this book I have four principal objectives. First, I explore the role these courts play in the CJS by looking in detail at how magistrates and DJs, the Crown Prosecution Service (CPS), defence lawyers, probation services, and court staff influence the outcome of criminal prosecutions. Second I explore the role of language in criminal proceedings by contrasting the "language of the law" (as found in legislation, legal documents, and published guidance etc.) and as spoken by legal actors in determining guilt/culpability with the everyday colloquial language used by defendants (Danet 1980; Mertz 1994). The issue of language is central to any examination of the law because the parties involved in a case argue about the appropriateness of the charge laid against a defendant, about how "the law" should be interpreted and applied and about the "facts" of the case. It is only through a detailed examination of the first two issues that it is possible to address my third objective, which is to assess the quality of justice in magistrates' courts where, regardless of a defendant's right to legal counsel, 70 per cent of defendants plead guilty at remand hearings and 85 per cent of defendants who plead not guilty are convicted at their trial. My fourth objective is to provide an ethnographic analysis of the courts that can be understood by members of the public who lack legal literacy and who are most likely to find themselves standing in the dock accused of a crime.

The courts and the 2011 riots in English cities

The objective of the CJS—the police, the Crown Prosecution Service, courts, judiciary, and prisons—is to maintain social and political order. The work of magistrates' courts, which is the lowest level of the CJS, provides a window through which to understand how the CJS works and its impact on the lives of Londoners. Regardless of the fact that 1.38 million residents of England and Wales were prosecuted in a magistrates' court in 2016/17, there is little public interest in these courts. This situation briefly changed in August 2011 when riots rocked London, Birmingham, Manchester, Liverpool, and six other English cities.[1] For four days the riots moved back and forth across England's cities: five people died, three hundred police officers were injured, 2585 commercial premises were attacked, and £500 million of damage was caused. By the time the smoke cleared, four thousand individuals had been arrested and charged with 5175 offences. In the days that followed—during which the Prime Minister stated that "anyone convicted of violent disorder would go to prison"—defendants were brought before magistrates' courts that convened at weekends and at night to prosecute offenders. By August 2012, some three thousand individuals had been tried. The offences that individuals were found to have committed included robbery (50 per cent of defendants), violent disorder (22 per cent),[2] "other riot offences" (10 per cent),[3] theft (16 per cent), and criminal damage (1 per cent). Only 68 per cent of defendants were found guilty and sentenced to custody, whereas just over 1 per cent received an absolute discharge, 1 per cent of offenders were fined, and about 14 per cent were given a community sentence (Home Office 2012a, Table 1.8).

---

[1] See: "Riots: tough justice in London's courts" (11 August 2011, *BBC News*); "Revealed: the full picture of sentences handed down to rioters" (18 August 2011, *Guardian*); "UK riots: the demographics of magistrate cases and convictions" (18 August 2011, *Guardian*); "Riot cases pose huge challenge for Crown Prosecution Service" (12 September 2011, *Guardian*); "The man accused of starting the 2011 riots—and what he did next" (26 June 2016, *The Observer*); "London riots 2011: 'We were getting hit all the time with missiles'" (6 August 2011, *BBC News*); "Timeline: Mark Duggan's death and the London riots" (8 January 2014, *ITV News*)"; "London riots photos August 2011" (9 August 2011, *Public Intelligence*).

[2] Violent disorder is defined under *The Public Order Act* (1986) and includes: violent disorder, riot, affray, causing intentional harassment, alarm or distress, assault with intention to resist arrest, common assault, and assaulting a police officer (see chapter 3).

[3] "Other disorder offences" include having an article with a blade or point in a public place, possession of offensive weapons without lawful authority, being in possession of a controlled drug.

Media coverage focused on the violence and to a lesser extent on the institutions—the police, the Crown Prosecution Service, and the courts—that dealt with the disturbances. By September 2011 media interest in the "riots" and the CJS ended. It only remained for the Ministry of Justice (Ministry of Justice 2012a, 2012b; House of Commons 2014) to finish sentencing the rioters. We know that magistrates' courts struggled to process cases. For example, Westminster Magistrate's Court in central London tried 922 individuals (one hundred were tried in one night) and that frequently, because the police had insufficient time to file evidence, neither the Crown nor defence lawyers had a case file for the accused when defendants were tried.

The events of August 2011 raise important and as yet unanswered questions about why the riots occurred (cf., Riots, Communities and Victims Panel 2012), about the work of the police (Metropolitan Police Service 2012), and about the role played by magistrates' courts. Were the accused tried fairly and justly sentenced? If police files were not available, how could defendants get a fair trial? Of the individuals brought to court,[4] 31 per cent of juveniles were charged and imprisoned whereas nearly 48 per cent of adults were charged and imprisoned. Why the disparity? Even though far larger numbers of males were arrested, the conviction rate for males (64 per cent) was lower than for females (78 per cent). Why? Finally, why were the average sentences given to "rioters"[5] (at 12.5 months) five times the length of sentences given to individuals charged for the same offence in 2010 (at 2.5 months)?

Part of the answer to the above questions comes from the "zeal" with which the CPS and the judiciary responded to the situation (Lightowlers and Quirk 2015). Thus the CPS appears to have abandoned its role as a disinterested prosecutor when it set up a special unit to deal with riot cases. The evidence for this conclusion comes from several sources. First, the CPS gave the police "a draft form of words" to put into case files, which explained that their enquiries could not be completed within the required time limit and that "charging decisions" should be based on the "lower standard threshold test" (seemingly abandoning the "evidential test"

---

[4] Substantial numbers of offenders under the age of eighteen were tried in magistrates' courts, not in youth courts (Lightowler and Quirk 2015, 73).

[5] Official statistics provide conflicting information. The Ministry of Justice (2012a, 10) reported the following figures on sentence length for rioters as opposed to individuals sentenced in 2010 for the same offence: violent disorder (25.5 months v 5.3 months); theft (8.3 months v 2.4); criminal damage (12.9 months v 7.7); robbery (31.2 months v 8.8); and burglary (15.7 months v 8.8).

that should have been undertaken).[6] Thus one duty solicitor working at Westminster Magistrate's Court on the night of 11 August reported that when detainees arrived at court

> it appeared that the rules had been rewritten . . . Good character counted for nothing; strong community ties were ignored and nearly all the detainees were remanded into custody and committed for trial at the Crown Court . . . it was clear that the prosecution were not open to discussion . . . that a strategic decision had been made by the CPS to apply for remand at the police station and at court in all riot-related cases, irrespective of circumstance. (Wright 2011)

Second, the individuals arrested during the riots were charged differently to what would normally be expected. In part this resulted in a failure to divert youths out of magistrates' courts (and into the youth courts) and many individuals were charged with burglary (which attracts a higher sentence) rather than theft.

The judiciary responded to the situation by adopting "informal guidelines" on sentencing, which guaranteed that sentences would be higher. The Magistrates Association called for its members' sentencing powers to be increased to allow them to impose sentences of one year. In any event, up to two-thirds of riot-related cases were sent to a Crown court to be heard and/or sentenced because offenders could be given lengthier sentences than magistrates could impose. As intimated, the result was a ratcheting up of sentences to periods of custody well above what would normally be expected.[7] As Wright observed at the time, the rules had been

---

[6] The CPS (2018a) is supposed to follow "the full code test," which specifies two tasks. In "the evidential stage," prosecutors "must be satisfied that there is sufficient evidence to provide a realistic prospect of conviction against each suspect on each charge. They must consider what the defence case may be, and how it is likely to affect the prospects of conviction. *A case which does not pass the evidential stage must not proceed, no matter how serious or sensitive it may be*." Prosecutors should also assess whether prosecution "is required in the public interest." This means that "A prosecution will usually take place unless the prosecutor is satisfied that there are public interest factors tending against prosecution which outweigh those tending in favour. In some cases, the prosecutor may be satisfied that the public interest can be properly served by offering the offender the opportunity to have the matter dealt with by an out-of-court disposal rather than bringing a prosecution" (my emphasis). See
https://www.cps.gov.uk/publications/code_for_crown_prosecutors/codetest.html.

[7] Lightowlers and Quirk (2015, 76) note that the authorities recommended that one hundred defendants should be deported and that individuals who resided in

rewritten, and the government, CPS, and courts were intent on sending a clear message of deterrence to offenders and to local communities.

The geography of crime in London

To understand the work of London magistrates' courts it is necessary to look at the wider urban context in which they operate. A review of urban policy and development in London over the past forty years shows that policy initiatives have simultaneously valorised local communities as part of the solution to local problems *and* undermined poor residents by creating urban regeneration programmes based on a "partnership" between the private and public sector (in which the latter was seriously constrained by profitability targets imposed by central government [Drozdz 2014]). These programmes exacerbated inequality across London and created differential access to housing, employment, and education; the programmes also contributed to sharply different levels of health/mortality and income for London's residents.

Central government used public-private partnerships to regenerate poor/deprived urban areas across the UK (variously referred to as "community development programmes," "City Challenges," or "New Deal for Communities" (NDC). Thus between 1999 and 2009, NDC programmes targeted thirty-nine areas/local neighbourhoods in an attempt to transform them. The programmes sought to achieve different objectives in different areas (Batty et al. 2010, 13).

Overall NDCs sought to achieve "holistic change" in relation to three place-related outcomes (crime, community, and housing and the physical environment [HPE]) and three people-related outcomes (education, health, and "worklessness"). The programmes also sought to "close the gaps between these thirty-nine areas and the rest of the country"; to "achieve a value for money transformation of these neighbourhoods"; "secure improvements by working with other delivery agencies such as the police, Primary Care Trusts (PCTs), schools, Jobcentre Plus (JCP), and their parent local authority"; to "place the community 'at the heart of' the initiative"; and to "sustain activity after NDC Programme funding ceased."

Poor residents in these development initiatives were marginalised in part because the projects were managed by officials and the middle-class "community planning elite" (Dillon and Fanning 2012). This was particularly the case in the areas of London that exhibited the greatest levels

social/council housing should be evicted. It is not clear whether either recommendation was followed.

of deprivation and poverty. The impact of these policies was not uniform, and they have had different outcomes depending on the location of the area, the focus of the scheme (i.e., refurbishing housing, services, etc.) and the degree of social stability/homogeneity in the area that was being developed (Batty et al. 2010). NDC interventions contributed to uneven urban spatial development, in particular improved services and housing gave rise to growing levels of gentrification that displaced poor residents.[8] Furthermore, when central funding ran out, local transformation stalled.

At about the same time public spending cuts occurred (after 2010 council budgets were slashed by 50 per cent),[9] a reduction of social/council housing stock (by almost 25 per cent since 1981) forced increasing numbers of people into the private rental sector or out of London altogether (Hodkinson 2011).[10] The benefit cap and the "spare bedroom tax," which were introduced in 2013, have, along with other welfare cuts, contributed to making an estimated 170,000 people homeless.[11]

The epicentre of the 2011 riots was Tottenham and Haringey, which, together with Newham and Tower Hamlets, were the most deprived boroughs in London (Trust for London 2011). Worryingly, they remain among the most deprived boroughs (though parts of these boroughs are being gentrified).[12] The Trust for London's (2017) analysis of inner-London points out that 43 per cent of children live in poverty and that 35 per cent of people in part-time working families and 9 per cent of people in full-time

---

[8] In early 2018, London councils granted property developers permission to build twenty-six thousand luxury flats priced at more than £1 million each, this follows the current construction of towers containing nearly 7500 luxury homes and existing rights to build a further 18,700 "high-end apartments and town houses." In contrast, only 6400 affordable homes were built in London in 2016/17. ("Anger as 26,000 new millionaire flats are given green light" (*Observer*, 4 February 2018).

[9] See http://www.londoncouncils.gov.uk/node/28157 (accessed 14 October 2017).

[10] So-called social cleansing, see http://www.independent.co.uk/news/uk/home-news/over-50000-families-shipped-out-of-london-in-the-past-three-years-due-to-welfare-cuts-and-soaring-10213854.html and https://www.theguardian.com/society/2016/may/22/councils-forcing-homeless-families-to-relocate-miles-away.

[11] See https://www.theguardian.com/uk-news/davehillblog/2016/dec/01/londons-homelessness-count-continues-to-rise.

[12] For information about ongoing gentrification, see https://www.theguardian.com/artanddesign/2015/mar/22/tottenham-regeneration-londons-most-deprived-spurs-stadium (accessed 13 October 2017) and for public opposition to gentrification see http://haringeyhousingaction.org.uk/no-gentrification-for-tottenham-the-threat-to-people-on-low-incomes-and-ethnic-minorities-from-haringey-councils-plan-for-tottenham/ (accessed 13 October 2017).

working families live in poverty. Furthermore, 32 per cent of households are in social housing.[13] At the same time 8 per cent of London's households are overcrowded (three times more than in the rest of the country; 16 per cent of homes in Hackney and 25 per cent of homes in Newham are overcrowded). The consensus is that poverty and deprivation are getting worse (Lesser 2016).

The 2011 riots exhibited elements of continuity with past public unrest, but they also raised new concerns about the rapidity and fluidity with which events occurred, the extent of looting and debates over policing, and the way that the "penal state" responded to the riots (Riots, Communities, and Victims Panel 2012; Newburn 2015). The majority of those arrested and prosecuted were young adults who have long expressed "discontent" with police "stop and search" methods and with police disrespect for local people. As already noted, 90 per cent of those arrested were males (of whom 46 per cent were black, 42 per cent were white, and 7 per cent were Asian). It is important to note that 76 per cent of the individuals arrested during the riots had previously committed twenty thousand criminal offences. The situation is deeply worrying because it reflects how the precariat, born out of persisting deprivation and racial disparities, is treated by the CJS (The Lammy Report 2017). The situation is generating conflict between urban youth and the police and courts.

Worryingly, at roughly the same time as the socio-economic situation was worsening in inner-city London, Parliament created four thousand new offences (Leveson 2015, ¶13), criminalising new areas of social life. Growing numbers of Londoners are being arrested and convicted for a variety of offences including begging, racist and religious assault, failure to pay council tax,[14] public order offences, and so on. As will become evident from the cases discussed in this book, in *at least* 20 per cent of the cases I observed, the defendant was impoverished if not destitute. The information on an appellant's economic status comes from an explicit acknowledgement during legal proceedings that the defendant was sleeping rough on the street, begging, already in debt to the court, or that s/he was

[13] This against a background in which 12,200 council homes were sold to tenants under right-to-buy schemes in England in 2015–16, but only 2000 replacement homes were begun.

[14] See "Thousands of UK's poor in court over non-payment of council tax" (*Guardian*, 18 October 2013).

compelled to have the court fine deducted from their income support/benefits.[15]

The ethnic identity of 181 of the defendants for whom I have data on is set out in Table I.1.

Table I.1. The ethnic identity of defendants whose cases I observed in magistrates' courts.

Ethnicity	Defendants by ethnicity
Black	46 (25%)
Asian	42 (23%)
White	81 (45%)
Other	12 (6 %)
Total	181

Identification of a defendant's ethnic identity was based on my visual assessment of a defendant; the category "other" is composed of individuals whose appearance did not easily fit into the principle categories (i.e., Middle Eastern descent). The large number in the "do not know" category arises because many defendants were not "produced" for their hearing, that is, they did not appear in court. The very high proportion of BME defendants (at 51 per cent) reflects the nature of policing in London, specifically the effect of "stop and search" police operations (see chapter 5) and urban poverty (see chapters 3 and 5).

In short, the cases I observed reinforces earlier research about the CJS, namely that a large proportion of the individuals arrested by the police and prosecuted in magistrates' courts are from BME communities and that many are "destitute" and vulnerable. Many defendants exist below the official income threshold entitling them to state support and their vulnerability is compounded by limited legal literacy, ill health, and low educational qualifications (McKeever, Simpson, and Fitzpatrick 2018; Wintersteiger 2015). In addition, it is worth noting that many of the proceedings I observed were prosecutions against young "adults." Specifically, the relative age of defendants was as follows: 24 per cent of defendants were between the age of eighteen and twenty-one; 63 per cent were over twenty-one years of age; in 13 per cent of the cases I observed, it was not possible to assess the age of the defendant. In short, many Londoners—in particular young men from a BME background and poor/destitute individuals—are very familiar with the police and the courts.

[15] Excluded from my estimate are the number of defendants who qualified for legal aid on the basis of having a low income and individuals prosecuted for failing to pay council tax.

Indeed, involvement in criminal proceedings is likely to exacerbate an individual's destitution/poverty and his/her propensity to re-offend.

The evolution of criminal justice policy

To understand what occurs in the courts we need to consider the evolution of criminal justice/penal policy in Britain and the role that magistrates' courts play in the CJS. As Garland (1997, 2018) and others have argued, as high crime rates became "a normal social fact," the direction of penal policy shifted. Because officials came to believe that the state could not control crime, there has been a corresponding shift in policy that has moved responsibility for crime reduction away from the state and on to citizens and "communities."

There is abundant evidence of this shift that has reshaped policing, prosecution, the courts, and prisons and that has been accompanied by sharp budgetary cuts.[16] With regard to the police, it has been apparent for some time that they are unable to control crime or secure convictions.[17] As table 1.3 (in chapter 1) indicates, not only did the police charge 16 per cent fewer offenders in 2017/18 compared with 2016/17, they continued to divert a high percentage of offenders away from court by using "out of court disposals" and/or by "dropping," that is, failing to prosecute, a very high percentage of cases that are "not in the interests of justice" to pursue.[18] Critically, in 2016/17 and 2017/18, between 49 per cent and 51 per cent of recorded cases were not prosecuted due to "evidential difficulties" encountered by the police. Official statistics on the number of adults remanded to magistrates' court by the Metropolitan Police (see table I.2) indicate that on average 233,000 criminal offences were tried in London magistrates' courts each year. Because some individuals are charged with multiple offences, it is not possible to know how many *individuals* were tried. The figures for each category of offence suggest that, apart from

---

[16] The most up-to-date figures have been published by the Institute for Fiscal Studies at https://www.ifs.org.uk/publications/9224.

[17] Reiner (2010, 244) states that "research shows the central role of the public (as victims and witnesses) in uncovering and clearing up offences" and that the police and popular culture "exaggerate the extent to which policing is concerned with serious criminal offences and overestimate the capacity of the police to deal with criminals by detection and deterrence."

[18] Sanders et al. (2010, chap. 3) note that a large percentage of those initially arrested are released without charge because the police follow different "working rules" depending on the situations they confront and their objectives, for example, to gather information, discipline, and so on.

summary non-motoring offences, the number of arrests and prosecutions is declining. Problematically, in 2016/2017 the crime rate increased as the number of police officers continued to decline (one CPS prosecutor told me that cuts to police budgets meant that fewer people were being arrested and prosecuted [IFS 2017]).[19] Furthermore, police "Sanction Detection Rates"[20] provide a similar picture: fewer than 14 per cent of all reported crimes result in a conviction. As will become apparent in chapter 1, the CJS is struggling to deliver justice.

Table I.2. Adults remanded into custody in London's magistrates' courts, 2012–16.[21]

	2012	2013	2014	2015	2016	Total (per cent average)
Indictable only	4,697	4,523	4,326	3,665	3,528	20,739 (1.7 %)
Triable either way	53,914	52,820	50,462	48,263	48,079	253,538 (21.7 %)
Summary non-motoring	107,470	97,829	92,837	96,237	104,866	499,239 (42.8 %)
Summary motoring	86,818	84,265	76,092	72,364	72,629	392,163 (33.6 %)
Total	252,899	239,437	223,717	220,529	229,097	1,165,679

Table I.3 shows the gendered nature of offending. First, looking left to right across different types of crime, adult women commit far fewer offences than men and they commit fewer serious crimes. Women commit on average about 1 per cent of "indictable only" offences, 16 per cent of "triable either way" offences, 50 per cent of "summary non-motoring" offences, and 18 per cent of "summary motoring offences." The statistics show that women constituted about 30 per cent of all criminal cases heard in London magistrates' courts for the period 2012 to 2016. The gendered nature of offending is also reflected in my fieldwork: out of the 238 remand cases I

---

[19] See "Crime rise is biggest in a decade, ONS figures show," *Guardian* (20 July 2017); "Knife crime up because gang warfare is becoming embedded in our culture," *Telegraph* (29 April 2017); "Huge rise in hate crime across London, new figures reveal," *Independent* (7 March 2017).

[20] See https://www.met.police.uk/sd/stats-and-data/met/year-end-crime-statistics/ (accessed 12 January 2019).

[21] Source: "Remand Magistrates" Pivot Tool; at https://www.gov.uk/government/statistics/criminal-justice-system-statistics-quarterly-december-2016.

Table I.3. Adult offenders by gender remanded into custody in London's magistrates' courts, 2012–2016.[22]

	2012		2013		2014		2015		2016		Grand Total
	Male	**Female**	**Male**	**Female**	**Male**	**Female**	**Male**	**Female**	**Male**	**Female**	
Indictable only	4,180	418 (0.1%)	3,994	410 (0.1%)	3,776	412 (0.1%)	3,189	337 (0.1%)	3,049	335 (0.1%)	20,100 (1.8%)
Triable either way	45,356	7,441 (16%)	44,814	6,962 (15%)	42,277	7,010 (16%)	40,303	6,849 (16%)	40,203	6,615 (16%)	247,830 (23%)
Summary non-motoring	65,709	33,068 (50%)	60,867	30,872 (51%)	56,481	28,393 (50%)	58,203	29,704 (51%)	62,152	28,278 (45%)	453,727 (42%)
Summary motoring	64,119	11,761 (18%)	66,892	12,215 (18%)	59,672	11,126 (18%)	56,206	10,740 (19%)	52,445	10,380 (20%)	355,556 (33%)
Females as total percentage of offenders	179,364	52,688 (29%)	176,567	50,459 (28%)	162,206	46,941 (29%)	157,901	47,630 (30%)	157,849	45,608 (29%)	
Total	232,052		227,026		209,147		205,531		203,457		1,077,213

[22] Source: "Remand Magistrates" Pivot Tool; at https://www.gov.uk/government/statistics/criminal-justice-system-statistics-quarterly-december-2016.

observed, 212 of the defendants (89 per cent) were male and 24 (11 per cent) were female.[23]

The magistracy is also under pressure due to the closure of growing numbers of courts,[24] a rapid decline in the number of magistrates, high levels of offending, and legislation that constrains the way they sentence offenders (e.g., by limiting their discretion in sentencing offenders, creating sentence enhancements, aggressive prosecution strategies, plea agreements, and so on). At the same time, the state contracted out responsibility to the private sector to run the probation service and prisons. This situation reflects a general shift in penal policy away from state responsibility for dealing with crime and crime reduction and the articulation of a policy of "responsibilising" citizens to protect themselves and their communities.

Studying magistrates' courts

Magistrates' courts provide a window onto the entire CJS because 94 per cent of offenders are initially arraigned, and their cases decided, in these courts. In looking at how these courts operate, it is possible to assess the role of the police, prosecutors, judges, lawyers, and other professionals whose work is essential to the functioning of the CJS.

"Summary justice"—proceedings that are carried out rapidly by omitting legal formalities required by common law—offers defendants a limited opportunity to defend themselves: today about 70 per cent of defendants plead guilty and are immediately sentenced without going to trial[25] and 85 per cent of individuals who plead not guilty and elect to be tried are convicted (CPS 2016/17). Why do most defendants plead guilty? What is the contribution of legal counsel to proceedings in which the majority of defendants are found guilty?

While historians have traced the appearance of lay magistrates—then called "justices of the peace" to the twelfth century—magistrates' courts in their current form came into being in 1971. It was at this time that government abolished "petty sessions" (which dealt with local matters) and "quarter sessions" (which dealt with legal affairs at county level) and created magistrates' and Crown courts.

---

[23] In one case, it was impossible to know the gender of the defendant as s/he was not produced in court.

[24] In the 1960s there were approximately 900 magistrates' courts; by 2011 the number had declined to 204 (Reichert 1973); a further 57 courts are earmarked for closure because of budget cuts and declining numbers of criminal cases.

[25] In the late 1970s 95 per cent of defendants pleaded guilty (McBarnet 1982).

Box I.1 lists criminal offences in England and Wales and where each type of case is heard. The jurisdiction of magistrates' courts is limited to "minor" criminal offences for which defendants are not entitled to trial by jury. Nearly all individuals accused of committing a crime have their initial/remand hearing in a magistrates' court. Individuals charged with "indictable-only offences" make their initial plea in a magistrates' court, which usually refers/remits the case to a Crown court to be tried by a judge and jury. Individuals accused of "either-way offences" can choose to have their case heard by magistrates or at a Crown court (if they opt for the latter and are found guilty, they can expect a lengthier sentence).

Box I.1. Criminal offences.[26]

Types of Offences	
Indictable only	Murder, manslaughter, rape, robbery, and serious fraud cases can only be heard at a Crown court.
Triable either way	These can be dealt with either by magistrates or before a judge and jury at the Crown court. These offences include theft, handling stolen goods, fraud, drug offences, domestic violence, sexual assaults on a minor, carrying a concealed/bladed weapon, assault on a police officer, GBH, etc. A defendant can insist on their right to trial in the Crown court. Magistrates can also decide that a case is so serious that it should be dealt with in the Crown court—which can impose tougher sentences if the defendant is found guilty. The maximum punishment for a *single* summary offence is six months in prison and/or a fine of up to £5,000.
Summary non-motoring	Minor assaults, theft, shop lifting, possession of drugs, public order offences, drink driving, threatening and abusive behaviour, racially aggravated assault, travelling on public transport without a ticket, begging, breach of bail, indecent exposure, fleeing arrest, etc.
Summary motoring	Motoring offences: causing injury, causing death, dangerous driving, driving under the influence, failing to supply the identity of the driver, other motoring offences, vehicle insurance offences, speed limit offences (not theft of vehicles).

Ethnographic approaches to the study of courts

Ethnographically informed researchers have adopted five potentially complementary approaches to study courts. First, it is sometimes useful to see courts as "ceremonies of situational transformation" that link and transform inter-personal disputes into issues of law suitable to be heard by a judge (Falk-Moore 1977; Felsteiner, Abel, and Sarat 1980–81). In this sense hearings/trials can be seen as a particular kind of social event in which

[26] See https://www.judiciary.gov.uk/you-and-the-judiciary/going-to-court/magistrates-court/.

legal actors, legal rules and procedures, and legal language dominate proceedings, often at the cost of "alienating" the parties to the case (Danet 1980; Mather and Yngvesson 1980–81).

Courts, and specifically trials, can also be viewed as "arenas" where legal battles are staged and performed (Carlen 1976; Goodwin 1994). Analysing the performance of law requires an understanding of the roles played by specific actors and the "language" they use. Specifically it is useful to focus on the *oral* nature of legal proceedings and to distinguish between the "language of law" (found in legislation and legal documents)[27] which is spoken during proceedings by legal actors[28] and the everyday colloquial language of defendants (which follows very different social and linguistic conventions). This distinction, which appears in the work of Conley and O'Barr (1998), Mertz (1994), Rock (1993), Danet (1980), and Gibbons (1999), among others, provides a useful way of examining the controlling nature of law, which attempts to "order social relations" and determine the possibilities open to defendants to contest/resist the hegemony of the law as they interact with prosecutors, lawyers, and the judge.

Edelman (1964), commenting on legal discourse, says: "It is precisely its ambiguity that gives lawyers, judges and administrators a political and social function, for unambiguous rules would, by definition call neither for interpretation nor for argument about their meaning" (cited in O'Barr 1981, 394). O'Barr has observed that "the language of the law is viewed as protecting the law and the lawyer" because defendants/litigants

---

[27] The language of the law as articulated/set out in legislation, statute, or legal rules is characterised by a highly technical vocabulary that uses colloquial terms in specialised ways, replete with lengthy noun phrases and the use of the passive voice, multiple negatives, complex grammatical structures, and multiple, embedded clauses.

[28] A good example of this is the requirement set out in s.174 of *The Criminal Justice Act 2003* which requires magistrates and District Judges to "state in open court, in ordinary language and in general terms, the court's reasons for deciding on the sentence. (3) The court must explain to the offender in ordinary language—(a) the effect of the sentence, (b) the effects of non-compliance with any order that the offender is required to comply with and that forms part of the sentence, (c) any power of the court to vary or review any order that forms part of the sentence, and (d) the effects of failure to pay a fine, if the sentence consists of or includes a fine." However, as my case summaries indicate, what is "ordinary" language for the court is incomprehensible to most defendants. See: http://www.legislation.gov.uk/ukpga/2003/44/part/12/chapter/1/crossheading/duty-of-court-to-explain-sentence.

cannot understand legal discourse and need a lawyer's assistance to give evidence and to interpret a decision (1981, 394).

Camiss (2006, 71–72) provides a more compelling argument about the tension between legal and colloquial language in courts. He argued that

> courtroom struggles are not limited to ascertaining the facts but extend to giving meaning to agreed facts: that is the participants struggle to have their view and interpretation of events accepted by the court. This struggle can lead to the mobilisation of different interpretations based upon alternative discourses.

The alternative discourses he refers to are what I have called the language of law as opposed to the colloquial language of defendants. He cites the work of Nobles and Schiff (2001), who argue that legal discourse is best understood as a form of autopoiesis that sees law "as a system of communication" in a society "made up of multiple systems of communication," where "[c]oordination is made possible by the use of common reductive terms, self-referential communication, and (at the level of discourse) widely shared values." Seen in this way, Cammiss (2006, 73–74) argues that the legal system is best described as being "normatively closed" yet "cognitively open" to communication with other discourses. For example, law is open to the language of anti-trust issues, market inefficiences, and so on. Fundamentally, however, "because the legal system is normatively closed, the engagement with alternative discourses operates in a manner that transforms these other discourses" into the language of law. In this way, law can "exclude and stigmatise—define out' alternative voices," thereby reproducing the legal/binary structure in legal language that selects legally relevant facts from different narratives to construct a case to be decided by the court. In this process law substantially changes participants narratives and it defines individuals as "autonomous agents able to participate fully in social relations" (ibid., 75).

A different way of putting this argument is provided by King (1978, 195):

> The use of stylized, ritualistic language as a mechanism of control lies not so much in its reflection of the power structure of the courtroom, as in the fact that it is not available to defendants. Some of them attempt, usually unsuccessfully, to imitate the language of deference, but the majority use their normal mode of expression. Thus, their attempts to question the police or argue an issue with the magistrate or clerk are likely to take the form of expressions of naked aggression with the defendant making accusations . . . Such behaviour is immediately ruled "out of court" and the defendant is reduced to a state of frustrated silence.

As a considerable body of research demonstrates, *legal procedure silences defendants who end up pleading guilty* (McBarnet 1981, 187–88). This happens because, as McConville and Baldwin (1981, 188) have argued, "criminal procedures in England are structured to produce convictions, within a framework of uncertain protections, confused and ill-defined responsibility, in which informal and even unlawful behaviour of various participants[29] is directly or indirectly legitimated." As my discussion of the *Public Order Act* (1986) in chapter 3 will make clear, the language used in the act to define offences (together with the abandonment of the need for proof) provides the police and the CPS with unfettered discretion to prosecute a wide range of public behaviours.

A third approach looks at how the design of courts—in the sense of a court's "segmented" physical layout—affects the staging of justice and constrains or controls participants. Remand hearings and contested trials can usefully be understood as a type of "performance" that is partly shaped by the spatial layout of a courtroom. While many observers portray courtrooms as neutral spaces, Mulcahy (2011, 1) has observed that

> Each time a section of floor is raised, a barrier installed or a segregated circulation route added it has the potential to create insiders and outsiders; empowered and disempowered participants in a space ostensibly labelled "public" in which the intricacies of civil liberties and participatory democracy are played out.

Mulcahy (2011) offers a rich and detailed analysis of the history of changing notions of privacy and due process, linkages between law and commerce, and the contribution of legal hubris that has contributed to the design and construction of courthouses and courtrooms. However, we also need to attend to elements of performativity that are apparent in criminal trials. In this regard, Umphry (2012, 122) draws our attention to the enunciations and citations made during a trial and to the repetitive, discursive frameworks, narrative strategies, and staged order of legal proceedings. She comments that

> Legal rules—both substantive rules defining the criminality of the acts at issue and procedural rules governing the introduction of evidence—do matter in creating and choreographing the context for the enunciation of the law: they shape the incriminatory and exculpatory narratives of fact and responsibility . . . At the same time though, its theatricality . . . renders the space of the trial a porous one in which legal rules can be inflected, overdetermined and even dismissed out of hand. Significantly, to succeed

[29] The reference is to the police.

> attorneys must appeal to competing versions of cultural common sense . . . in order to narrate stories that are internally persuasive.

While partitioning clearly supports the power of the judge over the proceedings, together with the force of legal rules, courtroom design reinforces the sovereign's right to try individuals, which creates a unique affective atmosphere of bodies, behaviours, roles, and technologies. In this book I seek to show how the legal process is performed and how legal procedure, legal language, and the design of the dock inhibit defendants from hearing proceedings and participating in their hearing/trial.

A fourth approach sees courts primarily as institutions characterised by a specific "legal architecture" (i.e., specific procedural rules and practice directions) that judges draw upon to manage hearings, ensure turn taking, and enforce their power (Spaulding 2012). Finally, a fifth approach looks at court "culture" in the sense that courts possess their own institutional procedures, tacit understandings and ways of conducting business (Yngvesson 1990). In what follows I draw on all five approaches to analyse magistrates' courts.

Analysis of legal proceedings

Legal proceedings in magistrates' courts are characterised by six features. First, magistrates are laypersons with limited legal training who, guided by a Legal Adviser, sit in judgement over fellow citizens. Limited legal training, I argue, ensures that magistrates fail to question police evidence and the arguments by the Crown prosecutor. Equally important, limited training ensures the development of a narrow "judicial vision" that focuses on a defendant's culpability/responsibility for a specific act without taking into consideration the wider social and cultural context that might help explain an alleged offence (this issue is taken up in later chapters). Second the spatial arrangement of the court, in particular the role played by the dock, reinforces the power of the court over defendants. Third, legal proceedings are brief: remand hearings last between four and forty-five minutes and contested trials last between fifty-five minutes and three hours. Fourth, and regardless of the "trivial" nature of the offences, the justice meted out to defendants lacks basic elements of due process. Fifth, while the offences that defendants are charged with may be trivial compared with offences referred to the Crown court (see chapter 2), the impact on defendants of being taken to court, convicted, and sentenced is far from trivial. Finally, the right of appeal against a wrongful sentence in magistrates' courts is fraught with procedural problems, uncertainty about the outcome, and high costs that effectively prevents/dissuades the majority of defendants from appealing against a wrongful conviction (Sanders et al. 2010, 613–17; Jacobson 2013).

Unpaid lay magistrates administering justice in local communities are supposed to serve two key roles in the CJS. First, magistrates[30]—there were approximately 28,700 in 1978 but by 2017 their number had fallen to 16,100—enable government to provide local-level justice at low cost (House of Commons 2016–17; Silverleaf 2017).[31] As one study has remarked, the purpose of summary justice is to provide "fast and effective justice" and "to produce the best justice at a reasonable cost and within an acceptable timescale" (Gibson and Gordon 2008, 14). Morgan (2008, 8) argues that magistrates' courts reflect the principle of proportionality, by which he means that "the level of criminal intervention, be proportionate to the seriousness of the offence." This principle means "that the more serious the offence, the more onerous the sanction" and the greater the procedural safeguards need to be "to ensure that justice is done."

The second function of magistrates' courts is "ideological." As Darbyshire (2002, 285) and others have commented, a principle justification for magistrates' courts is that they "give the citizen a part to play in the administration of the law" by entrusting citizens with the responsibility to decide minor offences in their communities. This argument is fundamentally flawed. First, magistrates, who were supposed to live within fifteen miles of the court's boundaries and be of "good character," do not reflect the diverse population served by the court. In 2016, and in the interests of efficiency, the Ministry of Justice reorganised Local Justice Areas to create large unified benches of magistrates who have no connection to the communities they serve.[32] Darbyshire (2002) found that magistrates were predominately conservative, white, middle class, and approaching retirement age (though a growing number are female). More recently, the Lord Chief Justice (2017, sec. 5) has reported that 54 per cent of magistrates are female, 86 per cent are over the age of fifty, and 11 per cent are black, Asian, or from an ethnic minority group. Sanders et al. (2010, 448) argue that as a

---

[30] In 2017 part-time unpaid magistrates were required to sit for at least thirteen days, or twenty-six half days, a year.

[31] In 2013, the government estimated the average cost of magistrates' courts per day to be £1,400 compared with £2,150 per day in the Crown court (see https://www.gov.uk/government/news/damian-green-reforming-the-role-of-magistrates [accessed 2 October 2018]).

[32] See "Explanatory Memorandum to the Local Justice Areas Order 2016 No. 941" (accessed 4 September 2018), https://www.legislation.gov.uk/uksi/2016/941/pdfs/uksiem_20160941_en.pdf.

result of the above factors, the magistracy "displays strong pro-authority attitudes and various forms of bias in all its decision-making."

Just as important is the argument that magistrates dispense justice. As McBarnet (1981, 1982) demonstrated long ago, legal procedure in magistrates' courts is characterised by the *lack of due process*. In particular, defendants lack adequate legal representation, the police are often the only complainant (and they fail to "investigate" an offence), a court record is not kept, and the "facts" in dispute are difficult for defendants to contest because of the "legal language" used to define and try offences.

In 1969, following a Royal Commission inquiry (Beeching Commission 1966–69), central government assumed control of court design. There followed the roll out of a standard court design in the form of a "segmented" courtroom that was used in all subsequent court construction (Mulcahy 2011, chap. 7). Segmentation—which occurred within the courthouse as well as inside each courtroom—reflects a clear hierarchy between different categories of court users. In courtrooms, segmentation is evident in the spatial layout and the use of barriers to create secluded zones. Thus, the judiciary sit on an elevated platform/bench and face all the parties; the legal adviser sits below the bench and faces the parties. Depending upon the size of the courtroom there are three to four long tables[33] behind which sit counsel for the defendant (on the left) and the Crown prosecutor (on the right) at the first table (facing the bench). In the second desk sit various legal and court staff; the desk furthest from the bench provides seats for counsel waiting for their case to be heard. A lockable, plexiglass dock (of varying size) is normally located along one wall of the courtroom,[34] and an open public gallery (which is normally empty) is usually located on the back wall of the courtroom facing the bench. A slightly elevated witness box capable of seating one person is located in front of and to the left or right of the bench. Fixed seating, and occasional tables, is available for other staff, for example, ushers, court administrators, and so on. In the mid-1980s, concerns about security[35] trumped other considerations and the dock became increasingly

---

[33] Fixed to the long tables are computer screens that do not work.

[34] Some courtrooms are linked directly to the cells in the basement of the courthouse from which defendants are brought up through a secure passage and placed, often in handcuffs, into a locked dock. They are accompanied by security staff who sit in the dock with the defendant during proceedings.

[35] Presumably this concern arose from the trial of individuals accused of involvement in IRA bombings. There is limited evidence that defendants pose a threat to the court, or that members of the public have sought to harm defendants (Justice 2015). Docks do not exist in the US, Ireland, the Netherlands, or in Australia, where defendants sit beside their lawyer.

fortified: the writing desk was eliminated; the dock was encased in glass/Perspex and defendants were locked in (Justice 2015, 6). As Mulcahy (2011, 56) notes, "architecture is complicit in the undermining of an active public sphere by creating docile bodies through segregation and the canalisation of circulation."

The key concern with a glass/Perspex dock is that defendants are placed on display in a "glass cage" in a manner that may prejudice the proceedings; glass docks restrict defendants' liberty by preventing her/him from speaking to their lawyers, from hearing what is being said, and from "participating" in their case in any meaningful way (this is much more pronounced at the Central Criminal Court [Tait 2011]). Research in crown courts has shown that the use of encased docks results in defendants' "passive acceptance" of the proceedings (Kirby, Jacobson, and Hunter 2016, 91–96, 191–96). The majority of defendants I observed were placed in an encased, lockable Plexiglas dock[36] (see figure 1.1) which seriously restricted their ability to "participate" in their hearing. The exception to this practice was at Highbury Corner Magistrate's Court where a "pleading bar" (and bench) was available for defendants located on the court-facing side of the encased dock (see figure 1.2). Wimbledon and Thames Magistrates' Courts also have a small number of courtrooms with open docks. It seems that rather than experiencing their time in court as one of realising justice, most defendants experience it as a form of "status degradation" that requires that they be isolated from other actors in the court and treated as a threat to security.

Before examining legal procedure, it is important to look at boxes I.2 and I.3, which set out what the Ministry of Justice refers to as the "committal path" between the police and the courts. Box I.2 shows that London police stations refer criminal offences to specific magistrates' courts to be heard. Box I.3 shows that each magistrates' court refers serious and either-way cases to a specific Crown court for trial (the asterisk indicates the courts in which I conducted fieldwork). The idea behind these "paths" is to ensure efficiency across the CJS in London. Fieldwork for this book was undertaken in thirteen magistrates' courts located in all but two "justice areas" in Greater London.

[36] If we exclude cases where individuals are brought up from the custody cells for their hearings, when individuals make a statutory declaration or when they register a new address, in nine of the twelve magistrates' courts that I observed, defendants were routinely placed in an encased dock for their hearing.

Box I.2. Committal pathways from police stations to magistrates' courts[37] (the asterisk indicates the courts in which fieldwork was undertaken).

London Magistrates' Courts		
Local justice areas	**Magistrates' courts in this local justice area**	**Police stations that refer prosecutions**
SW London Magistrates' Group	Lavender Hill* & Wimbledon* MCs	Wandsworth, Kingston, Wimbledon, & Richmond police stations
NE London Magistrates' Group	Barkingside* & Romford MCs	Ilford, Romford, Dagenham, & Barkingside police stations
SE London Magistrates' Group	Bexley & Bromley MCs	Bromley, Bexley, Plumstead, Lewisham, & Greenwich police stations
Central London Magistrates' Group	Westminster*, City of London* & Hammersmith* MCs	Charing Cross, Belgravia, Brewery Road, Central London (British Transport Police), & Hammersmith police stations (via Wandsworth & Acton)
NW & West London Magistrates' Group	Willesden*, Hendon*, Uxbridge*, Feltham, & Ealing MCs	Heathrow, Hillingdon, Ealing, Acton, Southall, Hounslow, Colindale, Wembley, Harrow (Kilburn police stations)
North London Magistrates' Group	Highbury* & Camden* MCs	Islington, Camden, Haringey, Stratford, & Forest Gate police stations
East London Magistrates' Group	Thames* & Stratford* MCs	Leyton, Stoke Newington, Hackney, Stratford, & Forest Gate police stations
South London Magistrates' Group	Croydon & Camberwell MCs	Brixton, Walworth, Croydon, & Sutton police stations

[37] Source for Box I.2 and I.3 is from FOI request no. 170926005 to the Ministry of Justice dated 17 October 2017.

Box I.3. Committal pathways from London's magistrates' courts to Crown courts.

Magistrates' courts	Crown courts
Highbury Corner, City of London, & Westminster Magistrates' Courts	Blackfriars
All London Magistrates' Court, City of Westminster, Thames, and City of London Magistrates' Courts	Central Criminal Court
Camberwell Green Magistrates' Court	Croydon
Hendon Magistrates' Court	Harrow
SW (Lavender Hill) & Wimbledon Magistrates' Courts	Kingston
Feltham, Uxbridge, Ealing, Hammersmith, & City of Westminster Magistrates' Courts	Isleworth
City of Westminster, City of London, & Hammersmith Magistrates' Courts	Southwark
Highbury Corner & Thames Magistrates' Courts	Wood Green
Bromley, Bexley, & Greenwich Magistrates' Courts	Woolwich
Barkingside, Bexley, & Greenwich Magistrates' Courts	Snaresbrook

Criminal courts are regulated by "procedure" and "practice" rules that magistrates, DJs, registrars, and circuit judges, are required to follow. The "overriding objective" of the procedural rules gives the court the power to "case-manage" a hearing/trial, that is, the rules are used to ensure that a hearing progresses to a just and fair conclusion.[38] Practice rules,[39]on the other hand, set out the procedures that magistrates/judges should use to manage judicial proceedings, hear evidence, pronounce sentence, manage appeals, and so on. These rules and directions are what Spaulding (2012) refers to as the "legal architecture" of the court, which is to say that they provide judges with the tools to hear and decide cases.

The existence of these rules does not, however, tell us much about how cases are actually heard and decided. To understand this, two factors need to be kept in mind: the role played by legal actors prior to and during a hearing (see my Prologue and Sanders et al. 2010, chapters 1–6) and the importance of legal procedure. The CPS, magistrates, and lawyers implicitly assume that a defendant is sufficiently competent and knowledgeable to

[38] See http://www.justice.gov.uk/courts/procedure-rules/criminal/docs/criminal-procedure-rules-and-criminal-practice-directions-complete-edition.pdf (accessed 2 September 2018).
[39] See http://www.justice.gov.uk/courts/procedure-rules/criminal/practice-direction/pd_consolidated (accessed 2 September 2018).

make decisions concerning the conduct of his or her case. However, to quote King (1978, 197), the rules not only determine the sequence of events that encompass defendants from charging through to sentencing, but also assume that

> the defendant is a free agent, capable of responsible, informed action in the conduct of his or her case . . . [whereas] The reality of the situation may be somewhat different. The defendant's freedom of action as well as freedom of movement may be very limited and his or her decisions, particularly if he or she is unrepresented, may be made on the basis of inadequate knowledge and imperfect understanding of his or her predicament.

At the outset of a hearing, and immediately following the identification of the defendant, the CPS lays a charge against a defendant where the offence is either stated in such general terms that the defendant is unable to offer a defence of his or her actions or is so narrowly defined in the statute/legislation that only a very specific defence is allowed. Frequently it is not clear which law is being used to charge a defendant. While poor defendants have a right to legal representation by a duty solicitor, there are serious questions about the effectiveness of these solicitors (see chapter 1). Problematically, defendants who represent themselves in court are uniformly found guilty and convicted. At the same time, remand hearings do not offer defendants an opportunity to address the court: defendants must speak "through" their representative who is supposed to have taken instructions from them before the hearing. Indeed, if a defendant speaks during proceedings, they are told to "shut up" and their sentence may be increased. While defendants who plead "not guilty" at their initial hearing are offered a contested trial, in fact magistrates/DJs do not assist defendants to give their evidence and the management of the hearing sharply constrains their ability to give evidence, which inevitably results in a conviction.

I have adapted McBarnet's (1981, 183) model (see box I.4) that identifies the different legal stages in remand hearings and extended it to include contested trials. The stages can be identified in part by ritualised enunciations of specific legal terms (set out in legislation, legal guidance, and other legal documents). However, as will become apparent, there are variations in the way that hearings and trials unfold. It is important to note that remand hearings and trials are *not* heard by a jury but by a "bench" of two to three magistrates *or* by a DJ.

Legal procedure in remand hearings and contested trials

Two observations are important. Once initiated, proceedings are frequently delayed because magistrates, DJs, and defence counsel have frequently not been given access to relevant case information—that is, they lack information about the case, the charges, and the defendants "previous" (i.e., the defendant's criminal record). Delays also arise due to the failure of the CPS and defence to complete the "Preparation for Effective Trial" (PET) form[40] before the hearing (the form contains a summary of key information about the case).

It is also important to note that the stages identified in Box I.4 do not follow in a sequence from stages 1 to 9 due to the way that magistrates case-manage proceedings.[41] For example at stage 1, not all defendants are present to be charged or to indicate their pleas. A defendant's absence may be due to their having been wrongly released from custody or from a secure hospital prior to their hearing, because they are mentally unwell and unable to attend (though only a small number of these defendants are excused from attending court), or because they have breached court bail and have failed to turn up.

When a defendant fails to attend court for his or her hearing, magistrates progress a case in one of three ways. First, the bench can list the case for trial (i.e., set a trial date) and make a "production order" requiring the defendant to surrender and appear at the next stage in the proceedings (i.e., the police are instructed to arrest the individual and place him or her in custody until the trial). Second, the court may decide to proceed in the defendant's absence, which results in a guilty verdict and the pronouncement of sentence (followed by the issue of an arrest warrant for the defendant). Less commonly at stage 2, a defendant may change his or her plea, which

---

[40] This six-page form is supposed to contain all the relevant evidence to facilitate a contested trial to hear the not guilty pleas. The PET form is available at https://www.justice.gov.uk/courts/procedure-rules/criminal/forms-2015#Anchor51 (accessed 2 July 2017).

[41] "Case management" means that the courts are mandated to follow specific procedures to "improve the way cases are processed through the system, for the benefit of all concerned within the criminal justice system." The objective of "robust" case management is to reduce the number of hearings, "maximise participation and engagement from every participant within the system," and ensure "efficient compliance with the Criminal Procedure Rules (and) Practice and Court Directions." At the core of these procedures is the PET form, which is critical to two major case management initiatives, namely the "uniform national Early Guilty Plea scheme and Crown Court Disclosure in document-heavy cases" (MoJ 2015a, 1).

Box I.4. Stages in criminal legal proceedings.

Stage	Remand hearings		Stage	Contested trials
1	The defendant confirms his/her identity.		1	The defendant confirms his/her identity.
2	The CPS reads out the charge(s) and the legal adviser takes the defendant's plea. If the defendant is charged with an "either-way" or indictable offence, a decision is made as to "mode of trial" for the case to be heard at a Crown court (the hearing ends at this point, though an application for bail may be heard). If the defendant elects to be heard at a magistrates' court or s/he is charged with a summary offence, the case proceeds in magistrates' court.		2	The prosecutor reads out the "facts."
3	Plea If the defendant *pleads guilty* to the offence(s), *proceedings skip forward to stage 6.*	Plea If the defendant *pleads not guilty*, the PET form is completed.	3	The prosecutor calls his or her witnesses, including police officers, to give evidence. Police evidence is submitted and examined (this usually takes the form of reading previously "agreed" summaries of the officers' interviews with the defendant and the victim). If available, CCTV footage is viewed.
4		A trial date is set.	4	A solicitor cross-examines prosecution witnesses.
5		A decision is reached regarding whether s/he should be bailed until the trial or remanded into custody. The case is then listed for trial.	5	The defendant gives his or her evidence and is cross-examined.
6	The Bench/DJ may "retire" before it announces the verdict: not guilty or guilty.		6	The Crown and the defence sum up their arguments regarding the guilt/innocence of the defendant.

7	The defendant's solicitor may offer mitigation to reduce the severity of the sentence. In DV cases, the CPS reads out the victim's impact statement.		**7**	The Bench/DJ may "retire" before announcing the verdict: not guilty or guilty.
8	The court may adjourn the case while the defendant is interviewed by a probation officer or the mental health team who will recommend a specific course of action for the court.		**8**	The defendant's representative may offer mitigation, and the court may adjourn the case for the defendant to be interviewed by probation or the mental health team who recommend a specific course of action for the court.
9	Sentencing. The court hears reports from probation and the sentence is announced.		**9**	Sentencing. The court hears reports from probation and the sentence is announced.

disrupts proceedings because an adjournment is required to allow his or her counsel to "take further instructions" before the hearing can proceed.

At stage 2, prosecutors ask the court to remit serious/indictable-only cases and some "either-way" cases to Crown court for trial. This stage is referred to as a "decision regarding the allocation of cases"—formerly "mode of trial" or "choice of venue"—and is discussed in chapter 2. If the court agrees that the case should be referred, the defendant's plea is usually not taken, and the proceedings end abruptly (the defendant may be remanded back into custody or they may apply for bail).

If a defendant pleads guilty to an "either-way" or summary offence the proceedings are transformed into an uncontested hearing aimed at sentencing the individual; proceedings skip to stage 6 when the court announces its verdict, at stage 7 mitigation is considered, then the court may send a defendant to be interviewed by probation (stage 8), which means that the case is adjourned and reconvened later for sentencing (stage 9).

However, if a defendant pleads not guilty at stage 3, the court completes the PET form. Magistrates take differing views about how much of a defendant's criminal record is read out in court. Not infrequently, because of IT failures, the bench asks the CPS to pass relevant parts of the case file—sometimes a laptop—forward to read key documents before it hears legal argument. A trial date is set (stage 4), then the court may consider applications for bail (stage 5), failing which the defendant is remanded into custody to await trial.

Turning to *contested trials*, it is important to note that legal proceedings vary depending upon: (a) whether the defendant is present, (b) whether witnesses are present to give evidence, (c) whether the defendant is legally represented, and (d) whether the trial is presided over by magistrates or a DJ. Having been warned about the consequences of not attending trial, most defendants attend either because of the penalty for failing to attend or because, as magistrates constantly tell them, this is their only opportunity to tell their side of the story.[42] If defendants fail to attend or if they are "excused"[43] from attending, the trial proceeds without them and takes a truncated form with proceedings skipping quickly to stage 3—defendants who are absent or who are not represented by a lawyer are at a serious disadvantage and are unable to challenge the prosecution's case[44]—then to stage 6 and to sentencing (stage 9).

If the defendant attends, prosecution witnesses, including the complainant, are called to give evidence (stage 3), following which they are cross-examined by the defendant's lawyer (stage 4). If defendants are not legally represented, the bench/DJ is under a duty to assist them to give their evidence (though this seldom occurs). Unrepresented defendants charged with sex offences or domestic violence are required to have a court appointed solicitor to cross-examine the claimant/witnesses giving evidence against them (stage 4).[45] In stage 5, the defendant provides his/her evidence and is cross-examined by the prosecutor. If witnesses fail to attend, proceedings may be temporarily disrupted because DJs tend to adjourn to find out whether they are on their way or why they are not present. If defendants provide no witnesses to support their case, this undermines their defence. However, if the complainant (on whose behalf the Crown initiated

---

[42] Out of the 238 cases I observed, nineteen defendants (8 per cent) failed to attend their hearing.
[43] See CPS guidance on "issuance of medical certificates" at: http://www.cps.gov.uk/legal/l_to_o/medical_certificates/ (accessed 20 July 2017).
[44] This happens because the lawyer is unable to take instructions from their absent client and cannot defend him/her. When this happens the lawyer "withdraws" from the case.
[45] See Part 23 of the Criminal Procedure Rules at https://www.justice.gov.uk/courts/procedure-rules/criminal/docs/2015/crim-proc-rules-2015-part-23.pdf (accessed 12 July 2017).

legal proceedings) or prosecution witnesses fail to attend,[46] the Crown's case is undermined. While the Crown may seek to continue the prosecution, the bench/DJ usually ends proceedings by issuing a verdict of "not proved" (stage 9).

At stage 6 both parties sum up their arguments regarding the guilt/innocence of the defendant and ask the bench/DJ to find in their favour. The bench may briefly "retire" (stage 7) to consider the evidence before announcing the verdict. At stage 8, a defendant's counsel offers mitigation in an attempt to reduce the sentence imposed on their client.

If a defendant is not legally represented, most magistrates do not give them an opportunity to offer mitigation or to suggest a different sentence to what the prosecution proposes. In 175 (66 per cent) of the 238 hearings for which I have data, defendants were legally represented; however, in 49 cases (20 per cent) defendants attempted to represent themselves.[47] When defendants are not legally represented, they are unable to defend themselves and are found guilty (cf., McBarnet 1981, 182–85). At this point, the court may adjourn for a probation assessment of the defendant to be undertaken (a case can be adjourned for a few hours or for several days or weeks). Once a report is ready, a sentencing hearing (stage 9) occurs at which the probation officer or a member of the mental health team orally present a report and recommendations, which may or may not be accepted by the bench/DJ; their report is immediately followed by pronouncing the sentence.

There are noticeable differences in court procedure depending on whether a trial is presided over by magistrates or by a DJ. When magistrates' courts were reorganised and brought under greater central control in the 1990s, a small number of "stipendiary magistrates" were appointed to sit full-time in areas with large criminal caseloads. These magistrates were subsequently appointed to full-time posts as District Judges to hear complex cases, but they may also sit with magistrates in youth courts.[48] Research has

---

46 In many cases, the absence of the complainant or of Crown witnesses is due to a failure by the CPS to issue a summons to ensure that complainants/witnesses attend court.

47 A small number of defendants had access to a lawyer under a section 36 order, which requires the court to appoint a duty solicitor to cross-examine key witnesses giving evidence against them. For the legislative basis of this provision see http://www.legislation.gov.uk/ukpga/1999/23/section/36

48 See https://www.judiciary.gov.uk/about-the-judiciary/who-are-the-judiciary/judicial-roles/judges/district-judge-mags-ct/ (accessed 18 July 2017) and "Magistrates and District Judges—two sides of the same coin?" at

consistently found that, compared with magistrates, DJs hear more cases, challenge and question all parties in a hearing, and exercise greater control over proceedings (Darbyshire 2002, 28–30; Morgan 2000, 2002). My observations support these findings: DJs do not rely on legal advisors—indeed their courts tend to be staffed by junior clerks—and proceedings are much brusquer and speedier because DJs "know the law" and because they frequently intervene to push cases forward to a conclusion. Despite the fact that DJs are legally qualified, I argue that magistrates and DJs exhibit a limited "judicial vision," manifested in a narrow focus on deciding individual culpability/responsibility for an offence, which involves stripping away nearly all relevant contextual information.

One reason why a contested trial is brief is because magistrates/DJs rely on the completed PET form, which sets out the charge, identifies witnesses (indeed whether witnesses even need to attend[49] or whether they can submit statements), and sets a time limit for the trial. It is difficult to establish from my data whether there is any correlation between whether a defendant was legally represented (or not) and the outcome of the case because so much depends on other factors, including the Crown's evidence, whether witnesses turn up to give evidence, and so on.

Table I.4. Hearings I observed, by gender and offence.

	Male	Female	Total (per cent)
Indictable only	28	2	28 (14 per cent)
Triable either way	45	10	60 (31 per cent)
Summary non-motoring	87	2	89 (46 per cent)
Summary motoring	20	3	23 (12 per cent)
Grand total	180 (92%)	17 (8%)	192

With regard to the hearings I observed (table I.4), 173 (72 per cent) of the 238 hearings for which I have adequate information were remand hearings (indicated as R1, R2 etc.). I observed 9 sentencing hearings (S1, etc.), 23 breach of bail hearings [BB1, etc.], 3 case management reviews (CM 1, etc.) and 8 legal applications (LA 1, etc.). I also observed 14

http://www.transformjustice.org.uk/magistrates-and-district-judges-two-sides-of-the-same-coin/ (accessed 1 September 2018).

[49] This can occur under Sec. 9 of the *Criminal Justice Act (2003)*, which allows the two parties to agree evidence to be submitted to the court rather than calling witnesses to give evidence.

statutory declarations (SD1, etc.), 17 requests for adjournment (A1, etc.), 5 video links (VL1, etc.), and 3 bail applications (BA 1, etc.). I also have data on 19 remand hearings when the defendant failed to attend, for which the court issued a summons for their arrest. In addition, I observed a small number of other types of cases. It often happened that a case was adjourned, sometimes for several days, for the defendant to be interviewed by probation or the mental health team; when this occurred, I was unable to attend the sentencing hearing.

With regard to extradition cases, I observed 6 extradition hearings (E1, E2, etc.) and 17 extradition bail applications (EB1, EB2, etc.) for which decisions were announced at a later date and I was unable to attend. Table I.4 sets out the number and type of remand hearings I observed and shows the distribution of cases in relation to the seriousness of the offence. The cases I observed are *not* representative of the range of criminal cases heard in magistrates' courts across London: I observed a far higher number of indictable offences, a slightly higher number of "either way" and summary non-motoring offences, and substantially fewer summary motoring cases. Even so, I have a sufficient number of each type of case to allow me to come to reasonable conclusions about how the court and different legal actors work, and how different types of cases are decided.

With respect to the 23 contested trials I observed (T1, T2, etc.), I have a record for 13 domestic violence cases, 4 cases of assault/criminal damage, 1 case alleging "intent to supply drugs," 1 case involving a motor vehicle accident, 2 cases held to vacate a trial date and set a new date, and several case management reviews that hinged on the failure of the CPS to disclose evidence before the trial. I draw on the trials I observed to provide greater insight about specific cases, the work of magistrates and DJs, how evidence is adduced, and how a verdict is reached.

The limitations of this study

A key problem arises because I was unable to observe "pre-trial procedures," that is, police interrogations, solicitor–client interviews, plea or charge bargaining (cf., Baldwin and McConville 1977; McConville and Baldwin 1981, 190 et passim; Baldwin and Feeney 1986; Sanders et al. 2010, chap. 9; Welch 2017). This is a limitation because events during the pre-trial stage can decisively shape the way in which "cases are constructed against defendants" by the police, because a defence solicitor may be unable to offer a defence for their client *or* because the offender's case is weak and would waste court time. This means that if the police pressured defendants to make a guilty plea and/or a defence solicitor did not take instructions or did not adequately prepare for their client's hearing, my understanding of the outcome of some prosecutions may be flawed.

Fieldwork was based primarily on participant observation, which means that I observed and took verbatim notes of everything that was said and done before, during, and after each case. I transcribed my handwritten notes into Word and key elements of each hearing/trial was entered on to an Excel spreadsheet, which has allowed me to quantify data and compare different types of hearings across fifty-eight different attributes from the sex and ethnicity of offenders, the type of hearing, offence, plea, and evidence proffered, whether they were represented, who presided over the hearing, the outcome, and so on. Normally I sat in the public gallery but sometimes I was allowed to sit in the "well" of the court to take notes. Sometimes I attended one court for an entire day; sometimes I attended a trial. Occasionally I was able to have informal conversations with judges, prosecutors, and defence lawyers. I have anonymised all the cases discussed in this book.

As McBarnet (1981, 189–90) found in her research in the 1970s, it is rare for anyone unconnected with a case to attend court. As she noted, "[T]he public in the lower court is an unusual phenomenon, and the purveyors of justice are somewhat sensitive to anyone seeing their particular brand of justice being done." I was frequently asked to state my business or whether I was a visiting magistrate. In one court where I brought post-graduate students to observe proceedings, magistrates laughed when told they were being observed by anthropologists.

The Metropolitan Police and the CPS declined my written requests to interview or talk with their staff. An attempt to set up meetings with magistrates to discuss their legal training and work was met with bureaucratic hurdles imposed by Her Majesties Courts & Tribunal Service; a similar request was ignored by the Magistrates Association. This situation is unfortunate and leaves potential gaps in my data, which I have attempted to fill-in by making Freedom of Information (FOI) requests and by examining official documents. As normally occurs when using FOI requests to understand how the government operates and what its policies are, official responses varied between providing helpful replies and being evasive (i.e., when officials seize upon key terms to rephrase or deny a request or by simply stating that my request would require far more time to answer than is allowed under the act justifying their refusal to answer).

It is important to note that where I report data that derives from a FOI request or where the source is an official Ministry of Justice or Home Office report, official data should be treated as provisonal. The provisional nature of official information arises because: (a) of the late reporting of many cases/statistics (a proportion of which are not included when each report is published); (b) it is the result of "data cleansing exercises"; and (c) subsequent publications do not adequately reconcile figures in earlier or alternative reports (UK 2012). In addition, government departments have changed the way they collect and report data, which creates gaps in data coverage.

I did *not* seek access to youth courts where similar cases are heard. In addition, I did *not* observe certain types of cases, for example the prosecution of government officials or police officers or the work of the UK Border Agency, which arrests and deports EU nationals who have no apparent means of support. Finally, given the limitations of time and resources, I did not follow cases that were referred by magistrates to the Crown courts because my purpose was to understand how magistrates' courts work and their impact on the lives of Londoners.

An outline of this book

Having set out my general approach to analysing magistrates' courts and legal procedure and in particular the vital distinction between the "language of the law" and the colloquial, spoken English relied upon by defendants, in chapter 1 I begin with a brief look at criminal procedure rules and at a typical court room "list" to clarify the daily workload of the courts. Next, I examine the different legal "actors" who can be observed in court, focusing primarily on magistrates/DJs, legal advisors, the Crown Prosecution Service, defence solicitors (including duty solicitors), Her Majesty's Courts & Tribunal Service officials, probation officers, and mental health teams. The chapter concludes by examining how summary criminal and motoring offences—and different types of legal "applications"—are processed; discussion highlights the roles and variable abilities of legal actors in a process marked by very quick hearings and high levels of guilty pleas.[50]

Magistrates' courts refer/remit indictable and some "either way" offences to the Crown court to be tried. Chapter 2 begins by sketching out the importance of the court's decision on "mode of trial"/choice of venue for a hearing, which results in either a case being referred to a Crown court for a jury trial or a speedy summary trial. To illustrate how serious crimes are processed, this chapter examines cases alleging homicide/murder,

---

[50] I do not examine sentencing guidelines. There are numerous studies about sentencing practices (e.g., Mews et al. 2015, etc.). To understand how sentencing guidelines are set, see the work of the Sentencing Council at https://www.sentencingcouncil.org.uk/consultations/.

assault/wounding, possession of a bladed instrument, sex offences, and theft. The cases provide insight into policing and decisions made by the CPS whose tasks have been substantially increased by new laws and whose work has been undermined by budget cuts and demands for efficiency. Analysis reveals that the government has consistently failed to address the underlying causes of crime, that large numbers of young black and ethnic minority defendants are being arrested and prosecuted (which was evident in the 2011 riots) and that many defendants were poorly defended.

Public order offences are offences that the police believe are intended to cause violence or to intimidate members of the public. Chapter 3 begins with a brief history of *The Public Order Act* (1986) and the language used in it and in related legislation to criminalise certain types of behaviour. I examine how the police and the CPS have used the act to successfully prosecute a very wide range of offences and "speech acts"; convictions have relied on the evidence provided by the police, not on independent evidence/corroboration. The successful prosecution of these offences also depends on technology—IT, phones, computers, and CCTV—rather than on detective work. I explore a range of cases—including Sec. 5 offences for uttering "disorderly and offensive words"—to illustrate the type of behaviour that is criminalised, the "evidence" used to convict/discharge individuals accused of these crimes, and the problematic way that judges assess "abusive" language.

Chapter 4 examines how domestic violence (DV) offences are prosecuted and decided. I begin by briefly reviewing the failure of the law and the courts to deal with this type of offence and cite statistics that show the very poor performance of the Metropolitan Police and the CPS in investigating and prosecuting these offences in London indicated, in part, by the very high number of cases dropped without being investigated or prosecuted. After setting out the law and legal guidance for the police and the CPS, I examine remand hearings and contested trials that strongly suggest that by adopting a narrow focus on individual culpability, the police, prosecutors, and magistrates fail to understand the history of the cases brought to court. This narrow judicial focus raises two further problems: whether the court can reach a just and sustainable decision (without a better understanding of a case) and whether a more serious prosecution should be mounted for "coercive control." What is also notable is that while the majority of DV cases occur in heterosexual relationships, this type of violence also occurs in same-sex relationships as well as against children, parents, and grandchildren. Indeed, the wide definition of "domestic violence" together with a focus on prosecuting a case even when defendants do not support a prosecution, raises questions about the need to rethink prosecution strategies and whether it is time to pursue alternative ways to address this type of abusive behaviour.

Chapter 5 examines how individuals are arrested and prosecuted for possessing cannabis, spice, ecstasy, heroin, and cocaine (I do not examine "complex" drug cases involving, for example, multiple-day trials of individuals accused of importing large amounts of illegal drugs). The cases that I examine illustrate Londoners' appetite for drugs, underlying levels of drug dependence, and how drugs are distributed/sold. As with public order offences, drug prosecutions raise important questions about "state-illegality relations" that reflect the social construction of crime, a process that selectively labels certain groups and behaviours as illegal while simultaneously ignoring the factors underlying such crimes, the selective policing of London using stop and search powers to arrest young men from BME communities, a focus on prosecuting possession (and an apparent reluctance to prosecute individuals for "intent to supply"), and evidence that individuals found guilty of the same offence receive different sentences.

Chapter 6 explores prosecutions for fraud (i.e., "victimless" crimes). These cases provide interesting insights into London as a metropolitan city and about how residents become caught up in different types of fraud. Fraud is a rapidly growing offence that has a huge social impact, but *very* few investigations and prosecutions are successful, largely because the state has consistently failed to set out and properly fund a national policy on fraud. I begin by examining how the government defines and prosecutes fraud and together with my observation of extradition bail applications and hearings, I identify potential links to organised crime that are not pursued by the police, the CPS/judicial authority, or the courts. As I found in DV and drug prosecutions, a narrow focus on individual culpability prevents the authorities from seeing the "wider layers of association," actions, and events that link individual defendants with organized criminal groups (OCGs). What is not seen is not investigated or prosecuted—only a small number of individuals at the lowest tier of OCGs are prosecuted.

I conclude by discussing the importance of four interrelated factors that have emerged from my fieldwork and that undermine the "over-riding objective" of the criminal justice system, which is to acquit the innocent and convict the guilty. The factors include the role played by key legal actors, the significance and impact of the legal language used to charge and try defendants, the impact of legal procedures specific to summary justice, and the narrow focus on individual culpability by magistrates and DJs. These factors, which have been exacerbated by austerity measures imposed by the government, have the effect of shunting problems from one part of the Criminal Justice System to another, all the while compounding delays and creating injustice. The book ends by proposing basic reforms to how magistrates' courts should work.

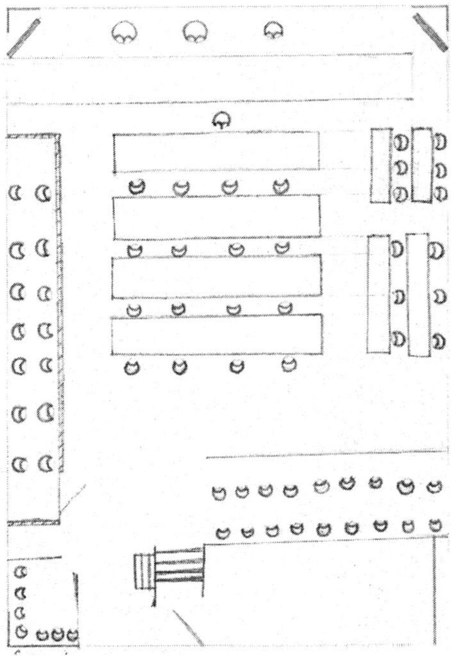

Figure I.1. Enclosed dock (left side): Courtroom no. 1, City of London Magistrate's Court © Alex Campbell.

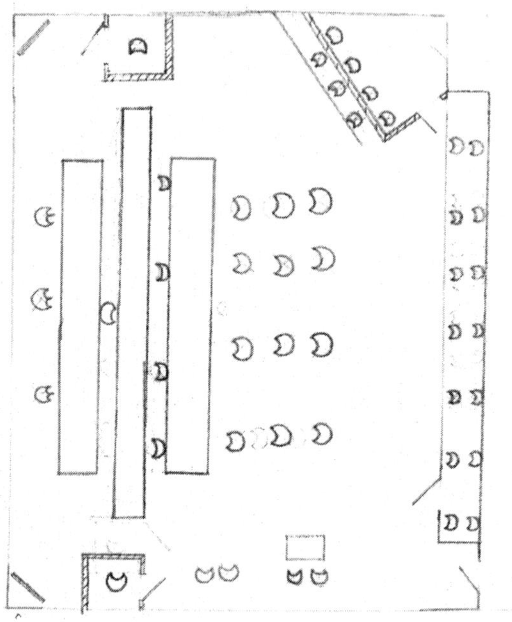

Figure I.2. Pleading bar and dock (top-right corner): Highbury Corner Magistrate's Court, London © Alex Campbell.

CHAPTER 1

MAGISTRATES' COURTS, LEGAL ACTORS, AND SUMMARY JUSTICE

In this chapter I examine the principal work of magistrates' courts, which is to apply "summary justice" to hear and decide "minor" criminal offences. It is important to recall that "pre-trial" processes undertaken by the police are responsible for bringing a defendant to court to be prosecuted (NAO 2016a; Sanders 2002).[1] The process begins with the police recording a reported incident as a "crime." Once this happens officers decide whether there is sufficient evidence to prosecute a case (if not, they "drop" the case). Alternatively, the police may deal with an incident by issuing an "out of court disposal" mechanism, that is, a "caution," a Penalty Notice for Disorder (PNDs),[2] and so on. Once the police record an incident as a crime, they are required to "investigate" it and to create a case file. Completed case files are passed to the CPS for legal advice and, at this point, a case may be discontinued/dropped, or it may be sent to a magistrates' court to be prosecuted. At the court the case is "listed" for a hearing. At each stage many cases are discontinued or dropped in a process that results in less than half of all reported incidents being listed for a hearing in a magistrates' court.[3] In addition, many cases that are prosecuted in a magistrates' court, including cases in which the defendant pleaded not guilty in anticipation of a trial, are also discontinued by the CPS.

The courts are expected to follow the Criminal Procedure Rules, and they are tasked with trying the cases that are listed near the entrance of every court. This chapter begins with an introduction to the "rules" and a discussion of court lists. In section ii, I outline the work of key legal

---

[1] See the quarterly and annual reports produced by the Ministry of Justice.

[2] See https://www.gov.uk/government/publications/penalty-notices-for-disorder-guidance-for-police-officers.

[3] Between June 2016 and June 2017 in England and Wales, only 10 per cent of recorded crimes resulted in a charge; 47 per cent "were closed because officers were unable to find the culprits." Police closed investigations into 2.2 million crimes (see "Millions of offences go unsolved," *Times*, 20 October 2017).

"actors," which includes magistrates, District Judges, the Crown prosecutor, the police, legal representatives/lawyers, HMCS court staff, and probation officers/the mental health team. In section iii I look at how summary cases are prosecuted to show how legal actors *perform* their work. I also look briefly at the importance of Statutory Declarations and other legal applications, including Applications in the Interest of Justice. I conclude by drawing attention to the way that defendants are "silenced" by legal procedure—aspects of which are explored in detail in subsequent chapters—which ensures quick, summary decisions.

i. Criminal procedural rules and the court "list"

The objective of the CJS is to implement the Criminal Procedure Rules (Ministry of Justice 2015b), which state that the "overriding objective" is that "criminal cases be dealt with justly." The Procedural Rules explain that this phrase should be understood to mean:

> (a) acquitting the innocent and convicting the guilty; (b) dealing with the prosecution and the defence fairly; (c) recognizing the rights of a defendant . . . ; (d) respecting the interests of witnesses, victims and jurors . . . ; (e) dealing with the case efficiently and expeditiously; (f) ensuring that appropriate information is available to the court when bail and sentencing are considered; and (g) dealing with the case in ways that take into account (i) the gravity of the offence, (ii) the complexity of what is at issue, (iii) the severity of the consequences for the defendant and others affected, and (iv) the needs of other cases.

Dealing with cases "justly" requires that *all* parties involved in the CJS work together to a high professional standard. Rule 3.2 specifically tasks the court with pursuing its overriding objective by exercising the power given to it by legislation and to apply the practice directions and interpret rules in a manner that allows it to "case-manage" the process to ensure that cases progress through the courts in an orderly and just fashion. In what follows I show what this means in practice.

Magistrates/DJs hear and decide the cases referred to the court by the CPS. They are not given information about the cases until the morning of the hearing, nor are they made aware of what steps the police and the CPS have or have not taken to construct and prosecute a case. Near the entrance of each court there is a central bulletin board on which is pinned the court lists for all courtrooms where hearings are scheduled; a separate list is also pinned on the door of each courtroom. A copy of the list for Courtroom 6 at Westminster Magistrates' Court for 22 August 2017 can be found in Box 1.1. These lists show very basic information about the cases scheduled for a hearing: the name of the defendant, the police unit pressing the charge, and the defendant's case number.

Box 1.1. Court list, Courtroom 6 at Westminster Magistrates' Court, 22 August 2017.

Public List for 02/08/2017
Westminster Magistrates' Court
181 Marylebone Road, London NW1 5BR

List	Name		Room	Case Number
10	Alexis, Phabrizio	MPHQ Units	06	1701976247
2	Bridgeman, Joshua Mr	MPHQ Units	06	1701934854
3	Burke, David	MPHQ Units	06	1701730221
1	Halliburton, C Mr	MPHQ Units	06	1701740529
4	Joseph, Mark	MPHQ Units	06	1701947110
5	Lemos-Thompson, J Mr	MPHQ Units	06	1701991718
11	Lyttle, Aron Mr	MPHQ Units	06	1701130991
6	McMahon, Claire G Ms	MPHQ Units	06	1701162324
7	Pardehar, Omid Mr	MPHQ Units/ Charing Cross CJU	06	1701874223
8	Puglisi AKA Michael Johns	MPHQ Units	06	1701672272
9	Santos, Lawrence Mr	MPHQ Units	06	1701944094

It is impossible to tell from the court list what crime an individual is charged with. Indeed, for some courts there are no lists (though an official may later assemble one). Indeed, some courts did not have a functioning electronic data system, which means that magistrates/DJs did not have access to the "papers" on a case until after the proceedings begin (in some courts the Crown prosecutor was asked to hand his/her laptop or papers up to the bench so that magistrates could see case documents).[4]

A list may identify between two and twenty individuals whose cases are to be heard, though each case is likely to raise a different legal issue. Indeed, the length of a list and the diversity of cases listed for hearing varies and depends in part on whether magistrates/DJs are scheduled to hear traffic or regulatory offences (in which cases the list may contain upwards of forty cases) or "custody" cases. Traffic cases are usually heard in one courtroom, whereas custody and bail cases are heard in a courtroom that is linked via a secure passage to the custody cells in the basement. Alternatively, the court may use a video link to a police station, a prison, or a secure room.

[4] In January 2019 the secure email went down, rapidly followed by the collapse of the Ministry of Justice's computer network linking lawyers, judges, probation workers, and court staff (see Owen Boycott, "Justice ministry knew court IT systems were 'obsolete', papers reveal," *Guardian*, 28 January 2019).

A more accurate idea about the number and diverse nature of cases that magistrates/DJs hear is provided in Box 1.2, which is taken from my field notes; this is a list of the cases actually heard in Courtroom 6 at Westminster Magistrates' Court on 22 August 2017. On this day thirteen defendants appeared. Some of the cases were on the initial list, some were "floats" (individuals whose names had been left off all court lists and that were allocated during the course of the day), and other cases were referred to Courtroom 6 to be sentenced.

Box 1.2. Cases I observed, Courtroom 6, Westminster Magistrates' Court, 22 August 2017.

Court opened at 10 am

1. A white male in his forties was remanded into custody to await trial for a criminal offence.
2. A young black male had been referred for a mental health assessment, but the report was not available, and the case was adjourned for a week.
3. An application was granted to "vacate" a trial date and set a new date.
4. The defendant failed to attend his hearing and a warrant was issued for his arrest.
5. A forty-year-old Asian male pleaded not guilty to theft and "assault by beating" and a trial date was set.
6. A male Indian national in his late forties was charged with committing fraud and was remanded into custody to await trial at a Crown court.
   Court adjourned for lunch from 1–2 pm.
7. A thirty-seven-year-old black male who had been found guilty of possessing cocaine was sentenced.
8. A white male in his fifties who had pleaded guilty to breaching bail conditions was "returned" to Bournemouth Crown court (where he had originally been tried) for sentencing.
9. A frail looking white male was sent for a mental health assessment under a Paragraph 5 order and his case was adjourned.
10. A forty-one-year-old white male was charged with breaching his bail conditions and was sent back to Portsmouth Crown court for sentencing.
11. A black male in his early twenties was sentenced for possession of class B drugs and for assault. Legal aid was transferred to a new solicitor who made an application to reopen his conviction (which was refused). He was found guilty of both offences, fined £650, sentenced to 150-hours unpaid community work and a community/restriction order was imposed on him.
12. A white male in his late forties had breached post-sentence bail and had been picked up by the police and placed in the cells. He was sent back to Brighton to be sentenced (where he had been tried).
13. A black male in his thirties from Mauritius who was not legally represented was referred for a full mental health assessment under Paragraph 5.
14. At least two cases initially listed for the court were transferred to another court.

Court adjourned at 4:38 pm.

ii. Legal actors

The administration of justice depends upon the ability of different public institutions to work together to ensure that justice is delivered. Each institution plays a specific role in the CJS and its work is taken forward by a designated official who appears in court. Indeed, defendants, witnesses, and victims are expected to work together to achieve justice.

Magistrates are supposed to be recruited from the communities that a court serves.[5] Most magistrates are white males in their fifties, though an increasing number of women (and to a much more limited extent, individuals from black and ethnic minority communities) have recently been appointed. Demographically speaking, magistrates are *not* representative of the communities they are appointed to serve: in 2018 about 55 per cent of magistrates were female, 12 per cent declared themselves BAME, and 4 per cent were under forty years of age; whereas, 55 per cent were aged sixty years or over (MoJ 2018a).

As unpaid "laymen" who are given minimal legal training, magistrates are required to administer summary justice in short legal proceedings. The jurisdiction and power of magistrates' courts are set out in Statutory Instruments made by Parliament or by the Lord Chancellor. A magistrate's role is to determine what the law is and, with assistance from a legal adviser and as set out in Procedural Rules and Practice Directions, to apply the relevant law in deciding criminal matters. For serious criminal matters, magistrates sit as a "bench" in twos or threes and are presided over by a "chair" who speaks for the bench (the justification for a bench is that by sitting together they minimise any errors of fact-finding and sentencing). Magistrates and benches vary considerably in terms of their experience and their ability to decide cases. Magistrates' decisions must be explained by setting out clear reasons. In addition to hearing and deciding criminal cases, magistrates/DJs also sentence defendants to a maximum of six months imprisonment for an either-way offence.[6] In addition they may release individuals on bail or "remand" them into custody to await a trial or for sentencing, release/discharge defendants, refer defendants for a mental

---

[5] Officially, magistrates must live within fifteen miles of a court; they must be adults under sixty-five years but need not be a British citizen. They must apply for the post and are required to be of "good character, understanding and communication, social awareness, maturity and sound temperament, sound judgement and commitment and reliability" (Darbyshire 2002, 294).

[6] See: "Magistrates' Court Sentencing Guidelines," at https://www.sentencingcouncil.org.uk/wp-content/uploads/Sept-2015-MCSG-pdf1.pdf (accessed 2 July 2017).

health assessment, grant police warrants,[7] and deal with civil matters (e.g., council tax payment[8]) (Gibson and Gordon 2008; Darbyshire 2002; Donoghue 2014; Gibbs 2016). As the cases cited in this book make clear, magistrates often address a defendant's "moral career," which is cited as a justification for the individualised sentence they impose in the belief that the court plays an important therapeutic role (King 1978, 212).

District Judges are qualified lawyers who are appointed[9] to sit in urban areas with high criminal caseloads. Individuals must apply and are expected to meet the same basic criteria as magistrates; individuals may be appointed to a full-time post or to a salaried part-time or fee-paid post. The characteristic feature of hearings presided over by a DJ is that while they sit over the same kinds of cases as magistrates hear, they decide cases alone. Gibb (2016, 4) reports tensions between magistrates and DJs; however, I did not witness a "mixed bench" in action and cannot comment on this issue. DJs frequently intervene in hearings, are better at case managing hearings, and are more likely to impose a custodial sentence. Because DJs know the law, they dispense with legal advisers and are serviced by a clerk, who takes notes of the proceedings.

Magistrates are advised on all legal issues by a *legal adviser* (or LA, this position was formerly called the court clerk). "Consultation" between the bench and the LA occurs throughout the proceedings. Legal advisers are qualified criminal solicitors or barristers who sit directly below the bench. LAs are expected to "know the law,"[10] to advise the bench on legal issues, provide guidance for sentencing defendants and to make a record of proceedings (Holvast 2016). Statutory changes in the role of the clerk/LA have resulted in "a blurring of their advisory and judicial roles" (Sanders et al. 2010, 514–18; Donaghue 2014, 942). As with all the legal actors I observed, LAs exhibit varying skills and degrees of competence: some regularly intervene during a hearing to "advise" the court, admonish the Crown, or cajole a witness, whereas others take a backseat during the

[7] The public is excluded from court when police ask magistrates for search warrants.

[8] For instance, on 16 October 2017 at Wimbledon Magistrates' Court seventy individuals were "listed" for a hearing in Courtroom 11 because they had failed to pay their council tax. Similar hearings were occurring across London. See "Thousands of UK's poor in court over non-payment of council tax," *Guardian*, 18 October 2013, and "Begging prosecutions increase dramatically across England and Wales," *Guardian*, 30 November 2014.

[9] See "Becoming a Judge," at https://www.judiciary.gov.uk/about-the-judiciary/judges-career-paths/becoming-a-judge/ (accessed 3 August 2017).

[10] LAs roles are set out in *The Access to Justice Act* (1999, amended) and in various Practice Directions and Guidelines.

hearing.[11] During proceedings, LAs intervene to keep cases on track and to prevent any breaches of the rules, particularly by defendants, who are told how to conduct themselves in court. When LAs interrupt defendants, for example to clarify their evidence, they "prompt" the defendant by suggesting a form of words that they should adopt to answer questions from the magistrates.

LAs decide all points of law raised during a hearing but they "must not play any part in making findings of fact" and can only assist magistrates whose responsibility it is to decide a case. Importantly LAs are expected to help unrepresented defendants by explaining what will happen in court, what the procedural rules are, and what a defendant's legal position is. I was told that LAs intervene if they feel the bench is relatively inexperienced; however, it was not always clear whether this was the case.

The *Crown Prosecution Service* (CPS) was created following the enactment of *The Prosecution of Offences Act* (1985) in an attempt to improve public confidence in the CJS by counter-balancing the power of the police and, pursuant to Art. 6 of the *European Convention on Human Rights*, to ensure "equality of arms" between the prosecution and the defence. The CPS is responsible for overseeing all criminal prosecutions, which means that in addition to stopping prosecutions going forward when there is "no realistic prospect of conviction" or when "the public interest" no longer requires a prosecution, they also prosecute cases on behalf of the state (cf., Sharpling 2006, 41).

Sanders has argued that because its structural position vis-à-vis the police is weak, "the CPS has rarely dropped cases that were evidentially weak" (2002, 157). He attributes this to "organizational pressures" to "win" cases (i.e., to get a conviction), that the CPS is not "completely independent" of the police, and that the powers of the CPS "are an inadequate match for the resources of the police" (Sanders 1994, 121–23; Sanders et al. 2010, chap. 7). The CPS relies on the cases that the police construct, but as Box 1.3 makes clear, the police fail to arrest and prosecute offenders for the majority of reported crimes. Sanders (2002, 123) notes that "[T]he point at issue here is that, since initial decisions to caution or take no action are the province of the police, crown prosecutors are generally presented only with cases which the police want prosecuted." Furthermore, case screening by prosecutors is perfunctory because they lack the resources to open up cases for investigation; this means that at best a case is scanned for internal inconsistencies that might undermine a prosecution.

[11] During the course of proceedings in one courtroom, the court's IT systems went down four times during the morning, which impeded the LA from keeping a record of proceedings.

Box 1.3. Police outcomes by year, 2016–18.

	Year ending March 2017		**Year ending March 2018**	
Outcome type/group	**Number of outcomes**	**Rate**	**Number of outcomes**	**Rate**
Charged/Summonsed	517,118	12.0	442,717	9.1
Taken into consideration[6]	10,087	0.2	6758	0.1
Out-of-court (formal)	116,211	2.7	87,597	1.8
Caution—youths	15,253	0.4	11,139	0.2
Caution—adults	83,224	1.9	63,608	1.3
Penalty Notices for Disorder	17,734	0.4	12,850	0.3
Out-of-court (informal)	142,358	3.3	127,587	2.6
Cannabis/khat warning	33,134	0.8	31,051	0.6
Community resolution	109,224	2.5	96,536	2.0
Prosecution prevented or not in the public interest	61,284	1.4	62,461	1.3
Offender died	1318	0.0	1819	0.0
Not in public interest (CPS)	3022	0.1	2112	0.0
Not in public interest (Police)	29,993	0.7	29,917	0.6
Prosecution prevented—suspect underage	6373	0.1	7623	0.2
Prosecution prevented—suspect too ill	11,528	0.3	11,909	0.2
Prosecution prevented—victim/key witness dead/too ill	1602	0.0	1716	0.0
Prosecution time-limit expired	7448	0.2	7365	0.2
Evidential difficulties (suspect identified; victim supports action)	449,093	10.4	434,500	8.9
Evidential difficulties (victim does not support action)	758,047	17.5	975,333	20.0
Evidential difficulties: suspect not identified; victim does not support further action	175,629	4.1	226,125	4.6
Evidential difficulties: suspect identified; victim does not support further action	582,418	13.5	749,208	15.4
Investigation complete—no suspect identified	2,098,367	48.6	2,316,610	47.5
Total offences	4,230,518	97.9	4,566.783	93.6

Recent research and news coverage have raised fresh questions about whether the CPS acts to realise an equality of arms between the state and defence counsel/defendants. For instance, Soubise (2018) notes that following the introduction of the "Optimum Business Model" in 2008—adopted in response to the need to be "more efficient" and save money—the CPS case management process has fragmented. Cases are no longer allocated to qualified Crown prosecutors but split up and allocated across a "team" with each member undertaking a limited task on a single case.[12] The division of tasks is split between charge, pre-trial hearings, trial, and sentencing; experienced prosecutors take "serious" crimes and less experienced Associate Prosecutors (AP)[13] are assigned to prosecute cases in magistrates' and youth courts.

Unlike Crown prosecutors, APs are not supposed to take "legal decisions"—that is, to alter or drop charges, to negotiate a plea, to disclose evidence or discontinue a prosecution, and so on—in the cases they are assigned to prosecute; they are supposed to seek advice from a prosecutor before taking any legal decision. However, weaknesses/evidential problems in a case often emerge during or after the hearing,[14] at which point it may not be possible to adjourn to seek advice. This means that APs make (sometimes wrongful) decisions on a case themselves. Serious problems can arise when defendants are not legally represented, if a defendant is unduly constrained to plead guilty (Helms 2019; and see chapter 3) or when a duty solicitor adopts a "passive role" by failing to question the Crown's evidence. Unfortunately, many duty solicitors adopt a passive role in court that legitimates the position pursued by the Crown: this situation is likely to arise when magistrates (rather than DJs) are sitting and when police evidence is not tested, perhaps because a defendant pleaded guilty.

In recent years the structural dependence of the CPS on the police, together with the impact of budget cuts on services and managerial oversight has led to a rising number of "miscarriages of justice"[15] (Sklansky

---

[12] Investigations by the National Audit Office (2006, 2016) have consistently highlighted problems at every stage of the police investigation and during CPS case preparation, trial, and sentencing, which have led to "cracked" trials, delays, and a failure to "resolve" cases at a time when there are growing financial pressures on the CJS (though defence lawyers also contribute to this problem).

[13] APs vary in the level of their experience and training; once appointed they are given a two-week training programme following which they are expected to pass a competence assessment and to "work shadow" a colleague before taking cases.

[14] For example, when trials collapse and when the Crown fails to disclose key evidence (see footnote 17). See: "Judge condemns court blunders" and "Failed CPS lawyers are paid off with public money" (*Times*, 20 October 2017); "Evidence disclosure failure rife in criminal practice, survey discloses" (*Law Society Gazette*, 27 February 2018); and "Police chief admits 'cultural problem' with evidence disclosure" (*Guardian*, 24 January 2018).

[15] See: "CPS criticized for 'wilful, calculated and prolonged disobedience' in trial" (*Bureau of Investigative Journalism*, 14 January 2014); "You must say no or 'rapist' may walk free" (*Evening Standard*, 22 January 2018); "More than nine hundred prosecutions collapse in a year over failure to disclose evidence" (*Telegraph*, 24 January 2018).

2017) that may be linked to a failure by magistrates to question CPS arguments. In addition, and as Table 1.1 shows, the CPS has discontinued and/or dropped large numbers of prosecutions before or during legal proceedings for reasons that are far from clear.[16] Furthermore, the police and the CPS have consistently failed to disclose key evidence to the defence before trial as required by law[17] (Baldwin and Feeney 1986; Plotnikoff and Woolfson 2001; Judiciary of England and Wales 2014).[18] While neither of these problems are new, the efficiencies that the police and the CPS are being asked to deliver in the face of continued budget cuts undermines their ability to cope with mounting case work, inadequate ICT systems, and tight deadlines (HMIC 2017).

Solicitors and duty solicitors (DS) represent defendants. My observations suggest that solicitors paid by a defendant spend more time taking instructions from their clients and provide better legal representation; they also appeared to actively defend their clients (when there was sufficient evidence) and they regularly offered mitigation following a guilty verdict.

---

[16] Prosecutors can terminate proceedings in a magistrates' court by discontinuance under section 23 of the *Prosecution of Offences Act 1985*, applying to withdraw the summons or charge, or offering no evidence. Prosecutions may also be discontinued if the Crown decides it is not in the public interest to proceed (CPS 2019c; CPS 2019/2020). "Discontinuance avoids the need for a court hearing and the unnecessary attendance of the parties. It enables a defendant in custody to be released immediately without the need to wait until the next hearing. For these reasons, and particularly where it is intended to discontinue the entire proceedings, the preferred method of termination is discontinuance whenever possible."

[17] Between 2014 and 2017 the CPS dropped or discontinued over 320,000 cases prior to prosecution in England and Wales. In London courts, 247,382 cases were dropped (FOI Request no. 7679, 30 April 2018 from the CPS). This is clearly a growing problem caused by a shortage of prosecutors, poorly trained police officers, and the growing importance of mobile phones, CCTV, laptops, and other digital information that has to be reviewed (see "CPS 'struggling to cope' with burden to disclose evidence to defendants," *Guardian*, 9 January 2020).

[18] In *R 238*, a "domestic criminal assault," defence counsel successfully argued that the CPS had repeatedly failed to disclose evidence before the trial. Counsel filed a "wasted costs" application. Similar arguments were made in *R 219*, in which the defendant was charged with stalking.

Table 1.1. Discontinued and dropped prosecutions by the Crown Prosecution Service in magistrates' courts, youth courts, and crown courts, 2014 to 2016.[19]

	2014		2015		2016		2017	
	Dis-continued	**Dropped**	**Dis-continued**	**Dropped**	**Dis-continued**	**Dropped**	**Dis-continued**	**Dropped**
London	3673	13,307	3979	13,690	4533	14,366	4,136	12,154
England & Wales	25,378	71,612	21,891	66,830	17,942	58,644	15,552	50,296

[19] Source: Reply to FOI Request 7679 dated 30 April 2018 from the Crown Prosecution Service.

However, most defendants rely on legal-aided duty solicitors who are attached to a court and who are paid on a pro-rata basis[20] for the number of clients they "assist," not for the quality of the service they provide their clients or the outcome of the case. The assistance provided by many duty solicitors appears to be minimal and may constitute little more than advising a defendant to plead guilty. Duty solicitors may do little more than attempt to negotiate a reduced or altered charge in return for a guilty plea or they may or may not offer mitigation following a guilty plea or verdict. In short, and as the cases discussed in this book illustrate, the quality of legal representation by some duty solicitors is questionable; many offer a passive defence and do not question the Crown's evidence (it is possible that this situation reflects limited pre-trial access to a defendant).

As McConville and Baldwin (1981, 190) found in their research at Birmingham Crown court, "police investigations are decisive in most cases, and the characteristic feature of the criminal justice system . . . is not public adjudication of responsibility but public proclamation of guilt," that is defendants plead guilty at the first opportunity during their remand hearing. This situation arises because,

> the need to build up the strongest case against the defendant requires the police to obtain the best evidence and it is understandable if they wish to do so in the least time-consuming and most efficient way. From the police viewpoint, confessions are the most convenient means of gaining convictions. Police work is, therefore, heavily geared towards obtaining admissions from suspects. (Ibid., 192)

In the past, police treatment of defendants has ranged from the offer of various forms of "persuasion" to plead guilty, to extended periods of confinement and using intimidation to secure a conviction. In parallel with pressures from the police, Baldwin and McConville (1977) found that some defence barristers were pressured by "deficiencies in the criminal justice system"—that is, the interrogation of suspects while in custody and the practice of allowing a discount in sentence for a guilty plea—to "negotiate justice" by convincing a defendant to plead guilty (perhaps because they have a weak case) rather than proceed to trial.[21]

---

[20] Unrepresented defendants are identified by custody officers or by a legal advisor who ask a duty solicitor to assist a defendant to prepare their case; this often means going into the cells to interview a defendant and "take instructions." Frequently duty solicitors take on multiple clients, which means they have limited time to prepare a case.

[21] Subsequent research by McConville et al. (1994) found that while defence solicitors often encountered situations in which they were unable to access their

Subsequent policy interventions in the CJS appear to have reinforced a trend towards the non-adversarial outcome of cases. Two key changes are important in this respect. First, in the late 1970s defence lawyers working in magistrates' courts disclosed their case to the prosecution in an attempt to understand the prosecution's case (Baldwin and Feeney 1986, 599f) even though disclosure[22] was not required and it might have undermined their ability to defend their client. It was not until 2005[23] that both parties were required to disclose[24] their case before trial in an attempt to cut costs and "improve efficiency." Second, in 2005 the "Narey reforms" introduced "plea before venue" to speed-up and streamline case management to reduce the time between arrest and arraignment. These reforms have put pressure on defence solicitors to expedite cases rather than act in their client's best interests (Sanders et al. 2010, 452).

---

client—in custody and at the early stages of case preparation—and were thus denied access to key information about the case, there were serious defects in the training and organisation of criminal defence practices. The situation gave rise to reactive rather than proactive practices in which "the defence trails the prosecution in adopting a strategy of case disposal through guilty plea" (276). See also Welsh (2013).

[22] "The meaning of disclosure, in simple terms, is the obligation of the prosecution to serve on the defence unused material which may reasonably be capable of undermining the prosecution case or assisting the defence. This must be done in a timely manner to assist the defendant in preparation for trial and the court in case management of the issues. It is not a one-way process. The defence must play their part, by identifying the issues in dispute, thereby helping the prosecution to make informed decisions" (UK 2014, ¶8).

[23] The key change occurred with the introduction of Criminal Procedure Rules in 2005 that compelled both parties to disclose their case before trial. The revised 2015 rule is I(A)1 (see https://www.judiciary.uk/wp-content/uploads/2015/09/crim-pd-2015.pdf, accessed 6 August 2017). While there has been research examining the quality of legal practice in the Crown courts (e.g., Hunter et al. 2018), no recent studies have been undertaken in magistrates' courts.

[24] I observed two contested trials for domestic violence that did not proceed as scheduled because the CPS failed to disclose its case to the defence. In case *T 12*, following the Crown's failure to make two deadlines to disclose, the court ordered the Crown to provide all the requested evidence by the morning of the trial (the defence threatened a "wasted costs application" if the Crown failed). In case *T 17* the defence threatened to make an application for "abuse of process" against the Crown and asked for the trial to be put back (which the magistrates did). Defence lawyers have few effective sanctions available to them when the Crown fails to disclose unused evidence and so on (UK 2014, 39–40).

In addition, Welch (2017, 584) has shown that legal-aid cuts[25] and the reintroduction of means testing[26] has deleteriously affected defence solicitors. She argues that "the remuneration regime means that the quality of legally aided defence services suffers, while the data suggests that changes brought about by introducing means testing have caused delay and uncertainty for lawyers, which also appears to have a negative impact on lawyer/client relationships." Given continued cuts in criminal legal aid for lawyers working in magistrates' courts, it is possible that the quality of legally aided work has declined (partly because barristers instruct their pupils to take up this work).

Probation Officers/Mental Health Teams are assigned to every court. My observations[27] indicate that magistrates refer a high percentage of defendants to probation officers/the mental health team to assess: a defendant's background, family, and employment situation; whether s/he has a drink or drug problem; to check their criminal record (and if so whether s/he is complying with reporting requirements); and to recommend suitable sentencing arrangements. A bench/DJ can accept or disregard the assessment.[28] Their important role was clearly stretched by staff shortages: depending on the court, sentencing was adjourned anywhere between an hour and 2–3 weeks to wait for a probation report to be produced.

The reason for these delays stem from reforms introduced in 2013 when the government decided to "open up service delivery to a wider range

---

[25] On 29 March 2018 the Criminal Bar Association, supported by legally-aided solicitors, called for solicitors and barristers to take "direct action" by refusing to take instructions or work for lower fees (see "'Direct Action' over cuts starts on Sunday, barristers announce," *Law Society Gazette* (accessed 2 July 2018).

[26] Access to a "legally aided" lawyer requires defendants to pass a means test to determine whether their income is low enough to qualify. The average income qualification for legal aid has been consistently lowered by the Government, which means that relatively few people qualify for legal aid; they must either pay for a lawyer or represent themselves in court. The guidance can be found at https://www.gov.uk/guidance/work-out-who-qualifies-for-criminal-legal-aid (accessed on 5 2 July 2018). Also see Sanders et al. 2010, 503f.

[27] Research strongly indicates that magistrates are not making use of their power under Sec. 47/48 of the *Mental Health Act (1983)* to refer individuals to a hospital for assessment or treatment, apparently due to the absence of information available to them and due to a lack of confidence in the effectiveness of community sentences (Magistrates Association 2019, paragraphs 16–20). The Centre for Justice Innovation (2018) reports a 22 per cent fall in the number of pre-sentence reports requested by the court.

[28] Probation Officers typically possess GCSEs, for a job description see: https://www.probationservicesofficer.co.uk/the-role.html.

of providers to achieve efficiencies, encourage innovation and extend rehabilitative provision to more offenders" (NAO 2014, 6). Trusts in England ceased operation in 2014 and were replaced by twenty-one "regional companies" and a reduced role for what was left of the National Probation Service (NPS). Subsequent reports by the Chief Inspector of Probation found that privatisation has "left the public at greater risk" (HM Inspectorate of Probation 2016). More recent evidence has emerged that private probation companies have failed to stop criminal re-offending because they are "doing little more than signposting and form filling."[29] In short, the privatisation of probation services has failed and is leaving large numbers of defendants with drug and alcohol problems to be sentenced without any prospect of treatment before or during their incarceration (Law Commission 2016; House of Commons 2018a).

Her Majesty's Courts & Tribunal Service (HMCTS) is an executive agency of the Ministry of Justice that undertakes a wide range of administrative roles in the courts and in tribunals. As with other institutions, their budget[30] has been severely cut. HMCTS staff members include legal advisers, clerks, ushers, administrators, IT-personnel,[31] court security, custody officers, and others. HMCTS is responsible for the poor quality of existing photocopy services, non-functional desktop computers, and the frequent failure of video links, which connect courts to a prison or to a secure facility where a witness can give evidence.

As with many institutions, much of their work is invisible to the public. This is particularly the case with managing the custody cells, which are located in the basement of magistrates' courts. A brief description of the custody suite/cells[32] at Hammersmith Magistrates' Court provides some idea about their work. In late 2017 I was given a tour of the custody suit by

---

[29] See "Probation service contracts unsustainable, say providers" (*Financial Times*, 12 October 2016); "Probation firms facing heavy losses" (*Times*, 21 March 2018); "Private firms 'failing to stop criminals reoffending'" and "Private parole companies 'lack resources for the job'" (*Observer*, 4 February 2018).

[30] Between 2010/11 and 2017 the government cut the budget of the Ministry of Justice by 40 per cent; the budget for HMCS was cut by 26 per cent. See "Cuts have left court system 'close to breaking point' and have left its credibility at risk, say MPs" (*Independent*, 26 May 2016) and "Public services face real-terms spending cuts of up to 40% by 2020" (*Guardian*, 22 November 2017).

[31] Despite plans for an expensive upgrade in court IT services in 2016, there was little progress to be seen in courts, which were experiencing problems with all aspects of court IT (see "Court IT upgrade complete by 2020, HMCTs chief," *Law Society Gazette*, 18 March 2016).

[32] Some idea of conditions in the custody suite is provided by an HMIC (2011) inspection report; the survey of prisoners is particularly interesting.

a serving officer; the suit was empty because the court was about to be closed.

In the basement of the courthouse there were thirty-six cells organised roughly in a U-shape, with men and women at separate ends of the corridor. There were two large holding cells for five to six individuals (one for men and a separate one for women), thirty cells for men, and four cells for women. Each wing had one toilet and one cell where detainees who "acted up" could be kept (these cells were slightly larger and differed from the other cells only in that they contained a toilet). Each cell was roughly the same size: nine feet by nine feet by ten feet high. Each cell contained a wooden bench attached to the wall on which was fixed a cushion. Each cell had a blue metal cell door with a peephole allowing officers to check on detainees. The walls were covered with yellow tiles. When the court was busy, as many as forty defendants could be held at a time. Detainees were brought to court at around eight a.m. and most were removed by six p.m., though some remained as late as midnight. Secure transport was provided by Serco and G4S, which are multinational companies contracted to provide key public services to government. All the staff—there were three present—were to be made redundant. My guide had worked in this suite for twenty years.

iii. The main work of the court: prosecuting minor summary offences

As Carlen (1976b, 42) and others have noted, "Magistrates are expected to dispose judiciously and lawfully of all matters brought before them; the other participants are expected to provide information which will assist the court in reaching its judicial decision." The "business" of the court requires that all "actors" play their part to bring a case to a conclusion, a process that begins with the police providing evidence of wrongdoing.

Table 1.1 lists the different types of "summary" offences that I observed. Summary motoring cases constituted approximately 39 per cent of all the initial/remand hearings I observed. These offences included failure to pay road tax, drink-driving, driving while disqualified, failing to insure a vehicle, and so on. Interestingly, the outcome of these cases is not a foregone conclusion. In this chapter I draw upon some of these cases to illustrate the role played by magistrates/DJs, the effect of "legal language" on proceedings, and the rapidity of the hearings. During a remand hearing, a defendant can only speak "through" their legal representative unless they decide to represent themselves (however, ignorance of the rules and of legal discourse prevents an effective defence). It is important to note that, as found in previous research, the courts exhibit "a fundamental caution and unwillingness to disbelieve the police and the Crown Prosecution Service" regarding the charge against a defendant (Sanders 2002, 332). This unwillingness creates a substantial difficulty for defendants to overcome.

The prosecution of drink-driving should, on the face of it, be straightforward because it depends on the existence of seemingly incontrovertible police evidence. However, this assumption is not borne out by the cases I observed. A charge of drink driving was prosecuted against a well-dressed, white middle-aged male (*R 15*) who pleaded guilty (he was not legally represented). The case began by identifying the defendant, after which the LA read out the charge: "On 14 January 2016 witnesses observed the defendant staggering around Marvin Gardens; he was later observed driving. Officers signalled him to stop but he was oblivious of their presence. The officers found him asleep behind the wheel. There were 'signs' of alcohol consumption. He was asked to provide a breath test, found to be over the limit, and was arrested and taken to the station. At the station he was breathalysed and found to have 85 mg of alcohol; the legal limit is 35 mg. . . . A court charge of £85 is suggested. He has no previous." The defendant stated: "I work . . . I was drunk. I won't do this again. . . ." In response the Bench condemned his behaviour and sentenced him: "Mr A, the courts take drinking and driving seriously. You were lucky there was no accident, or the severity of the sentence would be much greater. . . ." He was fined £613, disqualified from driving for eighteen months, and informed that he could reduce the period of disqualification if he registered immediately for a drink and drive course (which he did). The hearing took twelve minutes.

Drink-driving cases can play out in quite different ways depending in part on whether a defendant has legal representation. For example, in a nine-minute hearing (*R 18*), a middle-aged white male, who was represented by a solicitor, pleaded guilty. He had been breathalysed and found to have 102 mg of alcohol. His solicitor, who argued against the standard sentence for this offence (as given to *R 15*, above), stated that the appropriate punishment should be a community order. The solicitor informed the court that a medical report was being prepared and he asked the bench to refer the defendant for a probation report. Sentencing was put back three weeks for the report to be prepared, and the defendant—who was disqualified from driving—was released on unconditional bail until his sentencing hearing, which I did not attend.

Despite apparently clear evidence of drink-driving, a sixty-five-year-old unkempt and somewhat incoherent white male (*R 178*) was charged with three offences: drink-driving, driving a car that was not insured, and "driving otherwise than in accordance with a license" (i.e., without a license). In an eighteen-minute hearing in which the defendant represented himself, he pleaded not guilty.[33] He claimed that he had suffered a hypoglycaemia attack and that he had no memory of being at the wheel of a car or of having been arrested by the police. The court set a trial date and he was required to bring a medical report outlining his hypoglycaemia as well as an insurance certificate and his driving license.

In another drink-driving case, the defendant challenged police evidence of wrong-doing. The thirty-three-year-old black male (*R 79*) was charged with "being drunk in a black Mercedes" after he was found "slumped at the wheel." The defendant, who was legally represented, contested the entire case against him and pleaded not guilty. His solicitor—who at various points in the twenty-one minute hearing claimed that the defendant was making a statutory declaration *and* a not guilty plea—argued that: (a) the police had not provided any evidence,[34] (b) there were no witness statements, and (c) the officer who conducted the breathalyser test and the two arresting officers should be called to give evidence at the trial. The defendant was told to bring medical evidence to his trial (he claimed to have fallen asleep in his car while using a heat pad to alleviate back pain).

Table 1.2. Summary prosecutions I observed.

Summary motoring	**Number**
Applications	9
Summary motoring	24
Summary non-motoring	51
Application to adjourn	17
Application to issue a warrant for breaching bail conditions	11
Total	112

[33] Rumbold (2010, 23) notes that many defendants arrested for drink driving have subsequently been found to suffer from hypoglycaemia. He summarises the situation facing these defendants: "Testing of blood glucose and assessment of medical records will determine whether the person was hypoglycaemic. The level of education and history of compliance of the diabetic, in combination with expert evidence, will indicate how foreseeable the hypoglycaemic episode was. The type of offence together with the foreseeability of hypoglycaemia will determine how culpable the diabetic is for their incapacity. As a matter of policy, even those with loss of hypoglycaemic awareness will still be convicted of strict liability or negligence-based motoring offences, but sentences will be reduced where the defendant does not know he has loss of hypoglycaemic awareness, has done everything possible to reduce the possibility of hypoglycaemia and most importantly pulls over as soon as he feels unwell."

[34] A breathalyser test calculated that he had 66 mg of alcohol in his blood.

Eighteen of the twenty-four summary motoring cases I observed related to a charge of drink-driving; defendants included a mix of white, black, and Asian men (and two female defendants).[35] The cases, which were heard at different courts across London, illustrate the court's reliance on police evidence and a continuum in defendants' responses to being charged with this offence, which ranged from being fully compliant with the court, to redefining the circumstances of their arrest and contesting the charge. I was unable to speak to these defendants and can only comment that, compared to forty years ago when nearly all defendants pleaded guilty, today defendants appear to have lost their fear of the court. Part of this is undoubtedly explained by having access to a lawyer who is willing to actively defend a client. However, two other issues may also be relevant. First at the remand hearing police evidence is not made available to the court or to defendants—which means that if the evidence is contested a trial is required—and second if a defendant is found guilty at his or her trial s/he can expect to be fined and disqualified from driving. Note, however, that the court's ultimate sanction differs little between what it can impose at the remand hearing and what it can impose following a trial when a defendant is adjudged to be guilty. Perhaps this fact, together with access to a lawyer, explains why some individuals chance a trial.

Turning to summary non-motoring offences (see table 1.2), I begin by examining cases where individuals were prosecuted for failing to purchase a train/underground ticket.[36] Defendants ranged from students to the down-and-out, and the outcome of the hearing appears to reflect the court's perception of the defendant. For example, a thirty-four-year-old unemployed black male (*R 7*) was arrested at Oxford Tube/underground station for failing to purchase a ticket to travel on the tube; when he was arrested, he was found to be in possession of "a wrap of cannabis." He pleaded guilty to both offences. In a six-minute hearing, the DS only offered mitigation: the defendant had recently been released from his job; he admitted to not buying a ticket and to possessing cannabis but was "working for a charity" and was trying to start his own business. A custody order, said the DS, would mean that the defendant could not travel to the US to pursue his career. The DJ who heard the case accepted mitigation and, because the

[35] Some cases bordered on the bizarre, as in *R 138* where the defendant, an Asian male in his mid-thirties, was stopped by police because he was cycling erratically down a local high street. He admitted to having been drinking and showed officers a large machete which he pulled out of his trousers. He was charged with possessing a "bladed instrument" and faced twelve weeks in custody.

[36] At Westminster Magistrates' Court I saw court lists for twenty to thirty defendants who were being charged for travelling on the train without a ticket.

defendant had no previous convictions, imposed a fine of £175 and a community order.

The court took a very different approach to a poorly dressed and disabled white male in his late twenties or early thirties (*R 179*) who was arrested for travelling on a train without a valid ticket, an offence to which he pleaded guilty. While on the train he had been begging and had approached a plain clothes police officer who arrested him. At the police station the defendant made a "no comment" interview; however, he was found to be in breach of a community order[37] imposed for travelling on public transport without a ticket (in fact he had numerous convictions). During the ten-minute hearing the bench was informed by the DS that the defendant was living in a homeless shelter and was in receipt of benefits. Probation noted that the defendant had breached a community order, currently had a suspended sentence for assault, and had "mental health issues" (but was complying with a "DRR," a drink rehabilitation order). The bench accepted that the defendant was "engaging" with social services and imposed a £100 fine (which it deemed to have been paid "for time served," one day in gaol). He was released but warned, "If you breach bail conditions again, it ratchets up and you will end in prison. There is a community order in place. You must not be on public transport without a valid ticket. You are required to provide medical evidence for a (free public) permit. Please engage with probation and get your life in order. . . ."

A breakdown of the different types of summary non-motoring offences that I observed provides an indication of the range of these offences (see Table 1.3).

Below I analyse how the three most common offences I observed—common assault, shoplifting, and breach of bail—were prosecuted. As with my analysis of the motoring offences, these cases illustrate how, in contrast to more idealised accounts (e.g., Gibson and Gordon 2008; Donoghue 2014), magistrates/DJs manage and decide cases. The following cases also raise the issue of repeat offending, which underlines the failure of current sentencing practices to address the socio-economic problems that give rise to offending (many of these cases also illustrate the conditions in which the precariat live).

[37] The order required the defendant not to travel on public transport without a valid ticket, to refrain from drinking alcohol, and to report regularly to the police.

Table 1.3. Summary prosecutions of non-motoring offences I observed.

Type of offence	No.
Common assault	14
Shoplifting/theft	13
Breaching bail conditions	10
Failing to pay tube/bus fare	3
Failure to comply with the police[38]	5
Indecent exposure/photographing up girls' skirts	2
Request for adjournment	4
Criminal damage (for graffiti)	1
Application by probation to issue a warrant	1
"Interest of justice" application	1
"Closure" order	1
Statutory Declaration	16
Total	71

I begin with relatively straight-forward cases. The first case (*R 47*) concerns an allegation of assault made against a thirty-seven-year-old Lithuanian woman who was alleged to have attacked a co-worker at the hotel where they both worked. The defendant was initially charged with ABH[39] and was remanded into custody to await her remand hearing. Given the seriousness of the charge she could have been imprisoned for a lengthy period, however the DS[40] and the probation officer informed the bench about her history, her situation in the UK, and her remorse for her actions. In sentencing her at the end of a thirty-seven-minute hearing, the Bench stated: "I am giving you credit for your guilty plea and for your previous good behaviour. I have read the [probation] assessment report and I've heard from the probation officer. I am sorry you have suffered from illness. . . . You chose not to take the medication. Ms X [the victim] did not deserve to be treated as you did. You bit her and pulled her hair and pushed her down

[38] This includes obstructing/avoiding arrest and failing to provide a specimen for drink-driving.

[39] According to the CPS sentencing guidelines: "The offence is committed when a person assaults another, thereby causing Actual Bodily Harm (ABH). Bodily harm has its ordinary meaning and includes any hurt calculated to interfere with the health or comfort of the victim: such hurt need not be permanent but must be more than transient and trifling (*R v Donovan 25 Cr. App. Rep. 1, CCA*). It is an either way offence, which carries a maximum penalty on indictment of five years' imprisonment and/or an unlimited fine not exceeding the statutory maximum." See https://www.cps.gov.uk/legal-guidance/offences-against-person-incorporating-charging-standard.

[40] The duty solicitor used some of the victim's money to pay the initial fine to release her from custody; she also actively defended her by providing the court with a complete picture of the defendant's circumstances including her medical condition.

with your face very close to hers. There is no excuse for this. Taking everything into consideration, this is twelve-week imprisonment. But I suspend[41] it for twelve months. I am not imposing a 'requirements order.'[42] If in twelve months you commit another offence you will be liable for twelve weeks imprisonment plus charges for any new offence. You will pay a 'victim surcharge'[43] of £150 plus £300 compensation plus a fine of £85. A total of £500. I will reduce the fine by £195, which you have already paid the court. . . . Can you pay today?"[44] The defendant agreed to pay the fine immediately.

S 57 illustrates a more complex case of assault linked to other offences. This hearing was scheduled to sentence the defendant, a well-

---

[41] "When a court imposes a custodial sentence of between fourteen days and two years (or six months in the magistrates' court), the court may choose to suspend the sentence for up to two years. This means that the offender does not go to prison immediately but is given the chance to stay out of trouble and to comply with up to twelve requirements set by the court. These include: doing unpaid work; being subject to a curfew; undertaking a treatment programme for alcohol or drugs; being subject to a rehabilitation activity requirement. If the offender does not comply with the requirements or is convicted of another offence during the suspension period, they are likely to serve the original custodial term in addition to the sentence they get for the new offence." See https://www.sentencingcouncil.org.uk/about-sentencing/types-of-sentence/suspended-sentences/.

[42] The court may impose a "requirements order" as part of a community order that is set for a specific period of days when the defendant is placed under the supervision of "a responsible officer" and is required to attend an accredited rehabilitation programme. Defendants may be required to attend alcohol treatment or an "attendance centre"; subject to a curfew; subject to drug rehabilitation, an exclusion requirement, a mental health requirement, a prohibited activity requirement, a residence requirement, an unpaid work requirement, alcohol abstinence and monitoring (electronic tag), and a foreign travel requirement (Judicial College 2016, 4–14).

[43] "The Victim Surcharge was introduced in April 2007 and changes were introduced on 1 October 2012, 1 September 2014 and then again on 8 April 2016. When a court passes a sentence, it *must* also order that the relevant surcharge is paid. The amount of the surcharge depends on the sentence . . . and whether at the time the offence was committed the offender was an adult or a youth (under eighteen years of age), or if the offender is an organisation. Revenue raised from the Victim Surcharge is used to fund victim services through the Victim and Witness General Fund." See https://www.sentencingcouncil.org.uk/about-sentencing/types-of-sentence/other-orders-made-on-sentencing/what-is-the-victim-surcharge/.

[44] Whenever a fine is imposed there is limited negotiation with the defendant about his/her ability to pay and to agree a payment schedule (once an agreement is reached a court enforcement order is made in case the defendant defaults on their payment; in which case they find themselves back in court again).

dressed black male in his mid-twenties who had pleaded not guilty. He had been tried in his absence[45] and found guilty of "assault by beating" of an elderly man and for possessing class B drugs. The duty solicitor sought to make an application to reopen the conviction and to set a new trial date. The CPS argued against this application stating that the charge against the defendant was "found to be proved" and that the defendant had seventeen convictions from thirty-five offences. The DS argued first that his client was innocent of assault but admitted that his client did "show a pattern of violent offending." The bench decided that the defendant had been found guilty of assault in his absence and it imposed a twelve-month community order and 150 hours of unpaid work. In a thirty-seven minute hearing, the bench also imposed a fine of £200, compensation to the victim of £100, a court charge of £85, a victim surcharge of £85, a fine of £200 for possessing cannabis, and an indefinite restraining order to keep the defendant away from the victim's home. The defendant agreed that £10 a week would be deducted from his jobseekers allowance until the fine was paid.

Trials provide a much clearer insight into an offence, the offender, and the work of the court than can be learned from remand hearings. Case *T 24* raises a number of interconnected issues that arose when the police and the CPS insisted on prosecuting a person for assault (and secondarily, racial abuse) who failed to attend his trial. The defendant's solicitor stated that the defendant was homeless: "I suspect there are serious mental issues[46] and that he may need to be sectioned on this occasion rather than issue a warrant and then seek a retrial."[47] The bench decided to try the defendant in his absence, which led the defendant's lawyer to withdraw from the case because he could not take instructions from his client. The trial lasted fifty-four minutes, most of which was taken up hearing evidence from two Transport for London staff and the two police officers who arrested the defendant (stage 3). The defendant had been asleep in the exit of the station and, when awakened by TfL staff, he was alleged to have become abusive. He initially refused to leave the station and was said to have pushed the emergency stop for the escalators. He was also alleged to have called one PC "a nigger" and "a black monkey." After hearing the Crown's evidence,

[45] The defendant did not attend his trial and had "sacked" his initial solicitor. He had been sleeping in the corridor of the victim's apartment where the alleged assault took place.

[46] Many defendants exhibit signs of mental illness, which is not taken into consideration by the police, CPS, or courts in their approach to prosecuting crime. See Batty et al. (2010).

[47] He was referring to the possibility that the defendant might make a statutory declaration, which, if granted, would "reset the clock" and initiate a new hearing.

the Bench concluded (stage 7): "We are satisfied that the Crown's case has been proved. Can you [i.e., the CPS] issue an arrest warrant [for the defendant]?"

I turn to the prosecution of *shoplifting* and *theft*, which was the second most common offence I observed. The two cases discussed here indicate a preference by magistrates to sentence this type of offender themselves—rather than send them to the Crown court to be sentenced—and the cases also suggest that similar offences *are not* treated alike. Case *R 81* concerned a thirty-two-year-old black male who was charged with five counts of theft at or around Linen Hall Market (stage 2). The defendant, who was identified using CCTV, attempted to use stolen credit cards at an ATM; he was arrested in possession of two stolen handbags and the credit cards. He pleaded guilty to all the charges. The Crown argued that the defendant had been convicted of fifty-five of the ninety-nine offences he had been charged with between 1965 and 2017 and that he was currently in breach of a suspended sentence. The CPS suggested that the bench might wish to refer the case to the Crown court for sentencing, but the magistrates decided otherwise. After hearing mitigation (stage 8) on behalf of the defendant from the DS—primarily relating to the fact that he stole in order to pay his drug debts and that he was undergoing drug rehabilitation treatment—the bench stated (stage 9): "We are activating the suspended sentence for six months; we are also giving you two months for the two thefts in April and two months for each for the three thefts in September. A total of eighteen months! As you know, you would normally be released halfway through your sentence, but because you breached a suspended sentence, we are ordering that you be monitored for twelve months by probation once you are released.[48] If you fail to comply with probation there will be a penalty to pay. Regarding compensation and costs, we have taken account of your 'means' [i.e., your lack of income] and order no award for compensation, no court costs, and we remit your victim surcharge in recognition of your early guilty plea. If you had been referred to the Crown court, the sentence could have been much higher. I think that is all." The hearing lasted forty-two minutes.

In *R 42* the defendant, a black male in his late twenties who chose not to be legally represented, was charged with shoplifting. The Crown set out its case (stage 2) as follows: "He walked into House of Fraser and was being monitored. He picked up one watch and walked off, then picked up a second watch. He was stopped by store security who searched him and

[48] Bearing in mind the problems with the probation services, this requirement may not represent an effective means of dealing with repeat offending.

found both watches with the tags still attached. He said he was not guilty. He has seventeen previous charges for theft between 2010 and 2016. In fourteen of these offences he was convicted. . . . For the last offence of shoplifting he was sentenced to eight months . . . There is also a non-shoplifting charge and one suspended sentence which he breached twice." When asked by the DJ to respond to the charge (stage 3), the defendant was silent. He did tell the DJ that he was not working, had no fixed address, and was able to get "free food." The LA informed the court that the defendant owed the court over £4000 in unpaid court fines.[49] When the defendant failed to answer further questions, the DJ concluded (stage 9): "You need to get your life in order. You are guilty of the theft of the watches . . . You are sentenced to prison for ten weeks to serve five weeks . . . If you breach this condition you will be back. If there is a further offence you can expect a longer prison term. You will pay £85 court costs and a fine of £200. On October twentieth you will be released from prison and will appear in this court at 9:30 a.m. to discuss how you will pay the arrears.[50] If you do not attend, you will be arrested. This will give you some time to sort out your affairs." The hearing lasted thirteen minutes.

The offence of *breaching bail* was the third largest category of summary non-motoring offences I observed. These cases illustrate different approaches taken by the court towards defendants who had similar problems but who had committed quite different crimes. Thus *BB 46* concerns a homeless eighteen-year-old white male who was convicted of theft in Weymouth and given a conditional discharge and a date to report to police. He moved to London but failed to get in touch with the police, which led to a warrant being issued for his arrest; when police identified him, he was arrested and remanded into custody to await a hearing. In mitigation (stage 6), the DS argued that: "He is a young boy who has poor organisational skills and is vulnerable. He sleeps rough and eats from food dumps. He has a disorganized lifestyle . . . he needs assistance and probation can now provide him support." The probation officer pointed out (stage 8) that "We have rescheduled the meeting: he left school early, has been in custody twice, and will be referred to a local probation office who will help him join

---

[49]As of June 2017, defendants owed the courts in England and Wales a total of £895 million in unpaid court fines; in the second quarter of 2017, the courts imposed an additional £22 million in fines (MoJ 2017a, 6).

[50] This, and the following case, stand out as one of the few times in which a magistrate/DJ created a supervision order that required the defendant to return to court to discuss his/her progress in completing their sentence and/or how they were addressing their problems.

a GP[51] scheme and get support." The bench then addressed the defendant (stage 9): "Please stand up. I am taking a slightly unusual course of action. You are under lots of difficulties. I accept that you couldn't get to the probation office. I will say one day in custody is enough and issue an absolute discharge. It sounds as though you need help, so you need to prove this by cooperating. Failing that, it will be more prison for you. Alright?" He was released on continued bail. The hearing took ten minutes.

In contrast to the above case, the defendant in case *BB 49* was a fifty-year-old homeless white male who was charged with failing to comply with reporting conditions; his hearing lasted seventeen minutes. The Crown set out its case (stage 2) as follows: "The defendant is a sex offender convicted for an offence in 2003 who has not complied with reporting conditions. He is a high-risk offender of no fixed abode. There have been offences in 2004, 2007, and 2012 . . . He also failed to meet a suspended sentence order . . . When he was released, he failed to report. At the station he made a 'no comment' interview. This is the fourth breach this year and there were several breaches before that . . . The standard point of sentencing is eighteen weeks custody. Given his breach, it would be suitable to be remitted to the Crown court." The DS (stage 3) observed that the defendant's failure to comply was down to drug addiction and homelessness: "He gets short custody sentences, but no support . . . imprisonment is not working."

> DJ (stage 9): "Stand up. I am giving you credit for your guilty plea. . . . You know you were in custody for a sex offence which was imposed on you for a good reason?"
>
> Defendant: "Yes sir."
>
> DJ: "To stop further offences."
>
> D: "Yes sir."
>
> DJ: "You were supposed to report but you have breached that order twice in the past month. You are in need of a custodial sentence, possibly from the Crown court. I am going to take a pragmatic course of action. I am imposing a sentence of twelve weeks imprisonment with a further twenty-four weeks to serve from today. This is a total of thirty-eight weeks. You will serve half of this in custody. . . . If you don't comply with the order it is another offence and your bad situation will get worse. There is a victim surcharge of £115, but no court costs. There needs to be a "means" enquiry with this court in four months. You will appear again in this court to see if your situation can

---

[51] A general practitioner is a medical doctor.

> be reversed and to discuss your debt to the court of £2000. This is a serious order and the sentences will get heavier and heavier. Go with the officer."

I now look at different legal "applications" made to the court that illustrate the powers exercised by the judiciary. Sec. 14 of the *Magistrates' Courts Act* (1980)[52] allows an individual to make a declaration to the court that s/he "did not know of the summons or the proceedings" initiated against them and can, by making a valid declaration, have the original proceedings declared void. The effect of a declaration is to restart the proceedings to allow the defendant to attend court and give his/her evidence. The majority of applications I saw were traffic offences or for travelling without a ticket and involved a convicted offender completing a form and making a formal declaration to the court explaining why they did not attend legal proceedings; if the reason was accepted, the court scheduled a new hearing at the court that originally decided the offence.

Statutory Declarations are squeezed into the court's daily list. The individuals seeking to make a declaration are not legally represented, which means that the court must pause to explain the procedure, take their evidence, and sign the necessary form. Case *SD 150* concerns a statutory declaration made by a thirty-seven-year-old black female against a fixed penalty fine for theft of goods that was issued against her in 2010. The defendant stated that she first became aware of the fine when she received a letter from the National Compensation and Historic Debt Department[53] in 2017 stating that bailiffs would be coming to her home to seize property to the value of £350.00. The applicant presented her case so effectively that the bench decided to "remit the balance" of the payment, which, they said, would stop the bailiffs coming to her door. However, in the absence of a file from the police, the applicant would still have a criminal conviction. Individuals making these declarations—which typically take ten to fifteen minutes—uniformly declare that they were not informed of the charge against them and that they are innocent. However, I observed one person withdrawing a declaration after he was informed that he would still have to appear in court to answer the case against him.

I observed three other types of application being made that are worth noting because they indicate how the CPS and probation services use their powers to enforce the law, and conversely that the court can accept that it is sometimes "in the interests of justice" that a prisoner is allowed to challenge his or her conviction. Thus, in case *R 151* the CPS made a "bad

[52] See https://www.legislation.gov.uk/ukpga/1980/43/section/14.

[53] See https://www.gov.uk/government/news/hm-courts-tribunals-service-advice-to-debtors-on-unpaid-historic-fines (accessed 2 August 2018).

character reference" against a defendant who was currently in custody awaiting trial for a domestic violence offence. In the period between the original assault and the trial, the defendant was alleged to have assaulted his partner again. In a forty-nine-minute hearing, the bench heard arguments from the Crown and the defendant's solicitor regarding whether, under Sec. 101–4 of the *Criminal Justice Act (2003)*, the defendant's convictions and the second assault against his partner could be taken as evidence of a "propensity to commit further acts" of violence. The bench decided that the defendant's behaviour did demonstrate such a propensity. Their decision would be used by the CPS in the defendant's forthcoming trial and it would "make it easier for the prosecution to discharge the burden of proving the defendant's guilt."[54]

Case *LA 220* concerned an application by a probation officer asking the court to issue a warrant for the arrest of an individual who failed to fulfil his "rehabilitation requirement" to attend a "building better relationships course."[55] The application was granted by the bench. In contrast to the above two cases, case *A 217* was an "Interest of Justice" application made on behalf of a serving prisoner by a solicitor to secure legal aid. The prisoner was convicted of a fraud in 2017 involving the use of a debit card belonging to someone else. He was bailed but failed to attend the trial and was convicted in his absence. When he was arrested, he was found to be in possession of class A drugs (a charge that was subsequently withdrawn). The bench granted the application for the defendant to be given legal aid for a retrial. These applications provide a limited counterweight to the otherwise extensive power of the law over citizens as demonstrated in the following chapters.

Conclusion

In remand hearings only magistrates, the CPS, the DS, and solicitors speak, whereas defendants—regardless whether they are represented—are "silenced" by legal procedure (they have no right to speak). Indeed, defendants speak only to identify themselves, make a plea—either not guilty or guilty—and to negotiate payment of a fine, and so on. In trials, defendants are supposed to be assisted to give their evidence, but as will be evident

---

[54] See: "CPS—bad character evidence—legal guidance" at: https://www.cps.gov.uk/legal-guidance/bad-character-evidence (accessed 4 August 2018).

[55] Defendants are required to attend these courses following an early guilty plea or a conviction for domestic violence.

later, this seldom happens. Indeed, trials usually proceed even when the defendant is not present and even when s/he is not legally represented.

With respect to the prosecution of summary motoring offences, the vast majority of defendants entered a guilty plea, either because they are guilty or because they think that the Crown has sufficient evidence to convict them (at remand hearings the Crown's evidence is mentioned but is *not* made available to the court or to the defendant). Caught up in this situation, defendants adopt different strategies in dealing—perhaps ineffectively—with the case against them, ranging from acquiescence to contesting police evidence.

With respect to the prosecution of summary non-motoring offences, the decisions reached in remand hearings depends on the extent to which magistrates, District Judges, the CPS, solicitors, and probation/mental health teams work together to process cases. This "interdependence," which is widely observed and greatly valued by magistrates (Gibson and Gordon 2008, 23f), is hindered by the variable competence of the different actors to fulfil their designated roles, by the speed of proceedings, by the way in which proceedings are staged, the unintelligible "language of law" used, the frequent breakdowns of IT, and the belated provision of information to the bench/DJs. These problems are discussed in detail in the following chapters.

All the legal actors I observed demonstrated a varied ability to perform their assigned roles in court. Magistrates and District Judges are expected to "hold the ring" and to play an essential role in maintaining an "equality of arms" between the prosecution and the defence. However, magistrates are unable to do this when defendants are not legally represented and/or when duty solicitors play a passive role in defending their clients. The situation is exacerbated when poor and legally illiterate defendants attempt to represent themselves or indeed when they are not present at their hearings. In such circumstances, high conviction rates suggest either that a defendant's legal defence is ineffective or that some defendants are not fit to plead. The high percentage of defendants who are repeat offenders, homeless, and destitute strongly suggests that the Criminal Justice System is failing to address the socio-economic issues which underlie offending.

CHAPTER 2

THE PROSECUTION OF INDICTABLE AND EITHER-WAY OFFENCES

The offences dealt with in this chapter concern allegations of serious criminal offences that tend to attract considerable social and media attention and comment by politicians and officials. As indicated in the introduction, at stage two of a remand hearing if an individual is charged with an indictable or "either way" offence the CPS asks magistrates or a District Judge (DJ) to refer/remit the case to a Crown court for trial.

This chapter begins by briefly outlining the importance of the decision on the allocation of cases (formerly referred to as "mode of trial"). The remainder of the chapter examines the serious/indictable and "either-way" offences I observed. Unlike public order offences, these offences are clearly defined; however, a relatively small percentage of these crimes result in arrest and conviction. In 2017–18 police "sanction detection rates"[1]—where a suspect has been identified for an offence but not necessarily convicted, for example, they may have been issued a caution or fined—varied considerably.[2] Thus in only 67 per cent of murder cases was the perpetrator identified; in cases involving offensive weapons, 63 per cent of perpetrators were identified; in cases involving wounding/GBH, 22 per cent of perpetrators were identified; in cases involving "theft and handling" offences, fewer than 5 per cent of perpetrators were identified; in sexual offences, about 12 per cent of perpetrators were identified; in robbery cases, 7 per cent; in burglary cases, a mere 5.5 per cent; and so on. Indeed, less than half of all reported offences for serious crimes are prosecuted (see Table 1.3).

As pointed out in the introduction, the realization that the state cannot control crime has led officials to shift responsibility for crime reduction away from the state and on to citizens and "communities." While

---

[1] For a discussion of the statistics see, http://www.blog.murdermap.co.uk/the-justice-system/sanction-detection-rates/.

[2] See https://www.met.police.uk/sd/stats-and-data/met/year-end-crime-statistics/ (accessed 14 July 2018).

politicians continue to criminalise growing areas of social life by passing new legislation, the resources committed to supporting the police, the courts, and the prison system continue to be cut,[3] which means that decreasing numbers of offenders are arrested and prosecuted.

i. Allocation of case/mode of trial

Until the mid-nineteenth century all types of crime were indictable, and most offenders were entitled to a jury trial (Harris 1976). The situation changed following a series of decisions that began with the view that "young offenders" should not be indicted and tried, followed by a decision that "trivial charges" against individuals who "intended to plead guilty" should be heard by magistrates (though these individuals could still choose a jury trial). However, policy makers confronted a dilemma between sending a growing number of "trivial" cases for jury trial and the growing cost of jury trial. By the mid-twentieth century, a concern with reducing costs predominated and it was decided that "serious" crimes merited a jury trial whereas "trivial" cases should be heard by magistrates.

However, it became apparent to Victorian policy makers that it was impossible to differentiate crimes by their degree of seriousness. For example, while "theft" is clearly a serious matter, how was it possible to differentiate between theft involving goods worth £5 and the theft of goods worth a little bit more, and so on. The dilemma was addressed with a compromise: all individuals accused of a crime would be given "a summary of facts" that the prosecution would rely upon, and at that point a choice of venue would be made (Harris 1976, 186). Over time the rising costs involved in jury trials have pushed legislators and the judicial authorities to increasingly restrict the right to trial resulting in the current situation in which specific types of offences are designated as "indictable" and "either way" and are allocated for trial, while trivial summary offences were to be heard by magistrates (see box I.1).

However, and as research has repeatedly demonstrated, at stage 2 of their remand hearing a defendant is required to make a decision concerning mode of trial without understanding the implications that this decision will have for his or her case.[4] King (1978, 199f) summarised the situation in the 1970s: "not only are a large proportion of defendants

[3] For the most recent figures, see "Reality check: Is police funding falling?" at https://www.bbc.co.uk/news/uk-43699623 (accessed 4 July 2018).

[4] Indeed, it sometimes happens that neither magistrates nor legal counsel adequately explain to a defendant what this decision means (cf., *Rahmdezfouli) v Wood Green Crown Court [2014] 1 All ER 567*).

unaware of the full implications of their choice of venue, but also some of them do not even know they made a choice." This situation arose because most defendants are "not competent" to make this decision, perhaps because the decision was not clearly explained to them, or because the impact of legal proceedings caused them to withdraw and disengage (a situation that is not helped by being placed in the dock).

The regulations guiding "plea before venue" are set out in the *Magistrates' Courts Act (1980)* sections 17A–17C (as amended in 2013 and 2015[5]). The Act states:

> 7. The defendant is identified at the hearing and the charge is read out. The justices' legal adviser will check whether the defendant has received the initial details of the prosecution case. An adjournment may be granted, at the defendant's request, where he/she has not received the initial details of the prosecution case.
> 8. The justices' legal adviser will explain the plea before venue procedure to the defendant (if an individual), i.e.: (a) Will read the allegation of the offence to the defendant; (b) Will explain the allegation and the procedure for the hearing; (c) Will ask whether the defendant has been advised about the potential effect on sentence of a guilty plea; (d) Will explain that if s/he pleads guilty the court will proceed to hear the case as a guilty plea; but (e) Will explain that if s/he pleads guilty s/he may still be committed for sentence to the Crown court if the magistrates consider their powers of punishment insufficient.
> 9. The court will then ask the defendant whether s/he would plead guilty or not guilty. . .
> 10. The procedure outlined above will take place without hearing any representations from the prosecutor regarding the seriousness of the offence and whether the prosecution considers that the magistrates' powers of punishment are sufficient.
> 11. If the defendant indicates a guilty plea, then the prosecutor will open the case fully and the court will proceed as if the defendant had been convicted of the offence and consider sentence . . .

Research by Cammiss (2007) indicates that decisions in magistrates' courts on the allocation of the case are strongly influenced by local "rules of thumb"[6] relied upon by the CPS to identify specific cases

---

[5] See http://www.hse.gov.uk/enforce/enforcementguide/court/magistrates-mode.htm (accessed 14 July 2018).

[6] Sanders et al. (2010, 547) cites research that suggests prosecutors use CPS charging guidelines to minimise the level of violence involved in a case in order to charge individuals for summary offences rather than for an either-way offence. DV cases would be a case in point, see chapter 4.

which s/he asks to be referred to the Crown court, and by local "court culture" where magistrates/DJs take decisions. These factors may "subvert the national guidelines" by inconsistently referring serious and either way crimes to be decided locally or to the Crown court.[7] For defendants, the decision may also be influenced by "informal incentives" available to defendants to waive the right to trial, that is, the opportunity for immediate release from custody and a reduction in the time and cost involved in going to trial (Helms 2019). These factors may intersect with the vulnerability of poor and legally illiterate defendants[8] to unduly constrain their decision and thus their right to a trial. My research did not look at this issue. However, my observations of remand hearings suggest that decisions by magistrates and defendants on this issue are not carefully considered (see cases *R 194*, *R 24*, *R 63* below). As the cases discussed below make clear, a very high proportion of the individuals charged with serious crimes are young black and ethnic minority men who, if not unemployed, belong to the precariat.

ii. Case analysis

When serious criminal offences (see box I.1) are listed for a remand hearing at magistrates' courts, the CPS informs the bench that the allegation is too serious for them to hear. At this point the magistrates may or may not take the defendant's plea before referring the case to the Crown court. However, some serious offences are "triable either way," which means that magistrates can hear a case if the defendant asks them to and if the bench believes that it is competent to deal with the issue. If a defendant elects to have his or her case heard, the bench can try the case and send the defendant to the Crown court to be sentenced if magistrates feel that their sentencing powers are too limited.

Accurate statistics on serious crime are notoriously difficult to obtain. Police figures generally understate crime, can be misleading, and are subject to revision. In this chapter, I rely on statistics published by the Metropolitan Police on serious crime in London for 2016–18. To put these figures into perspective, in 2018 serious crime soared: the murder rate was up by 44 per cent, while youth murder, personal robbery, and home burglary were up by about a third. The figures from the Metropolitan Police indicate

[7] The extent to which the choice of venue adversely affects vulnerable defendants is taken up in the concluding chapter, see Jacobson and Talbot 2009.

[8] Helms (2019) noted that "informal constraints" on waiving the right to trial may be at play for defendants with "no fixed abode" and those accused of DV who may not have a home to go to; in both types of case without an address to be bailed to, magistrates will tend to remand the defendant into custody until their trial.

that the number of crimes in the year to March also showed a 23 per cent increase in gun crime, a 21 per cent rise in knife crime, and an 18 per cent increase in the number of rapes. Crime statistics need to be treated with caution: police statistics are sometimes contradicted by victim surveys or by data on violence provided by hospitals. Even so, police figures are usually the only available way to assess crime. Fieldwork in magistrates' courts allowed me to follow a range of serious offences (see Table 2.1), which I draw on to examine the work of legal actors and how legal procedures affect the way a case was heard and decided.

Table 2.1. Indictable and Either Way Offences I Observed.

Offence	No. cases observed
Murder	2
Attempted robbery	1
Theft	8
Acid attack	2
GBH	1
Aggravated assault	7
Proceeds of crime	2
Possession of a knife/offensive weapon	7
Unlawful wounding	1
Sexual assault against a minor	2
Indecent exposure/indecent images	3
Failure of sex offender to register	1
Obstructing police	1
Trespass	3
Other	1
Total	42
As a percentage of all observed cases	24%

Terrorism offences

Terrorism is the most serious offence that an individual can be charged with. CPS guidance[9] states that,

> Terrorism is the use or threat of action, both in and outside of the UK, designed to influence any international government organisation or to intimidate the public. It must also be for the purpose of advancing a political, religious, racial or ideological cause . . .

[9] See: https://www.cps.gov.uk/terrorism (accessed 16 July 2018).

> It is important to note that in order to be convicted of a terrorism offence a person doesn't actually have to commit what could be considered a terrorist attack. Planning, assisting and even collecting information on how to commit terrorist acts are all crimes under British terrorism legislation.

CPS guidance also states that:

> Terrorism crimes and terrorist-related offences are subject to the criminal justice system in the same way as all other crimes. The CPS reviews the case and makes a charging decision in line with the Code for Crown Prosecutors. However, terrorism offences are distinct from other types of crime in that individuals who commit terrorism-related offences have political, religious racial and/or ideological motivations, unlike typical criminal motivations, which may be personal gain or revenge, for example.

As the Home Secretary stated in 2018,[10] an attack in the UK was "highly likely" because the "security and intelligence agencies are, right now, handling over five hundred live operations, they have three thousand 'subjects of interest.' And there are a further twenty thousand people who have previously been investigated, so they may still pose a threat."

The police and the Home Office have two quite distinct procedures for handling allegations of terrorism. When the police possess sufficient credible evidence against an individual of involvement in terrorism, defendants are tried at Crown court. Alternatively, the Home Secretary can impose "control orders" on individuals whom the police and the Home Secretary believe are involved in terrorist-related activity. Control orders were withdrawn in 2011 and replaced by TPIMs that allow the government to impose a number of "restrictions" on individuals suspected of involvement in terrorist activities to protect the public while the individual is investigated.[11] The imposition of control orders/TPIMs against individuals are reviewed by the Special Immigration Appeals Commission (Jackson 2013; Campbell 2020).

All terrorist offences in England in Wales are referred to Westminster Magistrates' Court in London for an initial hearing where the Chief Magistrate sits (s/he and his or her deputy hear sensitive or complex cases including allegations of terrorism, extradition, and special jurisdiction

---

[10] See "Home Secretary announces new counter-terrorism strategy" (4 June 2018) at (accessed on 9 September 2018):
https://www.gov.uk/government/speeches/home-secretary-announces-new-counter-terrorism-strategy.

[11] See https://www.gov.uk/government/collections/terrorism-prevention-and-investigation-measures-act (accessed 10 September 2018).

cases).[12] Individuals can be charged with a wide range of terrorist offences including membership of banned organisations, directly or indirectly supporting Daesh, involvement in a terrorist attack (whether the attack was carried out or was being prepared), involvement with Turkish forces fighting Daesh, and so on. As with all criminal offences, the initial hearing is very short. Regardless of the defendant's plea, they are remanded into custody to await a police investigation and trial at a London Crown Court.[13] The number of individuals charged with terrorism-related offences has greatly increased in recent years.[14] I did not observe remand hearings of individuals accused of terrorism.

Homicide

Murder and manslaughter are offences that are prosecuted as homicide. The crime of murder is committed[15] where:

> a person is of sound mind and discretion (i.e. sane); if that person unlawfully kills (i.e. not self-defence or other justified killing) any reasonable creature (human being); if the human killed was born alive and breathing through its own lungs (*Rance v Mid-Downs Health Authority (1991) 1 All ER 801* and *AG Ref No 3 of 1994 (1997) 3 All ER 936)*; if the act was committed under the Queen's Peace (not in war-time) and with intent to kill or cause grievous bodily harm (GBH).

A second charge, normally manslaughter, would also be made against the defendant to ensure that the jury can hear as much evidence as possible.[16]

Between 1990 and 2003 the number of homicides in London averaged 173 per year, with a low of 139 in 1996, and a high of 204 in 2003. The number then fell between 2004 and 2014 to a new low of 83 but rose sharply to 118 in 2015, followed by a slight fall in 2016. In 2017 homicides

---

[12] See https://www.judiciary.uk/about-the-judiciary/who-are-the-judiciary/judicial-roles/judges/chief-magistrate/ (accessed 15 September 2018).

[13] Some sense of what occurs in these hearings can be gained from press reports, see, for instance, "Teenage girl accused in court of plotting terror attack in UK" (*Guardian*, 26 July 2017).

[14] In 2017, 400 individuals were arrested for terrorist offences; 115 were charged, 213 were released, and 60 were released on bail pending further investigation, see "Number of UK terrorism arrests hits record high" (*Guardian*, 7 December 2017).

[15] CPS guidance on this crime is set out at: https://www.cps.gov.uk/legal-guidance/homicide-murder-and-manslaughter (accessed on 5 October 2018).

[16] See https://www.cps.gov.uk/legal-guidance/homicide-murder-and-manslaughter (accessed on 5 October 2018).

rose to 131 (which included the victims of the Westminster Bridge, London Bridge, and Finsbury Park terrorist attacks). As of 31 December 2018, there were 132 homicides in London in 2018. In 2017/18 there was a 50 per cent increase in the number of murders before falling slightly in 2018/19. London's homicide rate is 18.4 per million people, the highest in England and Wales. In 2017/18, 263 of the 736 homicides in England and Wales involved a knife or sharp instrument. The boroughs with the highest homicide rates are Lambeth, Southwark, Newham, Hackney, Brent, and Haringey (areas associated with high levels of deprivation, poverty, poor housing, *and* the 2011 riots). The number of knife crime offences in London rose from 9.7 per thousand in 2015/16 to 14.7 thousand in 2017/18.[17] These incidents have led to repeated calls[18] for the government to address the issue. In April 2018 the government announced a "serious violence strategy" (UK 2018a) that focused on police enforcement but not with the causes of knife crime.

I observed one case that illustrates how homicide cases are heard in a magistrates' court and tried at Crown court. Cases *R 91* and *R 92* began as a "fight" in West London in 2017 that left a man dead from a knife wound. Two suspects, brothers, were identified from CCTV film and arrested. A third suspect fled the country but was arrested on return to the UK. During a search of the first two suspects' home, their mother lied to protect them and was arrested. The brothers appeared at a Magistrates' Court in September where they were brought up from the cells to make their plea.

In a nine-minute hearing the two black men were only asked to identify themselves—"D" was born in 1998 and "Z" in 1993. The charge was read out by the LA:

> "You are both charged with the murder of Mr X on 4 September. On 19 September officers searched your home address and found a large amount of diamorphine.[19] Take a seat. You are both charged with the murder of Mr X by stabbing. CCTV footage shows "D" holding the knife; he is jointly charged with stabbing and causing death. Drugs were found at your home address: four hundred packages of class A drugs . . . ; each packet was worth £20 to £30 each. Cash valued at £4500 was also found. The case involves

[17] See Metropolitan Police data at https://www.met.police.uk/sd/stats-and-data/met/crime-data-dashboard/ (accessed 26 August 2019) and House of Commons (2019b).
[18] In 2017, 40,000 offences involving knives or sharp objects were recorded across the UK, a 22 per cent rise on the previous year. See "Why is knife crime increasing in England and Wales?" (*Independent*, 27 April 2018).
[19] Diamorphine is a banned opiate, see http://www.drugstraining.co.uk/drugs_info_heroin.php (accessed 8 October 2018).

> drugs, murder and is an indictable offence which is in excess of this court's power to decide."

The defendant's solicitor replied: "In relation to Z, he pleads guilty to both charges. 'D' pleads not guilty to all charges. The defendants should be tried at Central Crown Court." The LA then asked each defendant to plead: Z pleaded guilty. The LA stated: "Under Sec. 3 [of the *Powers of Criminal Courts, Sentencing Act 2000*][20] this court does not have the power to hear these matters. Where do you wish to be tried?" Both defendants stated: "Crown court." The LA replied: "The matter is not suitable for this court to hear. A bail hearing is set for September 25." The bench ended the hearing by stating: "Both please stand. Your trial is set for the Central Criminal Court. Your bail hearing is on 25 September. The two other charges, money and drugs, are sent up alongside it. You are both remanded into custody." The defendants replied "thank you" and were taken down to the cells from where they would be transferred to prison to await trial.

"D" and a third suspect, "A" (but not "Z"), were tried the following year. For reasons that are unclear, the murder charge was dropped, and both "D" and "A" pleaded guilty to a charge of violent disorder and possession of a bladed instrument. The evidence against "D" appears to have come from his clothing (which was identified on CCTV) and the fact that he attended hospital on the same day as the stabbing with a knife wound to his leg. "A" was linked to the fight by CCTV and by phone and forensic evidence recovered from a car left at the crime scene. "D" was sentenced to four years in prison and "A" was sentenced to three-and-a-half years. The defendants must have been tried for possession of class A drugs separately.

This case illustrates the nature of the initial remand hearing: a quick hearing during which defendants are charged and make their plea; and at which little if any evidence is made available to the bench or to the accused, though the latter will have been interviewed by the police. In this case, due to the seriousness of the charge and an ongoing police investigation, both defendants were remanded into custody to await trial and/or the conclusion of police investigations. Murder has long been prioritised by the police and the justice system and is investigated centrally by the Homicide and Major Crime Command (HMCC) rather than by detectives in the London borough where the offence occurred. This means that because it investigates fewer cases than other units, HMCC can devote more manpower and money to analysing CCTV footage, mobile phone data, and forensic evidence. Nevertheless, despite the Crown's initial allegation

---

[20] See https://www.legislation.gov.uk/ukpga/2000/6/section/3A.

that both brothers were guilty of murder, none of the defendants were convicted for the death of Mr X.

Assault

Assault with injury, which comprises the offences of "assault occasioning actual bodily harm" (ABH) and "grievous bodily harm" (GBH), accounts on average for 40 per cent of all violence against the person offences within the Metropolitan Police area and 45 per cent of all violence against the person nationally. In England and Wales, "assault without injury" and "harassment" account for a further 38 per cent of crimes recorded within the "violence against the person" category.

The CPS[21] defines GBH as "really serious" harm and cites *DPP v Smith [1960] 3 W.L.R. 546*, which states,

> Ultimately, the assessment of harm done is a matter for the jury, applying contemporary social standards (*R v Golding [2014] EWCA Crim 889*). There is no necessity for an assault to have been committed before there could be an infliction of GBH. However psychological injury not amounting to recognizable psychiatric illness does not fall within the ambit of bodily harm for the purposes of the 1861 Act.

The offence of GBH is set out in Sec. 20 of the *Offences against the Person Act 1861* in the following terms: "Inflicting bodily injury, with or without a weapon. Whosoever shall unlawfully and maliciously wound or inflict any grievous bodily harm upon any other person, either with or without any weapon or instrument, shall be guilty of a misdemeanour." Initially the offence attracted a long prison sentence.[22]

Case *R 86* illustrates how the allocation of a case was decided by a bench of three magistrates in an eight-minute hearing during which the defendant, a young black male, was locked in the dock. The LA confirmed the defendant's name, date of birth, and address and read out the charge: "There are several charges amounting to 'grievous bodily harm.' On 6 July at Smith Road you attempted to steal a moped. On 6 July at Smith Road you unlawfully wounded Mr Y by throwing corrosive fluid in his face causing grievous bodily harm. On 6 July at Jump-off Road you were spotted by officers driving the stolen moped and were found to be in possession of class C drugs, cannabis." Turning to the bench, the prosecutor stated: "This case

---

[21] See CPS guidance at https://www.cps.gov.uk/legal-guidance/offences-against-person-incorporating-charging-standard (accessed 9 October 2018).

[22] See: http://www.legislation.gov.uk/ukpga/Vict/24-25/100/section/20.

is not suitable for this court. Some of the charges are indictable, those linked to stealing the moped and assault by throwing acid at the victim.[23] A device was also found on the defendant to create credit cards. The matters should be sent to the Crown court. These are serious matters." After an exchange between the LA and the defendant's solicitor regarding the evidence, the LA stated that the case would be referred to Crown court for trial. The passive role adopted by the defendant's solicitor was reflected in his failure to make an application for bail. At this point the prosecutor stated: "Regarding bail, we argue that the defendant will fail to surrender himself because of the likelihood of a lengthy sentence and because of his antecedents. He is also likely to commit further offences while on bail." The Chair of the bench immediately addressed the defendant: "Please stand. There are six offences linked together, some are indictable. The matter is committed to Isleworth Crown court on 1 October. We do not grant bail. The reasons are that it is likely that you will fail to surrender and that you will commit further offences on bail. You may go." The defendant was taken down to the cells from where he would be transferred to prison to await trial.

The prosecution of criminal offences can be delayed, sometimes indefinitely and with serious consequences for defendants who are held indefinitely in custody,[24] by the refusal of the Legal Aid Board to grant funding for an interpreter. This was the case in *R 154* in which a male Eritrean was arrested on an assault charge in an affray between Eritreans and Sri Lankans. The defendant and the victim both required interpreters (for Tigrinya and Sinhala), which the Legal Aid Board granted shortly before the scheduled trial. The solicitor for the defendant successfully applied for the trial date to be vacated and a new date to be set due to the delay by the LAA.

---

[23] In the *Theft Act 1968*, theft is defined as "(1) A person is guilty of theft if he dishonestly appropriates property belonging to another with the intention of permanently depriving the other of it; and 'thief' and 'steal' shall be construed accordingly. (2) It is immaterial whether the appropriation is made with a view to gain or is made for the thief's own benefit." Under Sec. 7, a person found guilty of theft "shall on conviction on indictment be liable to imprisonment for a term not exceeding seven years." See https://www.legislation.gov.uk/ukpga/1968/60/crossheading/theft-robbery-burglary-etc.

[24] In *R 241*, a man was charged with public indecency. His solicitor's request to the Legal Aid Board for a Tigrinya interpreter had been denied regardless of his assertions that due to a head injury his client needed a mental health assessment. The defendant had already been in custody for two months. A further delay of two days was granted to ensure that an interpreter would be at the trial.

"Acid attacks"[25] have become increasingly common in London and have increased in number from 77 incidents in 2012 to 465 incidents in 2017. The public outcry over these attacks,[26] which has been echoed in the press, has prompted numerous official statements. In July 2017 the Home Office launched a public consultation on the issue and the Sentencing Council issued guidance to judges indicating that the appropriate sentence for this offence was between three and seventeen years (Sentencing Council 2017). In August 2017 the CPS issued a statement setting out new guidance for prosecutors to use in prosecuting the offence. Finally, *the Offensive Weapons Bill*[27] was passed into law in June 2018 (House of Commons 2019b). Three points need to be made about this flurry of activity by the government. First, the police find it difficult to catch individuals who use acid in personal attacks or as part of a theft. Secondly, there is a serious gap between government rhetoric and its willingness to invest resources[28] to enable the police to arrest offenders. Finally, a sufficient basis in the law already exists without the need to introduce new laws.[29]

Wounding

CPS guidance for this offence states that

[25] Data on this type of offence comes from House of Commons (2017); "2017 was the worst year for acid attacks in London" (*CNN*, 26 January 2018); "Acid attackers will get life sentence even if they miss their targets, says CPS" (*Independent*, 4 August 2017).

[26] See "Acid attack menace set to cost Britain five hundred million pounds by 2020" (*Express*, 26 July 2018).

[27] The bill received Royal Assent in May 2019 and criminalises possession of a corrosive substance in a public place, makes a new offence of selling certain harmful corrosive products to under eighteens, and introduces new restrictions on online sales of bladed articles and corrosive products. The bill also introduce a new offence of possessing certain offensive weapons in public (the weapons concerned are already subject to restrictions on their sale, manufacture, and importation) and it would reclassify certain firearms as "prohibited weapons." See http://www.legislation.gov.uk/ukpga/2019/17/contents/enacted.

[28] As was made clear during the second reading of the Bill on 17 July by Louise Haigh (MP for Sheffield, Heely) who asked if additional resources would be provided to the police. See https://hansard.parliament.uk/commons/2018-06-27/debates/44FAE1BD-A3EC-4B2C-99C9-0743DB003606/OffensiveWeaponsBill.

[29] For example, section 29 of the *Offences against the Person Act 1861* specifically deals with the use of corrosive substances and carrying acid without lawful authority or reasonable excuse is an offence under section 1 of the *Prevention of Crime Act 1953*, which carries a sentence of four years.

> a "wound" means "a break in the continuity of the whole skin [citing *JJC (A Minor) v Eisenhower [1983] 3 W.L.R. 537*]. The definition of wounding may encompass injuries that are relatively minor in nature, for example a small cut or laceration. The charge of "wounding" is a Sec. 20 offence in the *Offences against the Person Act 1861* and should be reserved for those wounds considered to be really serious.

Between 2016 and 2018 the Metropolitan Police recorded nearly fifty-three thousand incidents of wounding/GBH in London (3 per cent of all recorded offences).[30]

House of Commons researchers (2019c, 16) found that:

> There were four thousand four hundred thirty-four finished consultant episodes (FCE) recorded in English hospitals in 2016/17 due to assault by a sharp object. This was an increase of 7.6% compared to 2015/16 and 21.7% higher than in 2014/15. The number in 2014/15 was lowest since 1998/99. The number rose from 1998/99 until reaching a peak of five thousand seven hundred and twenty in 2006/07. In later years the number decreased annually before rising again in recent years . . . *In 2016/17, of those admitted to hospital for assault by sharp object 15.5% were aged eighteen or younger. Around 91% of people admitted to hospital for assault by sharp objects are men.* [My emphasis]

Case *R 115* concerned an allegation of two offences against a twenty-five-year-old black male who was arrested and charged with unlawful wounding and possession of class A drugs following a fight in Finsbury Park at 3:30 am. During the fight the defendant "armed himself with a broken bottle and stabbed the victim in the back of the neck." The court referred both matters to Blackfriars Crown Court for trial and, presumably because he had no previous offences, they released the defendant on unconditional bail. He was warned by the bench that he was still on court bail, which meant that if he failed to attend his trial or if he committed further offences he would be arrested and jailed until his trial. The hearing took six minutes. If this case is compared with case *R 63* (below), it can be seen that there is a fine line between charging an individual with wounding as opposed to assault.

---

[30] See the Metropolitan Police "Crime dashboard" (accessed 12 February 2018) at https://www.met.police.uk/sd/stats-and-data/met/crime-data-dashboard/.

Assault

The CPS[31] defines common assault (ABH) as

> the use of a weapon of a kind likely to cause serious injury . . . ; a weapon is used and serious injury is caused; more than minor injury is caused by kicking or head-butting; serious violence is caused to those whose work has to be done in contact with the public or are likely to face violence in the course of their work; and [when] violence to vulnerable people, e.g. the elderly and infirm is caused.

The number of offences charged as "assault with injury" in London for the period 2016–18 was recorded as 106,792 (6 per cent of all cases).[32]

A typical case of wounding is illustrated in case *R 63*, an allegation of assault against a thirty-five-year-old white female. However, when the case opened, the defendant's solicitor spoke directly to the bench: "We do not intend to plead today. I am not wasting court time if I explain that I am attending with the defendant's mother and her psychiatric nurse. The defendant is suffering from early onset dementia . . ." The prosecutor asked for five minutes to read the file and the case was briefly adjourned.

When proceedings resumed the CPS stated:

> "The case is not suitable for summary trial. This is a Sec. 20 case.[33] Prison is a possibility. The issue is about culpability aggravated by alcohol. There is a possible sentence of one to five years . . . These are the facts. There was an attack on a female at a pub at 11:40 p.m. when the defendant came up to the victim and blew into her face. The defendant started to shout at the victim saying: "why are you looking at my man?" The defendant then punched the victim in the face, got on top of her and started pulling her hair out. At this point the landlady asked the defendant and the victim to leave, and the victim went to the hospital for treatment. Subsequently the victim and her friends were able to identify the defendant by looking on Facebook following which papers were served on the defendant and she was charged with GBH. The victim's statement indicates that she was badly bruised, suffered hair loss, a

[31] See https://www.cps.gov.uk/legal-guidance/offences-against-person-incorporating-charging-standard.

[32] See the Metropolitan Police "Crime dashboard" (accessed 12 February 2018), https://www.met.police.uk/sd/stats-and-data/met/crime-data-dashboard/.

[33] He was referring to Sec. 20 of the *Offences against the Person Act 1861*. Such offences are framed as somewhat less serious than GBH but more serious than ABH (actual bodily harm). It is used to prosecute defendants with psychiatric illnesses; the maximum sentence is five years imprisonment. See http://www.legislation.gov.uk/ukpga/Vict/24-25/100/section/20.

> dislocated nose, and damage to the eye requiring continued treatment. Here are photos of the wound. The defendant was interviewed and provided a witness statement. The case is appropriate for summary treatment."

The defendant's solicitor stated that she had no representations to make. The bench conferred amongst themselves and concluded that the case was suitable for the court to hear. At this point, the legal adviser asked the defendant: "This case can be heard at this court or a Crown court, which do you prefer?" The defendant, carefully watching her solicitor, stated "Crown court." The bench referred the case to Inner London Crown Court and clarified bail conditions: specifically, no contact with the victim. The hearing took nineteen minutes. Her decision to be tried at a Crown court may or may not have been well advised because if she is found guilty there, she could face the maximum sentence.

Trials provide a clearer insight into how criminal offences are prosecuted, argued, and decided. *T 22* involves the trial of an Indian national for assault. Before the trial opened, the defendant's solicitor informed the DJ that his client was not present, having left for India, and he requested that the trial be put back one month. The DJ refused the application saying: "The incident occurred two months ago. It is unacceptable that he took himself out of the court's jurisdiction." The judge told the solicitor that the case would proceed; at this point the defendant's solicitor withdrew from the case,[34] which meant that the defendant was not legally represented.

When the case began, the prosecution witnesses and the victim/claimant were called into court and the CPS began by outlining the case (stage 2). The incident arose between members of a cricket club in south London who were arguing about the outcome of a match between India and Sri Lanka. The men left the club and returned to one of their homes were the argument continued for a little over an hour until they left for a mosque. On their return, the argument was resumed and the defendant hit the victim on the head, knocking him out. In his written statement, the defendant claimed that the others "were making fun of him" and that he hit the victim in "self-defence." He also claimed that he was injured in the altercation, though he did not provide evidence to support either claim. The case proceeded quickly because, in the defendant's absence, the witnesses' evidence was not contested. Two witnesses, who took an oath on the Koran, were questioned by the Crown and provided corroborating evidence (stage 3) supporting the victim. When the witnesses finished their evidence, the DJ

---

[34] The basis on which solicitors can withdraw from representing their clients are set out in Rule 2 of the Solicitors Code of Conduct, see:
http://www.sra.org.uk/documents/code/rule-2-client-relations.pdf.

stated (stage 7): "The defendant's identity is accepted; the summary of the evidence is accepted . . . I am satisfied that the defendant Mr S assaulted Mr L on June 4th. There is evidence of an injury [i.e., photos]. A warrant will be issued for his arrest on return from India." The hearing, which had lasted thirty-three minutes, closed.

Possession of a knife

Public awareness of the extent to which young people in London carry and use knives has increased in step with the number of incidents and growing media coverage.[35] Knife crime in London has increased every year since 2009; in 2017/18, nearly fifteen thousand incidents were recorded in London, the highest level in ten years (House of Commons 2019c). Worryingly, police data on annual "sanction detection rates" is lower for knife crime than for other violent offences, that is, by 20 to 30 per cent. Published data indicate that less than 35 per cent of reported cases were prosecuted between 2009 and 2018 (House of Commons 2019, Table 9). At the same time the number of cases that the police dealt with by cautioning juvenile offenders declined during this period even though convictions for the offence and the average length of custody increased to 30 per cent and six and a half months, respectively. The increase in sentencing followed a decision in the *Court of Appeal (R v Povey [2008] EWCA Crim 1261)*, which stated that magistrates should normally sentence those convicted of knife crime possession offences at the top end of the range. The length of sentences increased again in 2015/16 following the coming into force of the *Criminal Justice and Courts Act 2015*[36] which introduced a minimum custodial sentence of six months for those aged eighteen or over and for repeat offenders.

As has occurred in relation to the rise in acid attacks and moped-related theft[37] in London, the government responded by introducing

---

[35] See for instance, "Knife crime: News headlines are predictable—but they don't have to be" (*Guardian*, 8 April 2019).

[36] See http://www.legislation.gov.uk/ukpga/2015/2/part/1/enacted. This increased sentences for all "serious crime" and redefined the role of parole boards and their ability to release prisoners.

[37] The Metropolitan Police recorded twenty-two thousand crimes in London enabled by scooters, mopeds, and motorcycles from June 2017 to May 2018, 50 per cent more than the same period in 2016/17. However, in late 2017 the number of these crimes began to decline. See: https://fullfact.org/crime/moped-crime-rising-london/?gclid=EAIaIQobChMIteaI4dLf3AIVmed3Ch0ZQA70EAAYAyAAEgJrIPD_BwE (accessed 6 October 2018).

minimum sentencing, electronic tagging, and greater control over the release of prisoners on parole. This "get tough on crime" approach has not addressed the causes of rising knife crime nor does it appear to have resulted in increased central government funding to the police, courts, or prisons for detecting, trying, or rehabilitating offenders.

The *Guardian* newspaper[38] reported the response by the authorities to rising crime in the following terms:

> Commenting on the figures, the Met's Assistant Commissioner, Martin Hewitt, raised the issue of funding cuts. "The Met continues to experience a very busy and challenging time against the backdrop of significant reductions in resources," he said. "I am very concerned about the rise in crime in the capital, particularly murder, violent crime and knife crime." He added: "We are doubling our targeted anti-knife crime activity with hundreds more officers on visible patrols in affected communities. But despite our continued focus on reducing knife crime, prevention and diversion will always be key."
>
> The Mayor of London, Sadiq Khan, said: "These statistics show once again that crime, and violent crime in particular, is rising at an unacceptably high rate across the whole of England and Wales, including London. This is clearly a national problem that requires national solutions from the government."
>
> Louise Haigh, shadow policing minister, said the government was failing to protect the public. She said: "Whether it's Windrush citizens or victims of violent crime, the Home Secretary has repeatedly refused to acknowledge the evidence staring her in the face. "The Tories have axed twenty-one thousand police officers, and neighbourhood policing, which help to prevent crime . . . Our communities are now exposed and we have a government unwilling or unable to put it right."

Case *R 99*, discussed in chapter 1, shows that bladed instruments are routinely carried and used to threaten violence against the person. Arrests for knife-related offences often occur haphazardly. Thus, in case *R 224* the police arrested a thirty-year-old black male who appeared to behave suspiciously in Waterloo Station and who was found to be carrying a twelve-inch knife. When officers searched him, he was also found to be carrying a three-inch lock-knife.[39] When he appeared in court his solicitor stated:

---

[38] See "Surge in knife and gun crime in England and Wales" (*Guardian*, 26 April 2018).

[39] The Crown charged him with an offence *either* under Section 1 of the *Prevention of Crime Act 1953* for a person to have with him in any public place any offensive weapon without "lawful authority or reasonable excuse" *or* under Section 1(4) of

> "Mr J is in supported accommodation under a psychiatrist's care. There was an incident at the home which has caused him "fear." The house was immediately reorganized to prevent contact between the two persons. This is the basis for his "fear" which led him to carry the knives. He is a quiet, non-violent person. There is no violence in his history. I suggest the lowest category, a community penalty. I need a pre-sentence [probation] report and a report from his care worker. His new care worker is present in court."

Asked by a magistrate where Mr J had obtained the knives, his solicitor said: "The internet." The probation officer who was called to provide a report asked for at least five days to interview and report to the court. The court adjourned the hearing to receive the report; however, the officer returned to say that it would take at least three weeks to provide a report. The bench released the defendant on unconditional bail to his care worker until his sentencing hearing. The case took twenty minutes to hear.

Similarly, in case *R 233* the court took seven minutes to hear the case of a nineteen-year-old black male who pleaded guilty to possessing two weapons: a wooden bat and a metal knuckleduster. The Crown read out the charges (stage 2): "On 15 July officers became aware of his reaction to their presence [on the street], so they searched him and found a bat. He said it was for his own protection. He also had a bag inside of which was a metal knuckleduster. He was arrested at this point. I am not able to provide photos of the two weapons."

In mitigation (stage 6) the duty solicitor stated:

> "This is a nineteen-year-old with a few assault convictions which he received as a youth. . . . He has pleaded guilty at the earliest possibility and has been upfront with the police. He has been fully co-operative and should be given credit for this. He had no plans to use the weapons; there was no intention to use. The second was in a bag. He has recently been released from juvenile detention; he supports himself and has no parental support at all. He hopes to establish a clothing line and would like to attend a management course. There are no serious connections to gangs. He is not taking drugs or alcohol. These are not deadly weapons. I realize that possession is an aggravating factor, but this did not take place in a public

---

the 1953 Act that defines "offensive weapon" as "any article made or adapted for use for causing injury to the person or intended by the person having it with him for such use by him or by some other person"; *or* under (ii) Section 139 of the *Criminal Justice Act 1988* that states that it is an offence for a person to have with him in a public place any article which has a blade or is sharply pointed, except a folding pocket knife with a cutting edge of three inches or less, without good reason or lawful authority.

place. I suggest this is a category 1 offence and it requires a report by probation. I suggest a community order at a very low threshold."

The bench arranged for the defendant to be interviewed by probation (stage 8) and put the sentencing hearing back several days to allow for a probation report. He was released on unconditional bail and told to attend his sentencing hearing.

Sex offences

The Metropolitan Police recorded over sixteen thousand rape offences (0.009 per cent of all recorded crime) and more than twenty-five thousand "other sexual offences" (less than 1.5 per cent of all recorded crime) in London between 2016 and 2018.[40] I did not observe any cases alleging rape (they are sent to a Crown court to be prosecuted).[41] Sexual offences can be charged under the CPS *Violence against Women and Girls (VAWG) Strategy (2018a) (UK 2019a)*, which is

> an overarching framework to address crimes that have been identified as being committed primarily but not exclusively by men against women. The crimes include domestic abuse, rape, sexual offences, stalking, harassment, so-called "honour-based" violence including forced marriage, female genital mutilation, child abuse, human trafficking focusing on sexual exploitation, prostitution, pornography and obscenity.

---

[40] See the Metropolitan Police "Crime dashboard" (accessed 12 February 2018) at https://www.met.police.uk/sd/stats-and-data/met/crime-data-dashboard/. Rape is defined as "the penetration of the vagina, anus or mouth of another person with a penis, without the person's consent, where the perpetrator does not have reasonable belief there was consent." Sexual assault "is defined as a person intentionally penetrating the vagina or anus of another person with an object, or part of the body other than the penis, without their consent, and without having reasonable belief in consent." While the police must investigate both types of offence, the CPS will only prosecute a rape case if it is satisfied that the case can be proved "beyond all reasonable doubt," a very high standard. For further information see: http://www.rasasc.org.uk/independent-sexual-violence-advocate-service/criminal-justice-system/.

[41] Studies suggest that one in ten rapes or attempted rapes reported to police in England and Wales are brought to trial. Research from 2013 estimated that between one in twenty and one in thirty rape cases end up at trial. See https://fullfact.org/crime/how-many-reported-rapes-go-to-trial/ (accessed 12 February 2018). The CPS reports that rape was successfully prosecuted in 57.6 per cent of cases across England and Wales; in London the rate was 54.7 per cent (CPS 2016–17, 87).

I observed cases alleging sex offences that were considered pornographic in nature and that could be prosecuted under either Section 1 of the *Protection of Children Act 1978* (PCA 1978) or Section 160 of the *Criminal Justice Act 1988* (CJA 1988). The common elements of this offence are that the charge concerns indecent photographs or pseudo-photographs of a child, which is an either-way offence punishable on indictment with a maximum of ten years imprisonment. If the charge is made under Section 62 of the *Coroners and Justice Act 2009*, which created the offence of possession of a prohibited image of a child, it is triable either-way and punishable on indictment with a maximum of three years imprisonment. The following cases indicate the seriousness with which magistrates dealt with these case—all were referred to a Crown court to be heard—and as with domestic violence cases (see chapter 4) they show how violence is directed at females.

Case *R 16* concerned an allegation against a young Asian male for taking photos up a girl's skirt in central London. The defendant initially decided to defend himself and he pleaded guilty. After the defendant identified himself (stage 1), the prosecutor read out the allegation (stage 2):

> "The defendant was observed using a mobile phone camera in Top Shop on Oxford Street; he was photographing up the skirts of girls. He has pleaded guilty to a charge of indecency.[42] He was photographing young women going up the escalator. The arresting officer seized the device, but as the defendant was not scheduled for a hearing the officer has not gotten back to me. The case was to be heard later … The specific pictures are of a girl aged twelve to fourteen years. The matter is serious."

The magistrate informed the defendant that the court was waiting to hear from the police about an "ancillary charge" and that it was adjourning the case to await a police report. At this point the defendant stated that he wanted a duty solicitor to represent him.

Twenty-five minutes later, the case resumed with the LA handing the magistrate a copy of the police report confirming that photos of a young woman which were found on the defendant's mobile phone. The solicitor informed the court that the defendant had been carrying out this type of

---

[42] Sec. 1 of the *Protection of Children Act 1978* states "Indecent photographs of children. (1) Subject to sections 1A and 1B, it is an offence for a person—(a) to take, or permit to be taken [or to make], any indecent photograph [or pseudo-photograph] of a child or (b) to distribute or show such indecent photographs [or pseudo-photographs]; or (c) to have in his possession such indecent photographs [or pseudo-photographs], with a view to their being distributed or shown by himself or others. . . ." See https://www.legislation.gov.uk/ukpga/1978/37.

activity—it is referred to as "upskirting"[43]—for two years. The evidence and the admission of guilt led the prosecutor to state: "We have concerns about the appropriate government rehabilitation program. It may appear to be fairly onerous, but the offence is low-level. The victims were unaware of the offence. That is why we are asking for the second and third condition on the 'Harms statement.'[44] The minimum period is five years."[45]

The LA told the court: "You need to consider access to IT property—phones, camera, and computers—at his property; and the sentence needs to be practical in terms of policing." Asked to comment on his offence, the defendant stated: "I am sorry for my actions. I have no plan to repeat them. What does the order mean?" The LA and the magistrate explained that a minimum order of five years duration was to be imposed on him during which he cannot use IT devices in public and that the police will be installing an "app" on all his IT devices to monitor him. If he violates the order, he will breach the conditions of his sentence.

While an appropriate rehabilitation programme was being identified, the magistrate passed sentence:

> "Mr C please stand. We note you pleaded guilty in the first instance. And for that there will be a community order for twenty-four months. You are required to attend an accredited programme for sex offenders. Successful rehabilitation will reduce the period for up to forty days. You must comply with all the directions. If you fail to comply it will be a breach[46] and you will come back to court where the sentence may be increased, or you may be re-sentenced and given a heavier sentence. You must inform the court if you

---

[43] There is no specific offence for this act that used to be prosecuted as an "Offence of outraging public decency," which was triable either way under Sec. 320 of the *Criminal Justice Act 2003*. In 2019 a specific offence for upskirting was created as a triable either-way offence with a maximum imprisonment of two years under the *Voyeurism (Offences) Act 2019: Implementation of the Voyeurism (Offences) Act 2019.*

[44] See Sec. 103A–103K of the *Sexual Offences Act (2003)* at http://www.legislation.gov.uk/ukpga/2003/42/part/2/crossheading/sexual-harm-prevention-orders-england-and-wales.

[45] Mandatory sentences for sex offences have continually been revised upwards over the past ten years. Current guidelines for this offence can be found at Sentencing Council (2016b, 75–80).

[46] A common breach of a criminal offence of this type is failure to register with the police. In *R 77* the defendant, a young black male in his early thirties, had recently been released from prison for a sex offence but had failed to register with the police and sign the sex offenders register because he was homeless and sleeping rough in different areas around London. He was given a twelve-week suspended sentence and fined £200 (which was to be deducted from his benefits).

change your address. If you can't attend the program for a medical reason, you must provide a medical certificate. You are being given a "sexual harm order," which means you cannot have unsupervised contact with anyone under the age of sixteen. If you find yourself in contact with under sixteens, you must inform their parents. Any IT, phone, or computer you own is subject to confiscation by the police. You must allow the police to install monitoring equipment on your devices. The period is for five years. You must pay a victim surcharge of £115 and court costs of £30. Can you pay the fine today?"

When the defendant agreed to pay, the magistrate concluded by stating: "A payment order will be made for seven days. If you fail to pay, the bailiffs can come to your home and seize property to cover that cost and their costs." The hearing took thirty-six minutes.

Case *R 107* concerned an allegation regarding possession of pornographic images[47] to which the defendant, a forty-three-year-old Asian male, pleaded guilty. He had been on bail for two years prior to the hearing, presumably to allow the police time to complete their investigation, which was linked to an "intel operation." After the defendant confirmed his name, date of birth and address, the LA read out the charges:

LA: "Between 8 and 16 of September 2016 you were in possession of 123 indecent images of children, still photos and moving images. This is a category A offence. Between 8 and 16 September you were in possession of 46 additional images, category B. In April 2009 you were in possession of 97 images of indecent photos; category C. The case is not suitable for magistrates' court. The defendant was in possession of category A images aggravated by the possession of category B and C images. He was arrested,

[47] Prosecution was based on the *Criminal Justice and Immigration Act 2008*, which states at Sec. 63. "Possession of extreme pornographic images." "(1) It is an offence for a person to be in possession of an extreme pornographic image. (2) An 'extreme pornographic image' is an image which is both—(a) pornographic, and (b) an extreme image. (3) An image is 'pornographic' if it is of such a nature that it must reasonably be assumed to have been produced solely or principally for the purpose of sexual arousal. (4) Where (as found in the person's possession) an image forms part of a series of images, the question whether the image is of such a nature as is mentioned in subsection (3) is to be determined by reference to—(a) the image itself, and (b) (if the series of images is such as to be capable of providing a context for the image) the context in which it occurs in the series of images. . . ." Sec. 69 identifies the sentence for a conviction as "on summary conviction, to imprisonment for a term not exceeding the relevant period or a fine not exceeding the statutory maximum or both; (b) on conviction on indictment, to imprisonment for a term not exceeding 3 years or a fine or both." See: https://www.legislation.gov.uk/ukpga/2008/4/part/5.

> and his home was searched where the police seized computers, images, and a server. I make an application to deal with these offences consecutively."

His solicitor observed the seriousness of the case against his client and the bench noted that sentencing guidelines indicated that the minimum sentence would be one year. The defendant's solicitor and the prosecutor corrected the bench by noting that one year was the starting point for possessing category A images. The bench declined to hear the case and referred it to the Crown court where it was listed for a hearing in four weeks. The solicitor and the Crown were asked to complete the PET/trial form, following which the bench addressed the defendant: "Mr P, please stand up. You have pleaded guilty. Your trial will be at Wood Green Crown Court; your next appearance will be in one month at the Crown court. You are released on conditional bail on the condition that you do not have any contact with individuals under the age of eighteen without the explicit consent of the child's parent or guardian. Do you understand?" The hearing lasted ten minutes.

Case *R 111* concerned an allegation of sexual assault against a minor.[48] The defendant was a twenty-three-year-old white male dressed in a suit jacket who pleaded not guilty to two offences. The Crown began by stating that the case was not suitable for summary trial given the nature of the assaults, which occurred in 2014. He read out the allegation:

> Prosecutor: "The assaults occurred when the victim was fourteen years old. The defendant held a position of trust in the family.[49] He committed a number of offences including sexual assault; he touched her breasts through her clothing; he attempted to kiss her; his hands were under her top while he was in the family home. These are category 1–2 offences involving psychological harm and sexual assault. The starting point for sentencing is three years."

---

[48] *R 65* is a very similar case where the defendant is alleged to have sexually abused a young girl over a period of five months in her family's home.

[49] This appears to be a prosecution under Sec. 9 of the *Sexual Offences Act 2003*, which states that "Sexual activity with a child (1) A person aged eighteen or over (A) commits an offence if—(a) he intentionally touches another person (B), (b) the touching is sexual, and (c) either—(i) B is under sixteen and A does not reasonably believe that B is sixteen or over, or (ii) B is under thirteen. Sec. 9(3) states that a person guilty of an offence under this section is liable—(a) on summary conviction, to imprisonment for a term not exceeding six months or to a fine not exceeding the statutory maximum or both; (b) on conviction on indictment, to imprisonment for a term not exceeding fourteen years." See https://www.legislation.gov.uk/ukpga/2003/42.

The defendant's solicitor stated: "I concur with the Crown. However, I haven't seen any evidence.[50] This is a category 2 matter; category A with culpability with sentencing in the range of two years. It is a matter for the Crown court." The magistrates agreed to remit the case and, with a look towards me sitting in the gallery, they noted that there were "lifetime reporting restrictions" in place that prohibited details of the case from being published.

The prosecutor noted that the defendant had been brought to court by way of a requisition/summons. Furthermore, there was a "no contact" order in place with the victim and her family. "He is not to go to the victim's residence. . . . He is not to instigate any contact with persons under the age of eighteen in an effort to replicate the conditions [that gave rise to the offence] without the permission of the persons' parents or guardians." Having determined that the defendant was "happy to comply" with the bail conditions and that no evidence had been served on him, the bench addressed the defendant:

> "Please stand. You have pleaded not guilty to this offence. A trial has been set at Wood Green Crown Court with a first meeting in two weeks. You are required to attend the hearing. You are released on conditional bail [they repeated the three conditions]. If you fail to attend, you may be arrested and may find yourself in jail. If you breach conditions of your bail, you will be brought back to court and there will be no bail. Do you understand?"

The bench reiterated: "no contact means no contact at all. Do you understand?" The defendant promised to attend court. The hearing lasted seventeen minutes.

Theft

Between 2002/2003 and 2008/2009 there was a gradual decline in the number of robberies across London; however, in 2009 cases of theft began to increase. For the period January 2016 to January 2018, theft[51] constituted 27 per cent of all offences in London.[52]

---

[50] This statement appears to indicate an attempt by the lawyer to comply with procedural requirement to assist the court to "case manage" his client's case. See my discussion of this in Chap. 1.

[51] There are four main types of theft that the Metropolitan Police record, listed in terms of largest to smallest in number of offences, these are: "other theft," "shoplifting," "theft from person," and "bicycle theft."

[52] See the Metropolitan Police "Crime dashboard" (accessed 13 February 2019) at https://www.met.police.uk/sd/stats-and-data/.

In September 2017 the Home Office issued a "Crime Assessment Guide"[53] to the police that set out details regarding the types of crime that the police should *not* pursue due to cuts in government funding. These crimes included "crimes involving a loss of under fifty pounds, [that] car crime and some assaults will not be investigated unless a suspect is already identified, and that CCTV should only be analysed for crimes committed in a twenty-minute time frame." The policy represents a decisive step back from protecting the public.

Prosecutions for theft accounted for 19 per cent of the cases I observed and illustrate the different ways that individuals, particularly poor, homeless individuals, become inextricably entangled with the law. In case *R 194* the defendant, a homeless, white male in his forties, was charged with violating a Criminal Behaviour Order and "attempting to steal a motor vehicle." He pleaded guilty to both offences. The Crown read out the charge:

> Prosecutor: "There are two matters. Attempted theft of motor vehicles. Between 21 and 27 July the defendant attempted to steal from two Mercedes Benz by opening their doors; he was caught on CCTV. On 11 November he was found within a prohibited zone: he was convicted in October 2017 and a CBO was issued for two years banning him from entering the area due to three previous breaches. This is his fourth breach. It was imposed in relation to thefts. He had a DRR imposed and received a suspended sentence. The suspended sentence was activated in May and he was given eight weeks custody; you may wish to activate it. There is some suggestion that you may wish to think again about the effectiveness of the ban to prevent him from stealing. The exclusion zone was redefined from a situation in which he was not able to be in the zone to one which allowed him to attend appointments if he could verify the appointments. We ask for £85 costs."

The defendant's duty solicitor clarified the case against her client and offered mitigation:

> "Both cars were parked in the driveway; that's the incident. Sentencing should be on a lower scale; the area in which it occurred was not within the zone . . . [I suggest] category 3; there was no planning. Regarding the CBO, there are issues in terms of the wording of the CBO which were clarified in October. He is allowed in the town centre for appointments, but he needs to have written evidence. There is no evidence that he is guilty of breaching the CBO. There is no suggestion of criminal behaviour. He needs to be given credit for his early guilty plea. Drugs are an ongoing issue here. . . . Could

---

[53] See "Met Police to stop investigating some 'low level' crime £400m funding cuts" (16 October 2017, *Independent*).

you consider a suspended sentence? He is applying for benefits but has none at the moment. I ask that you deal with him today by way of a penalty."

After briefly conferring amongst themselves, the bench addressed the defendant:

Magistrate: Please stand up. We are sending you to prison for four weeks. The offence is so serious that only custody can be justified. This is the fourth breach of the CBO. You have a substantial criminal record during 2017; your record is lengthy. We have taken into account your early guilty plea and reduced custody from six to four weeks. The surcharge of £115 is discharged by two days custody. We make no order for costs because you are going into custody and because of your circumstances."

The defendant was taken back to the cells from where he was transferred to prison.[54] The magistrates clearly disregarded the DS's information about her client and the request that her client should pay a fine rather than be imprisoned. The entire hearing lasted nineteen minutes.

The extent to which theft is an opportunistic crime is illustrated in case *R 44* in which an allegation of theft and breach of trust was made against a young black male. The LA confirmed the defendant's name, date of birth and residence. She then informed the bench that "all options are open, including custody." The prosecutor set out the case against the defendant:

"On 25 May at Charing Cross Station the victim, Mr F, entered a train and occupied two seats. When he reached his stop, he picked up what he thought were all of his things and left the train. However, his phone was missing. He went to SE Rail and asked whether his phone had been returned but was told to return later. He checked with his phone service who said that the phone was turned off, and he reported it missing. A week later he reported the incident to SE trains who examined CCTV; they discovered that an employee who had been sitting near the victim pocketed the victim's phone. The defendant's home was searched, but the phone was not found. When later interviewed by the police the defendant admitted to having taken the phone but, because he could not open it, he discarded it. His employer . . .

---

[54] In *R 106*, a thirty-year-old black defendant—who was currently serving a seven-year sentence in prison for burglary—was charged with attempting to break into a domestic dwelling, an offence that carried a minimum sentence of one year. Via a video link to the court, he pleaded not guilty to the offence and asked to be tried at a Crown court. According to the prosecutor the defendant, who had prior offences for burglary, was caught on CCTV. The bench referred his case to the Crown court for trial.

> saw his actions as a breach of trust. We seek £85 costs plus £632 compensation for the victim."

The duty solicitor disputed the amount of compensation and offered mitigation, namely that the defendant was likely to lose his job if he were to be convicted and that the defendant and his wife were struggling to pay their bills. A claim by the lawyer that the CCTV had not been made available to him was countered by the prosecutor who stated that: "When it was shown to the defendant, he changed his account. It was a calculated act." There were further discussions about the costs incurred by the defendant, the lack of insurance for the phone and the cost of replacing it. At this point the District Judge turned to the defendant:

> DJ: "Stand up Mr Y. I have been listening to the evidence. I note that you pleaded guilty after you were shown the CCTV. This was an opportunistic theft. I take note of the pre-sentence report by Probation. This is a case where you appear to have thought about it. You tried to use the phone but couldn't. You didn't hand it in, and you chose to destroy it. There is also an abuse of trust. I have taken into account what your representative has said. I am sentencing you to eight weeks in prison; sentence suspended for one year. You must do one hundred hours of unpaid community work. If you fail to turn up, you will find yourself back in court for breach of bail conditions and will be sent to prison for eight weeks. You will pay a victim surcharge of £115, costs of £85, and compensation of £484; a total of £684."

The defendant's offer to pay £10 a week was rejected by the DJ because the fine was "meant to be a punishment." The offer to pay £20 a week was accepted, and he was released with a warning to speak to probation on his way out of court. The hearing took thirty-one minutes.

VL 24 was also an opportunistic theft: an allegation of theft at a disco. The defendant, Mr B, was a Syrian asylum seeker in his early twenties who gave evidence via a video link from a police station to Westminster Magistrates' Court (because the interpreter and the defendant's representative were in court, communication with the defendant was difficult).[55] The LA began the hearing by confirming the defendant's name, date of birth, and address and noted that the language spoken by the defendant was French: "An incident occurred on 1 November at a disco in central London at which the defendant stole a phone and credit cards the value of which is unknown. The defendant is Mr B. How do you plead?" Mr B replied: "not guilty."

---

[55] A police officer was in the video booth with the defendant, but it was not possible to see the defendant's face due to the angle of the camera. The quality of the sound was poor.

The prosecutor then set out the case:

> "The Crown submits that this matter is suitable for trial. Ms A was in a nightclub with friends. A bag went missing and the phone and credit cards were taken. She used a friend's phone to locate hers, the phone rang and was in the possession of the defendant. The incident was recorded on CCTV though the tape is not with the court. The defendant was arrested in relation to the theft of the phone and credit cards. This is a category 4 offence,[56] which points to twelve weeks [imprisonment]. He has no previous convictions. You have sufficient authority to deal with this matter."

For reasons that are unclear, the defendant opted to be tried at Crown court. His solicitor then stated: "Why is he still in custody? There are no previous convictions. He did not fail to surrender himself. Isn't that a sufficient test for custody?" While the interpreter was translating the solicitor's request to the court, the prosecutor stated: "the Crown is content with conditional bail [providing that] the defendant stays at a known address." Asked to verify the defendant's address, his solicitor stated that he had been on bail for two months.

> "He attended his appointment at the police station and was detained. There seems to be some misunderstanding. He has been given advice and will attend court. He understands. He lives with a cousin, a UK national, at a verified address. He attends the police station fortnightly. He is a Syrian national. He is doing everything he is supposed to do. Unconditional bail is appropriate. He has no plans or resources enabling him to move. Please grant unconditional bail."

The LA identified a date for the trial, which was confirmed with the Crown and the defendant's solicitor. The magistrates then intervened to stop the defendant from speaking:

> "Save your arguments for Crown court. Mr B your trial will be at Suffolk Crown Court, a pretrial hearing will occur on 8 March. You need to be there at 9:30 a.m. Until that time, you are on conditional bail: you are required to sleep and live at 1 Bail Street. If you breach bail you will be brought back to court and there will be no bail. If you fail to attend court it is an offence under the Bail Act; a fine or a sentence or both may be imposed. If you do

[56] The Sentencing Council's "Theft Offences Definitive Guide" (2016a, 6) identifies a category 4 offence as suitable for a conviction for "Low value goods stolen (up to five hundred pounds) and little or no significant additional harm to the victim or others." The appropriate sentence is a medium level community order or thirty-six weeks custody.

> not attend court, it will be much more serious. The police will arrange for your release. Can you take note of the date and place of hearing?"

The video link was closed; the hearing lasted twenty minutes.

Conclusion

Several observations are in order. First, it should be clear that the government has criminalised "new offences" but it has failed to commit additional resources to the police or CPS to arrest and prosecute offenders. Second, the government has failed to address the underlying causes of crime while at the same time it has criminalised young (black) people in London. Third, many young defendants do not appear to fear the consequences of their actions; far from seeing their hearing as a form of "status degradation" (King 1978; Benson 1990), an appearance in court now appears to be viewed as a rite of passage into adulthood.

With respect to the "serious" offences I observed, my data suggests that a large percentage (forty-eight percent) are young black or Asian men (see table 2.2), which supports findings in the government's "Race Disparity Audit" (UK 2017) indicating a clear disparity in the arrest and prosecution of young males from black and mixed ethnic backgrounds.

Table 2.2. Gender and race of defendants in observed cases.

Gender		Ethnicity		
Male	**Female**	**White**	**Black**	**Asian/other**
15	1	3	9	4

Without exception, the key piece of evidence supporting the prosecution of defendants charged with a serious/either way offence is the availability of CCTV evidence or some form of photographic evidence. As table 2.3 shows, CCTV/images provided independent corroborating evidence in seven of the thirteen cases I observed. It should be clear that the police and CPS rely heavily on CCTV evidence to secure a conviction.

Table 2.3. Availability of CCTV/images to prosecute serious offences.

Yes	No	Unknown
7	4	2

I have limited information about the victims of the offences analysed above, in part because victims do not attend remand hearings. However, analysis of the cases fails to show a clear relation between the race of the defendant *and* his or her victim. Three cases were "victimless" in the sense that the police arrested individuals for possession of weapons and so on rather than for an offence against a person.

Turning to legal procedure, the rapidity of proceedings means that frequently neither the LA, the prosecutor, or the magistrates clearly state the statute/legislation that a defendant is being charged with. In as much as the police and the CPS exercise considerable leeway in how they charge a defendant, this means that even if a defendant has competent legal representation s/he will still find it difficult to provide an acceptable defence (as set out in legislation).

Finally, I saw little evidence that the defendants were legally, much less educationally, literate. Defendants appeared to shut down during proceedings, which means not only that they fail to understand what is happening to them—a situation compounded by the reliance of legal actors on arcane legal language—but also that they are at the mercy of the CPS because magistrates rely heavily on the arguments of prosecutors whereas duty solicitors tend to provide a fairly passive defence for their clients.

CHAPTER 3

THE PROSECUTION OF PUBLIC ORDER OFFENCES

Linguists have long debated how best to understand speech and "speech acts." Many have followed the work of Austin (1962) and Searle (1965) in defining a "speech act" as "a specimen of linguistic communication" that involves a linguistic act containing a basic or minimal unit of meaningful linguistic communication. In attempting to take this distinction further, linguists have found it necessary to devise a number of rules and propositions to identify the "meaning" of very basic speech acts. In contrast, politicians have had no qualms in criminalising what they see as "threatening, abusive, or insulting words" and behaviour that are said to be offensive, that is, which challenges social order. However, the criminalisation of speech has only increased the need for a careful analysis of the four inter-related elements of speech acts: action, speech, intention, and impact. This task has been taken up by the courts who lack linguistic training and who have been loath to provide guidance to magistrates' courts regarding how they should interpret and adjudicate such matters. This chapter looks at the criminalisation of speech acts and the problems this creates in a diverse and democratic society in which citizens have a right to freedom of expression that is guaranteed by Art. 10 of the *European Convention on Human Rights*.[1]

The *Public Order Act* (hereafter, the PoA) was proposed during Margaret Thatcher's second term of office, a period marked by deep social division and years of cuts to public services, rising unemployment, urban

---

[1] "1. Everyone has the right to freedom of expression. This right shall include freedom to hold opinions and to receive and impart information and ideas without interference by public authority and regardless of frontiers. This Article shall not prevent States from requiring the licensing of broadcasting, television or cinema enterprises. 2. The exercise of these freedoms, since it carries with it duties and responsibilities, may be subject to such formalities, conditions, restrictions or penalties as are prescribed by law and are necessary in a democratic society. . . ." See: https://www.echr.coe.int/Documents/Convention_ENG.pdf.

decay, and unrest. In its second reading in Parliament in January 1986, MPs voiced concerns about the miners' strikes (both the right to strike and violence between strikers and the police), "festivals" at national monuments, rising levels of violence in or around football stadiums, the 1981 Brixton riots and the 1985 Tottenham "riots," and rising levels of "hooliganism" and vandalism.[2]

The bill was preceded by a 1985 government White Paper that reviewed the *Public Order Act (1936)* and a report by the Law Commission (1983) that looked specifically at Sec. 5 offences in the POA (1936).[3] The Government used its Parliamentary majority to pass the bill and introduce new police powers, newly defined offences, and harsh sentences. The introduction to the POA (1986)[4] sets out its objective as:

> An Act to abolish the common law offences of riot, rout, unlawful assembly and affray and certain statutory offences relating to public order; to create new offences relating to public order; to control public processions and assemblies; to control the stirring up of racial hatred; to provide for the exclusion of certain offenders from sporting events. . . .

The Act was intended to strengthen the ability of the state to control behaviour and "speech acts" performed in public places that allegedly challenged the authority of the state. As Gibbons (1999, 156) has remarked: "Law is language . . . it is a profoundly linguistic institution. Laws are coded in language, and the processes of the law are mediated through language." The cases examined in this chapter focus on language—written and spoken—which is central to understanding how the police and the Crown use the PoA to regulate wide swathes of public life.

Section (i) examines the "language of law" in the Act that defines criminal offences, particularly section 4 and section 5 offences (but also the closely related offences of assault,[5] "drunk and disorderly" (Sec. 91 of the *Criminal Justice Act 1967*) and criminal damage (*Criminal Damage Act 1971*). I discuss how the police, CPS, and courts use the Act in an attempt to control public behaviour. Section (ii) analyses the public order offences I observed in magistrates' courts in 2017/18 to show how these cases come

---

[2] See http://hansard.millbanksystems.com/commons/1986/jan/13/public-order-bill.

[3] A discussion of the White Paper occurred in the House of Lords in May 1985, see http://hansard.millbanksystems.com/lords/1985/may/16/public-order-legislation-review#column_1277.

[4] See https://www.legislation.gov.uk/ukpga/1986/64/introduction.

[5] The offence of assault exists in different legislation; see the CPS charging guidelines on assault at https://www.cps.gov.uk/legal-guidance/offences-against-person-incorporating-charging-standard.

to court and how individuals were prosecuted. My analysis of remand hearings shows how "legal discourse" dominates a hearing and how "legal language" marginalises defendants who cannot understand it, leaving them unable to defend themselves. Section (iii) looks at the judicialisation of criminal language by examining how the appellate courts have decided whether and when words spoken in public are "threatening, abusive or insulting." I argue that the POA provides substantial discretion to the authorities to interpret and use the Act to prosecute a wide range of quite distinctive behaviours for which independent proof is not required to convict a person and because the statute provides defendants with very limited legal ground to defend their actions.

i. The language, scope, and use of public order offences

In the bill's second reading (UK 1986), Mr. Kaufman (MP for Manchester, Gorton) claimed that the "breadth of scope and lack of clarity" in the Public Order Bill opened the way for a serious erosion of civil liberties. Kaufman and his Labour colleagues were principally concerned that the bill would politicise the police (by giving them the power to regulate picketing) and that the Act would undermine the right of assembly. Sec. 5 of the proposed Act was also criticised because it "provides the police with extended and permissive powers of arrest" that the Association of Chief Police Officers had requested. As Scraton (1985, 389) commented at the time,

> The combination of "disorderly words or behaviour" with the causing of "alarm or distress" exemplifies the discretion embodied in the new proposals. As to what constitutes a "disorderly word" or what personal condition demonstrates "distress" is not clear. What is clear is the permissiveness and the breadth of this offence which effectively criminalizes any form of disorderly behaviour—real or imagined.

The passage into law of the Act, along with related legislation, has ensured that public protests and strikes have been tightly regulated and controlled.[6] I did not observe any cases that arose out of strikes/public protest nor did I observe anyone being charged with "riot."[7] In this chapter I focus on three issues that were raised during the bill's second reading and which, I argue,

---

[6] In the period between 2008 and mid-2018, there were only four arrests in London for the offence of "riot." Source: reply to my FOI request by the Metropolitan Police, Adhoc reference number 12498, dated 28 June 2018.

[7] See my discussion in the introduction about how the police and courts dealt with the "riots" of August 2011.

are apparent today in the way that the Crown uses the Act. The issues are the broad language used to define a public order offence, the abandonment of proof to prosecute an offence, and the discretion that the Act gives to the police and the CPS to prosecute a wide range of minor crimes/misdemeanours.

The government made it clear that the Act was intended to strengthen the power of the police and that the offences were drafted to secure convictions. However, rather than carefully defining specific offences[8] the Act used general, undefined terms to set out offences that can be used to regulate diverse forms of behaviour, in quite different contexts, which might be said to cause or threaten violence or distress. For instance, the principle distinction between the offence of riot, violent disorder, and affray concerns the number of offenders allegedly involved, not specific types of behaviour. Thus, the offence of "riot" refers to the purported actions of twelve or more persons, the offence of "violent disorder" refers to the purported actions of three or more persons, and the offence of "affray" refers to the purported actions of a single person.

Furthermore, and in contrast with most criminal legislation, the PoA states that "victims" are not required to give evidence because, at the time, the government argued that members of the public were afraid to give evidence. Instead it is sufficient for the court to take the word of a police constable who is authorised to "arrest without warrant anyone he reasonably suspects is committing an offence under this section." In short, the Act "abandoned the requirement of [independent] proof." However, even though this specific clause was repealed in 2006, individuals continue to be arrested and prosecuted on the evidence of a police officer.[9] It is worth noting that the police *only* collect evidence to support a prosecution, not to prove innocence (Sanders 1994, 2002).[10]

---

[8] Contrast this with US legislation that attempts to draw very clear boundaries designed to identify, arrest, and punish "sex offenders" (Small 2017) with the problems that arise when there is no clear definition of an offence. According to a recent report by the CPS Inspectorate and the HM Inspectorate of Constabulary, in England and Wales "The absence of a single accepted, consistent definition of stalking is said to be a 'very significant contributory factor to the unacceptably low number of recorded crimes and prosecutions'" ("Stalking and harassment crimes routinely badly handled, UK report says," *Guardian*, 5 July 2017.

[9] Police evidence comes before the court either in a written statement that has been agreed between the prosecution and the defence and is simply read to the Court, or in the form of oral testimony from the arresting officer.

[10] This occurs even though the *Criminal Procedure and Investigations Act 1996* (Sec. 23[1]) Code of Practice sets out the obligation of the police at ¶3.5 to "pursue all reasonable lines of enquiry [in their investigation] whether these point towards or away from a suspect." See MoJ (1996).

In 1989—three years after the PoA was implemented—research by the Home Office found that there had been a 70 per cent increase in the number of prosecutions for summary public order offences (UK 1994, 2). Specifically, the study found that

> the increase in prosecutions for sections 4 and 5 offences was partly explained by *increased use of these provisions* in preference to the offence of drunk and disorderly and arrest for common law breach of the peace and, additionally in London, to offences under the *Metropolitan Police Act 1839* . . . The research also suggested that there had been a *net-widening effect* and that some forms of low-level disorder were for the first time being drawn within the ambit of the criminal law. One by-product of the new summary offences was that *the police were able more easily to intervene where they themselves were the victims of offensive conduct*[11] *or where the victim was a hypothetical one*. (UK 1994, 3, my emphasis)

How was net-widening possible? It was found that in about one-third of the cases examined, the police were the sole "victim." Just as importantly,

> sec. 5 was at the time employed *as a kind of catch-all offence which was easy to use because of the relative ease of proof.* It was also popular because it frequently led to the offender being put before the court rather than cautioned or released. The situations in which *arrests* were *made ranged from ones differing little in substance from drunk and disorderly to domestic disputes and cases of indecency*. (Ibid., 3, my emphasis).

During the 1980s the CPS prosecuted 90 per cent of cases in which the police charged an individual for a Sec. 5 offence. In only 4 per cent of cases did the CPS discontinue proceedings, and in only 1 per cent of cases were proceedings terminated (UK 1994, 46). Furthermore two-thirds of defendants were found guilty in magistrates' courts; 10 per cent of the cases were dismissed, and approximately 19 per cent of defendants agreed to be "bound over"[12] without the case going to trial (ibid., 47).[13] As Sanders et al. (2010, 160) noted, "[t]he imprecision of public order laws enables them to be used as a resource for the police. Enabling rules are contained within the

---

[11] The police routinely arrest individuals who use "offensive language" against an officer.

[12] Magistrates can "bind over" a person by requiring them to enter into a recognisance, with or without sureties, to keep the peace or be of good behaviour towards the complainant. In short, these defendants are not tried, sentenced, or fined.

[13] A subsequent Home Office study found that 23 per cent of defendants charged with a public order offence chose not to request legal advice, a decision that would have been critical to the outcome of their case (UK 1998, 61).

law itself, allowing—but not requiring—arrest in a very wide spectrum of circumstances." In short, arrests and prosecutions authorised by the PoA have proved to be a very effective way for the police to deal with a wide range of public behaviours that are deemed to "threaten public order" and that are enforced by relying upon normal "working rules" to deal with disorder on the basis of demeanour and/or disrespect shown by individuals towards officers and their suspicion of the intentions of members of the public.

As noted earlier, the police do not investigate cases: for the most part they interview victims and the individuals accused of a crime and they may submit CCTV/body camera footage.[14] Historically defendants are under pressure to plead guilty, which many defendants do. A guilty plea occurs because of the pressure placed on defendants by the police and their solicitor (Baldwin and McConville 1977).[15] Defendants may plead guilty for three reasons. First, it may be in their interest to plead guilty if their case is weak. Second, because the language of the law defining an offence is very broad, defendants have limited scope to defend their actions (indeed when only the police are involved, the behaviour of the accused is described in the exact terms spelled out in the offence).[16] Finally, they may plead guilty at a remand hearing to secure a reduced sentence.

The language used in the PoA makes it clear that individuals accused of an offence do not have to cause harm. All that is required is for

---

[14] This situation is ironic because body cameras were introduced to increase the accountability of officers to the public (see "Police with body cameras receive 93% fewer complaints—study," *Guardian*, 29 June 2016). Murphy (1999, 41) summarises the legal status of "visual recordings" in criminal proceedings as follows: "The courts have demonstrated an uncharacteristic willingness to accept visual recordings as evidence in criminal proceedings, perhaps by virtue of the applicability of rules of admissibility developed over many years with regard to photographs and audio tape. On the whole these principles extend equally to digital images which, although this technology is not used by the majority of CCTV systems in the UK, will thus be admissible as an increasingly valuable source of evidence in criminal proceedings."

[15] In the mid-1990s "about half of suspects pleaded guilty when interviewed. . . . Relative use of charge and caution varied according to a range of factors. Females rather than males, juveniles rather than adults, and those with no prior record rather than those with previous convictions were more likely to be cautioned and released. White suspects were more likely than black or Asian suspects to be cautioned" (UK 1998, xix–xv).

[16] Individuals may also plead guilty "at the earliest opportunity" because they did not seek legal advice (only 23 per cent of individuals charged under the Act in 1993 sought legal advice [UK 1998, 61]).

the police to provide evidence[17] that would allow a judge, magistrate, or jury "to infer" common purpose from their conduct. An inference is defined[18] as:

> A truth or *proposition* drawn from another which is supposed or admitted to be true. A process of reasoning by which a fact or proposition sought to be established is deduced as a logical *consequence* from other facts, or a *state of facts*, already proved or admitted. (My emphasis)

"Common purpose"[19] is understood as follows:

> common purpose, common design, joint enterprise, or joint criminal enterprise is a legal doctrine in some common law jurisdictions which *imputes criminal liability on the participants to a criminal enterprise for all that results from that enterprise*. A common incidence of the application of the rule is to impute criminal liability for assaulting a person with a knife, on all the participants to a riot who knew, or were reckless as to knowing, that one of their number had a knife and might use it, even when the imputed participants did not actually have knives themselves. (my emphasis)

The PoA (1986) applies to behaviour in public places and at public events, to conduct in "the common parts" of private "dwellings," specifically landings, shared entries, and so on, and in private dwellings. While the Act creates a limited "defence"[20] and differentiates degrees of seriousness, nevertheless the range of potential forms of behaviour that is prosecuted is immense. Thus, an offence can occur by displaying, publishing, or distributing material or for possessing certain types of material. In addition, Sec. 5 offences can occur within a private home if "emergency workers" are

---

[17] The CPS Charging Standard guidance on "affray" (CPS n.d. c) indicates that "mere words are not enough," nor does "the expression 'present together' . . . require any degree of cooperation between those using or threatening violence." Furthermore, and with regard to affray, "[T]here must be a person within the sight or hearing of the suspect who is likely to be caused harassment, alarm or distress by the conduct in question. A police officer may be such a person, but remember that this is a question of fact to be decided in each case by the magistrates."

[18] See https://thelawdictionary.org/inference/ (accessed 3 May 2018).

[19] See https://www.definitions.net/definition/common+purpose (accessed 5 June 2018).

[20] CPS Charging Standard guidance states it is a defence if a defendant "had no reason to believe that there was any person within hearing or sight who was likely to be caused harassment, alarm or distress, or that he was inside a dwelling and had no reason to believe that the words or behaviour used, or the writing, sign or other visible representation displayed, would be heard or seen by a person outside that or any other dwelling, or that his conduct was reasonable."

obstructed, hindered, or "threatened." Indeed "disturbances" on NHS premises can be charged as a Sec. 4 offence (see *R 108*, below).

Three observations are in order. First, the authority to implement the Act is delegated to the police who exercise wide discretion in deciding whether to detain, release, warn, fine, arrest, or prosecute a person (see chapter 4 for statistics on the policing of domestic violence). Second, at remand hearings the victim does not attend, and "evidence" is not submitted (it is only adduced at the trial). Finally, Sec. 5 of the Act was intended to control "speech acts" (cf., Danet 1980, 458). In the cases discussed below I examine the tension between the "language of the law," how the police and the CPS use the law to prosecute individuals, and the constrained nature of the evidence provided by defendants who attempt to defend themselves.

Table 3.1 sets out statistics for the number of prosecutions under the PoA between 2011 and 2017 for all London boroughs. This data shows significant differences in the number of prosecutions by year (with prosecutions rising sharply after 2014) and by borough. The boroughs with the highest number of prosecutions are: (1) Westminster, (2) Ealing, (3) Lambeth, (4) Camden, (5) Southwark, (6) Lewisham, and (7) Brent (in that order).[21] These boroughs are in central London where public protest occurs (CPS 2010, 6). What is not clear from the table is that in each borough the police force cites/relies upon different sections of the PoA to charge individuals for essentially the same behaviour. For instance, police in Barking and Dagenham charged individuals using twelve different offences (though most individuals were charged using only seven), whereas in Barnet the police used eighteen offences (though most were charged using eight offences) and in Westminster the police used twenty-six different offences (though most individuals were charged using just eleven offences). Clearly different police forces use the POA differently in their efforts to achieve fairly broad policing objectives. It is also important to note that the number of offences markedly increased in 2014/15 presumably following guidance issued by the College of Policing on hate crime (Home Office 2018/19, 2) clarifying the kinds of incidents that can be charged. A breakdown of the offences during this period indicates that the proportion of harassment-related offences as opposed to hate-crime related offences varied by borough from a low of 46 per cent to 76 per cent of all offences.

[21] A full examination of this data will have to await a detailed analysis. However, it should be clear that differences in charging relate in part to variations in police practice (discretion) between different London boroughs.

Table 3.1. Public order offences in London, 2011–18[22]

Borough	2011	2012	2013	2014	2015	2016	2017	2018*	Grand Total
Barking & Dagenham	599	522	613	781	952	944	1,050	358	7,789
Barnet	709	632	743	1,102	1,330	1,558	1,731	619	10,908
Bexley	362	418	469	584	729	839	990	392	6,292
Brent	1,477	1,348	1,206	1,409	1,514	1,646	1,736	733	14,239
Bromley	774	691	805	1,148	1,441	1,408	1,407	629	11,375
Camden	1,190	1,189	990	1,322	1,576	1,762	1,931	761	15,811
Croydon	740	900	944	1,320	1,713	1,878	2,008	740	12,664
Ealing	1,506	1,230	1,227	1,418	1,791	1,798	1,974	778	16,950
Enfield	626	545	718	996	1,118	1,290	1,282	551	8,837
Greenwich	847	863	885	1,147	1,471	1,684	1,747	652	12,485
Hackney	814	906	988	1,333	1,654	1,808	1,883	679	13,000
Hammersmith & Fulham	1,032	1,088	1,055	1,263	1,419	1,585	1,484	598	13,190
Haringey	521	590	610	1,107	1,299	1,696	1,833	683	10,172
Harrow	403	410	475	566	655	616	708	352	5,386
Havering	557	574	620	745	937	1,024	1,074	454	7,628

[22] Source: Freedom of Information Request to Metropolitan Police Adhoc request no. 12498, 28 June 2018.
*First four months of 2018.

Hillingdon	739	811	842	1,282	1,406	1,482	1,551	635	11,953
Hounslow	1,038	946	905	1,197	1,356	1,473	1,586	622	12,347
Islington	1,293	1,319	1,072	1,626	1,832	1,897	1,761	651	15,165
Kensington & Chelsea	468	474	483	798	1,132	1,237	1,154	506	7,790
Kingston	212	383	347	463	602	651	735	261	4,445
Lambeth	1,048	1,199	1,261	1,865	2,218	2,019	2,094	794	16,420
Lewisham	1,191	1,013	1,082	1,235	1,556	1,627	1,568	652	14,813
Merton	392	407	418	543	709	743	837	370	6,231
Newham	1,040	943	803	1,201	1,505	1,597	1,683	685	12,980
Redbridge	882	713	674	992	981	1,100	1,196	496	9,377
Richmond upon Thames	391	449	405	482	670	738	757	280	5,788
Southwark	948	1,108	1,148	1,506	1,670	1,772	1,939	722	15,314
Sutton	229	393	391	537	616	691	807	299	4,837
Tower Hamlets	976	1,051	1,272	1,505	1,819	2,222	2,288	938	15,043
Waltham Forest	623	713	809	1,070	1,233	1,303	1,296	512	9,883
Wandsworth	661	802	751	997	1,409	1,381	1,481	587	10,278
Westminster	1,779	1,636	1,644	1,868	2,170	2,582	3,193	1,256	22,114
Grand Total	26,067	26,266	26,655	35,408	42,483	46,051	48,764	19,245	361,504

Statistics on recent Sec. 5 prosecutions are set out in table 3.2, which gives some idea of the variable way that different offences are used by the police and how police prosecutions change over time (it is worth recalling my discussion in the introduction about how the authorities dealt with rioting in London in 2011). The statistics, which show very clear differences in charging individuals for the use of threatening words and so on, raise important questions about the wide degree of discretion exercised by the police and about the role of the CPS in prosecuting defendants.

Table 3.2. Prosecutions in London for Section 5 offences.[23]

Offence	2014	2015
Use of threatening words/behaviour	797	31
Displays of writing/sign, visible representations that are threatening	3	-
Use threatening or abusive words/disorderly behaviour	2292	2183
Display threatening/abusive writing, signs. Visible representation likely to cause harassment, alarm, distress	10	9
Total	3102	2223

Table 3.3 summarises the public order-related offences that I observed (which constituted 19 per cent of all cases) and that I draw upon in this chapter.

Table 3.3. Public order prosecutions I observed.

Affray	Sec. 4	Sec. 4A	Sec. 5	Other charges			
				Criminal Damage	Assault	Drunk & Disorderly	Multiple Charges
1	2	2	8	2	22	2	7

ii. Affray

The offence of affray, as defined in Sec. 3 of the PoA, occurs *if a person "uses or threatens unlawful violence towards another and his conduct is such as would cause a person of reasonable firmness present at the scene to fear for his personal safety."* Alternatively, "Where two or more persons use or threaten the unlawful violence, it is the conduct of them taken together that must be considered for the purposes of subsection (1)." It is notable that, for this act, *a threat cannot be made by the use of words alone,*

[23] Source: an unnumbered FOI request to the Metropolitan Police dated 2 March 2018. The numbers refer to "custody records" and exclude cautions and warnings; they do not indicate the actual number of prosecutions.

however *no person of reasonable firmness need actually be, or be likely to be, present at the scene*. Finally, "a person guilty of affray is liable on conviction on indictment to imprisonment for a term not exceeding three years or a fine or both, or on summary conviction to imprisonment for a term not exceeding six months or a fine not exceeding the statutory maximum or both."

Affray is an "either-way" offence that can be prosecuted in either a magistrates' court or a Crown court depending on whether a defendant elects for a trial or if magistrates decline jurisdiction. Between 2008 and mid-2018, just over twenty-two thousand individuals were prosecuted for affray across London.[24]

For example, in case *R 67* the defendant was a twenty-two-year-old black female who was arrested[25] following an altercation on a busy street. At her arraignment she pleaded not guilty to the charge of affray against "D," a black male[26] in his mid-twenties who had previously assaulted her. The CPS, citing CCTV film (which was not shown)[27] said that the defendant pulled out a knife and stabbed "D" in the neck and that she had grabbed his hoody and pulled him. Both individuals were said to have assumed a fighting position and a tussle ensued. At one point "D" rushed up and hit her. The defendant—aware of the CCTV recording of the incident—confessed that she saw her boyfriend and "D" in a verbal argument, became angry, and "went after" him. She apologised for her behaviour.

The defendant pleaded not guilty and asked for her case to be heard by magistrates.[28] The court, which was clearly sympathetic, decided to join the two cases—the attack against her and her assault on the same individual—

[24] Source: Freedom of Information Request to the Metropolitan police of 22 June 2018, Ref. no. 2018060000927 (copy in my possession).

[25] To see how police officers are trained to perceive affray, see the "Special Constabulary Trainers Blog—Affray," at https://scontutor.wordpress.com/tag/affray/ (accessed 5 May 2018).

[26] The "victim" was awaiting trial for a previous assault against her.

[27] At the remand hearing, the Crown presents the facts that are recorded on a MG5 case summary and cites the evidence that it will rely upon. Often that evidence is not available at the first hearing. If a defendant pleads not guilty, the Crown is obliged to disclose the evidence that it will rely on, and any other evidence that may assist the defence or undermine the prosecution, by a date set by the Court as part of the trial preparation process.

[28] The defendant knew that she could not pretend innocence because the affray was filmed. She pleaded not guilty presumably in the hope that the court might find that she had been provoked by Mr. D. This strategy, no doubt suggested by her lawyer, appeared as if it might be successful.

into one hearing to hear evidence from both parties, see nine minutes of CCTV footage, and hear evidence from witnesses. The defendant was released on conditional bail to await her trial and, very unusually, the CPS was asked to review the case to "see whether she had a case to prove." The facts of the case fit the offence of affray: there was a public altercation caught on CCTV and "unlawful violence" involving a weapon occurred. I was surprised to hear the magistrates ask the CPS to consider dropping the charge against the defendant (the hearing lasted twenty-two minutes; I did not attend the trial and do not know the court's decision).

iii. Section 4 offences

A section 4 offence[29] is concerned with the "fear or provocation of violence." A person is guilty of this offence *if* he or she

> *uses* towards another person *threatening, abusive or insulting words or behaviour, or distributes or displays to another person any writing, sign or other visible representation which is threatening, abusive or insulting, with intent to cause that person* to believe that immediate *unlawful violence* will be used against him or another by any person, or to provoke the immediate use of unlawful violence by that person or another, or *whereby that person is likely to believe that such violence will be used or it is likely that such violence will be provoked* (my emphases).

This offence "*may be committed in a public or a private place*, except that no offence is committed where the words or behaviour are used, or the writing, sign or other visible representation is distributed or displayed, by a person inside a dwelling and the other person is also inside that or another dwelling." Finally, "a person guilty of an offence under this section is *liable on summary conviction to imprisonment for a term not exceeding six months or a fine* not exceeding level 5 on the standard scale or both" (the emphasis is mine).

The cases I observed suggest that there is a very blurred line between how the police charge an individual for assault/affray as opposed to a section 4 offence. Thus, in case *R 28* an allegation was made against a white male in his mid-fifties who was arrested following an incident at Liverpool Street train station. The prosecutor began by stating: "You are charged with causing distress and disorderly behaviour under Sec. 4."

---

[29] Fifty-six individuals were charged with this offence in London between 2008 and early 2018. Source: Freedom of Information Request to the Metropolitan police, 22 June 2018, Ref. no. 2018060000927.

Following the defendant's not guilty plea, the prosecutor read out the charge:

> "The charge is assault and battery and an intention to cause harm. On [date of alleged offence] 'F' was commuting to London on the train. At the [ticket] barrier he noticed that another man had not provided a ticket. The defendant challenged him. The man swore at him and an altercation occurred. They were separated by the police and the victim walked away. However, that evening another altercation occurred on the platform when the defendant demanded the same man's identification. When the man refused, 'F' tried to use his phone to photograph him. The man knocked his phone out of his hands and 'F' threatened him with a closed fist. Staff had to separate them."

The defendant spoke to confirm his identity and he asked to be tried in a magistrates' court. A three-hour trial was scheduled to hear four witnesses and see CCTV footage. The defendant, who was legally represented, was released on bail until his trial. The hearing lasted twenty-five-minutes. The defendant's case would rest on providing an explanation for his behaviour to the court and contesting the evidence against him.

Contrast the above case with *R 108*, which concerned an allegation against a young black male in his mid-twenties who worked as an orderly in a hospital. The prosecutor stated: "The defendant was working in the ward of X hospital. On [date] he was assaulted by a patient. After staff restrained the patient, the defendant punched the patient. His actions went beyond self-defence. The defendant may need an intermediary[30] to assist the victim to give evidence. The Crown would like a report on the victim. This is a straightforward trial issue." The defendant, who had been suspended from his job, pleaded not guilty and the magistrates scheduled a three- and one-half-hour trial to hear the evidence and view CCTV footage. The defendant was released on conditional bail to await his trial. The hearing took twenty-eight minutes during which the defendant was only asked to confirm his identity and make a plea. Even though the charge left little scope for the defendant to explain his behaviour, and he was advised about the value of an early guilty plea by his lawyer, he pleaded not guilty. Both cases involved "threatening" behaviour that occurred in a public place, but only one of the defendants actually hit someone.

---

[30] Because defendants cannot question victims, an "intermediary" must be appointed to help the victim give their evidence. Two of the defendants work colleagues were to be called to give evidence against him. In this case either the police or hospital staff called the police and initiated the charge.

iv. Sec. 4A offences

A Sec. 4A offence is defined as intentional harassment, alarm, or distress. It is caused when a person intentionally "*uses threatening, abusive or insulting words or behaviour*, or disorderly behaviour, or (b) *displays any writing, sign or other visible representation which is threatening, abusive or insulting*, thereby causing that or another person harassment, alarm or distress." As with Sec. 4 offences, this offence may *be committed in a public or a private place*, except that no offence is committed where the words or behaviour are used, or the writing, sign, or other visible representation is displayed, by a person inside a dwelling and the person who is harassed, alarmed, or distressed is also inside that or another dwelling.

It is *a defence* for the accused to prove "that he was inside a dwelling and had no reason to believe that the words or behaviour used, or the writing, sign or other visible representation displayed, would be heard or seen by a person outside that or any other dwelling, or that his conduct was reasonable." Finally, "a person found guilty of this offence is *liable on summary conviction to imprisonment for a term not exceeding six months or a fine* not exceeding level 5 on the standard scale or both" (the emphasis is mine).

All of the Sec. 4A cases I observed were "speech acts" in which prosecution hinged upon the use of specific "words" allegedly performed with the intention of causing harassment, alarm, or distress. As Danet (1980, 513) has argued, in some societies "the mere utterance of critical words is regarded as offensive; in others, intention is relevant. Sometimes the affront must directly address the injured person."

I begin with the case of a minor [*R 131*]—a young black girl—who shouted "abusive language" at an adult on the street; the case was mistakenly listed to be heard at a magistrates' court from where it was referred it to a youth court. Another case, [*R 159*] began as a Sec. 5 offence but during the hearing the prosecutor altered the charge to a Sec. 4A offence. An allegation of "harassment" was made against a thirty-nine-year-old homeless white male who tweeted a female CNN reporter over a four-month period; he regularly went to the victim's office and followed her through the shops. During a forty-three-minute hearing, which was adjourned for fifteen minutes to allow the duty solicitor to take instructions for a bail application, the prosecutor argued that there were substantial grounds for believing that the defendant would commit further offences if he was bailed (the defendant had already been granted conditional bail and had been ordered not to go to the victim's office; he already had a criminal record for theft/shoplifting). The District Judge refused the defendant bail and he was returned to prison to await trial. When the defendant attempted to address the court from the dock he was told to "shut up." A trial date was set to hear from the victim, assess a printout of the "tweets" and hear evidence from security at CNN and from the defendant. This case is similar to case *R 219* (below) and once again underlines the very blurred distinction between a Sec. 4A offence and a stalking offence. Indeed, as his duty solicitor suggested, he could have been issued with a police caution.

v. Section 5 offences

The original wording in Sec. 5 of the PoA targeted "threatening or abusive words or behaviour, or disorderly behaviour." The wording in this section was amended by the *Race and Religious Hatred Bill (Part 3A, 2005)* to differentiate between racial and religious hatred *regardless of the intent of the defendant*. The number of individuals charged with "Racially or religiously aggravated intention harassment, alarm or distress" in London between 2008 and early 2018 was 33,500.[31] Before 2013 it was enough for a prosecution to proceed by arguing that a person was guilty if s/he used threatening, abusive, or insulting words or behaviour (UK 2013). In 2013, following a lengthy public campaign[32] that arose when a number of questionable prosecutions were dropped, the Home Secretary removed the word "insulting" from Sec. 5 and stated that prosecutions under this section would proceed on the basis of "guidance" from the CPS.[33] The Home Secretary's decision was intended to allow the courts to decide whether particular words or behaviour were criminally abusive or merely insulting, but the courts have been loath to provide guidance (Goodall 2007).

---

[31] Source: Freedom of Information Request, adhoc reference no. 12498, MOPAC Ref No. 2018060000927, 28 June 2018.

[32] See: "'Insulting' to be dropped from sec 5 of Public Order Act" (*Guardian*, 14 January 2013).

[33] CPS (n.d. c) guidance now states: "The amendment is intended to enhance the protection of the right to freedom of expression under Article 10 of the European Convention on Human Rights (ECHR). Words or behaviour that are merely 'insulting,' or the displaying of writing, signs or other visible representations which are merely 'insulting,' within the hearing of someone likely to be caused harassment, alarm or distress, will no longer constitute a criminal offence under section 5(1). More serious, planned and malicious incidents of insulting behaviour could still constitute an offence under section 4A. . . ." See https://www.cps.gov.uk/legal-guidance/public-order-offences-incorporating-charging-standard (accessed 14 May 2018).

While the Home Secretary's decision was welcomed, it left the courts with the difficult task of evaluating police evidence about whether a defendant's behaviour was "insulting" or "offensive." Methven (2017) notes that while legislation does not identify specific "prohibited words" as "insulting" or "abusive," nevertheless the police tend to arrest individuals who utter specific (normally four-letter) words in their presence; critically, police evidence forms the basis of these prosecutions. As the cases analysed below make clear, *Sec. 5 prosecutions target "direct speech acts" and focus on the "utterance of critical words*" (i.e., *not* on their meaning or "contextual anchoring" [Danet 1980, 513; Searle 1975; Mertz 1994, 439]). This approach is frequently at odds with normal standards of speech and it may also conflict with an individual's right to exercise "freedom of speech" in a plural and diverse society.

A sec. 5 offence is concerned with "Harassment, alarm or distress." This offence arises if a person "*uses threatening words or behaviour, or disorderly behaviour, or* (b) *displays any writing, sign or other visible representation which is threatening*, within the hearing or sight of a person likely to be caused harassment, alarm or distress thereby." Here to, this offence "*may be committed in a public or a private place*, except that no offence is committed where the words or behaviour are used, or the writing, sign or other visible representation is displayed, by a person inside a dwelling and the other person is also inside that or another dwelling."

It is *a defence* for the accused to prove

> that he had no reason to believe that there was any person within hearing or sight who was likely to be caused harassment, alarm or distress, or that he was inside a dwelling and had no reason to believe that the words or behaviour used, or the writing, sign or other visible representation displayed, would be heard or seen by a person outside that or any other dwelling, or (c) that his conduct was reasonable . . .

Finally, a *person* who is convicted for this offence "*is liable on summary conviction to a fine* not exceeding level 3 on the standard scale" (the emphasis is mine).

Sec. 5 prosecutions illustrate the variable way that the police make use of the PoA to arrest and prosecute diverse forms of behaviour. In the cases discussed below, it appeared that the key issue was whether the accused uttered abusive words, which required magistrates to assess the significance of the context in which the alleged words were spoken.

For example, case *R 230* concerned an allegation against a well-dressed, middle-aged white male[34] who pleaded not guilty to a Sec. 5 charge of racially aggravated assault and a second charge of assault arising out of an incident at Covent Garden. The defendant identified himself, pleaded not guilty and asked for his case to be heard in magistrates' court. At this point the LA noted that the charge of "racially aggravated assault" was "barely understandable," to which the CPS replied that he would "rewrite it." The insulting word allegedly used was "immigrant"; he was also alleged to have spat on two black security guards. The defendant's solicitor complained that evidence for thirty-eight minutes of the alleged event had not been supplied. The magistrates accepted jurisdiction, completed the PET form, and scheduled a five-hour trial to hear the evidence, which included viewing footage from the body cameras worn by two police officers, listening to the evidence of the officers and two security guards, and listening to the evidence from the defendant and a character witness for the defendant.[35] The hearing lasted 15 minutes.

Case *R 198* concerned an event in a hotel at which the accused, a fifty-year-old Asian male, was arrested for three public order offences involving "assault" against three police officers and "criminal assault" against a hotel employee. The CPS indicated that this was an either-way offence. The defendant was brought into court from the custody cells where he had spent the night. He was asked to plead to all four offences and replied not guilty to each. The defendant was legally represented, and he asked to be tried in a magistrates' court. As the PET form was being completed it became apparent that the defendant had "previous" and that the Sec. 5 assault against the police officers involved the use of "abusive words" (though precisely what words was not clear). The trial, which was scheduled for three-and-a-half hours, was to hear evidence from a witness and four police constables and to view CCTV footage. The defendant, who made a "no comment"[36] interview at the police station, was also to give evidence. He was released on conditional bail—a no contact order with the police

[34] The defendant was alleged to have been drunk at the time of his offence; it is likely that he wore a suit to his hearing to play the part of an upright, law-abiding citizen. In short, it is not only legal actors who perform in court.

[35] I went to Hendon Magistrates' Court to observe the trial, but it was not listed to be heard. When I asked the CPS why, he said: "This is the kind of case that could have been dropped."

[36] A "no comment" interview indicates that he refused to answer questions. The right to silence while being questioned ended in 1994 when Sec. 34 of the *Criminal Justice and Public Order Act (1994)* came into force. The court is allowed to draw adverse inferences from "no comment" interviews.

officers was issued and he was excluded from the hotel where the incident took place—until his trial. The hearing lasted twenty-one minutes (most of which was taken up with completing the PET form; I did not attend his trial).

In the above two cases the inference seemed to be that the incidents were drink related. If this was the case, then the police could have charged both men for being "drunk and disorderly," which, under Sec. 91 of the *Criminal Justice Act 1973*, would have carried a maximum penalty of a Band C fine rather than a jail sentence and a much larger fine (Sentencing Council 2017). The police, and the CPS, deal with assault against a police officer in different ways depending upon their view of the "seriousness" of the offence. The defendant could have been charged under sec. 89 of the *Police Act (1996)* and sentenced for between one to six months imprisonment and/or fined between £1000 and £5000. In this case, the defendant was charged under either Sec. 4 or Sec. 5 of the POA (during the hearing the CPS did not state which section of the legislation he was using). The use of an alternative charge might also have avoided the cost of a five-hour trial.

Case *R 190* involved an allegation of "racially abusive language"—an offence charged under Sec. 28–30 of the *Crime and Disorder Act (1998)*[37]—against a white unemployed male in his mid-forties who chose not to be legally represented. The prosecutor stated:

> "On [date of offence] you were seen by members of the public assaulting a cab driver and you were employing racially abusive language. You were seen punching 'M' and calling him a 'black cunt.' No specific injuries were indicated by the victim. At the station you accepted that your behaviour was wrong. You have no previous. . . . The racially abusive charge results in an 'uplift'[38] of sentence. We ask £85 costs and compensation to the victim as the court deems appropriate."

When asked to explain his behaviour the defendant said: "I was stupid, I apologise. I am not normally racist . . . I have friends who are black and Asian." The hearing was adjourned to allow the defendant to be interviewed

---

[37] Sec. 28(1) states that "An offence is racially or religiously aggravated . . . if—(a) at the time of committing the offence, or immediately before or after doing so, the offender demonstrates towards the victim of the offence hostility based on the victim's membership (or presumed membership) of a racial or religious group; or (b) the offence is motivated (wholly or partly) by hostility towards members of a racial or religious group based on their membership of that group."

[38] This means that the sentence is automatically increased. See "CPS guidance on 'Racist and Religious Hate Crime'" (2019a).

by a probation officer prior to sentencing. Magistrates kept "all options"[39] open for sentencing (I was unable to attend the sentencing hearing). The hearing lasted seven minutes.

The other Sec. 5 prosecutions I observed exhibited similar features to the above cases. The victim and defendant are usually interviewed, but the principle evidence relied upon by the police and CPS was CCTV footage or social media posts. Most defendants plead not guilty (despite having been warned about the value of an early guilty plea) and ask for their case to be heard in a magistrates' court. If a defendant pleads "guilty" on arraignment, s/he is sentenced in a very short hearing. If the defendant pleads not guilty, the hearing is slightly longer and is given over to completing the PET form for the trial. Defendants uniformly sit in a glass dock (where they cannot hear what is being said) and are only asked to identify themselves and make a plea.

The following remand hearings and trial illustrate how the CPS and magistrates deal with individuals charged with multiple offences, including Sec. 5 offences. In case *R 99*, the defendant was a Sikh male in his early 30s who, despite having lived in England for nine years, did not speak English. The charge laid against him was that: ". . . he went to his employer's house and said he would kill him and his family, and that he had a knife. The police arrived and found that he had an axe in his bag . . . he said the axe was not his, someone else put it in his bag." The defendant was also said to have phoned his employer of nine years threatening to kill him and his family, and of going to his work place carrying a "bladed instrument."[40] At his hearing, which lasted thirty-one minutes, the defendant pleaded guilty to "making offensive messages"[41] but "not guilty" to carrying a bladed instrument. The defendant was given a "no contact" order and bailed to appear at his trial (which I did not attend). The defendant will have had

[39] The phrase means that the magistrates will consider imposing custody, fines, and a community order depending on their view of the probation report.

[40] The legal term is "a bladed article," which can refer to any sharp instrument. The defendant was in possession of a knife and an axe. The police and CPS can charge individuals under different legislation including Sec. 1 of the *Prevention of Crime Act (1953)* or Sec. 139 of the *Criminal Justice Act (1988)*. See CPS Guidance "Offensive weapons, knives, bladed and pointed articles" (2018b). Depending on the seriousness of the offence, defendants can be sentenced from twelve weeks to six months custody.

[41] This is an offence under Sec. 127 of the *Communications Act (2003)*. On conviction a defendant can be imprisoned for a term not exceeding six months or to a fine or to both. See https://www.cps.gov.uk/legal-guidance/communications-offences (accessed 6 June 2019).

difficulty establishing his innocence because he was arrested in possession of an axe and he admitted to threatening his employer.

Cases *R 128* and *R 129* were linked cases in which the defendants, two white unemployed males in their early thirties, were arrested outside a hotel where police were called to deal with an incident. The LA (stage 2) read out four charges—racially aggravated assault, damage to a police vehicle, drunk and disorderly, and assault against a police officer—to which both men pleaded "guilty." The prosecutor then read out the indictment:

> "On [the date of the offence] there was an incident at Hotel X caused by three drunken males. The charge sheet states that the males were drunk, disruptive, and refused to leave the hotel. When the police arrived one of the defendants[42] attempted to grab his Taser. He was arrested for being drunk and disorderly. He made threats to the PCs and assaulted PC Y by kicking him in the testicles. Mr 'H'[43] was involved in the same incident; he was drunk and when he was asked to leave he refused. He was also abusive[44] towards the PC. He was led outside but refused to leave; he exposed his ass to the police and returned to the hotel. He was 'warned' again and there was an altercation; he was arrested on a Sec. 5 public order offence. While being transported to the station he said he was going to be sick and was taken to hospital where, once again, he was abusive. At five a.m. as he was being taken to the police station he peed in the van."

At their duty solicitor's request (stage 7), sentencing was adjourned to allow them to be interviewed by a probation officer. Probation reported that "C" "took responsibility for his actions" and that "H" was "embarrassed" by his actions but because he was in cuffs, he "couldn't hold out" from peeing in the van. The probation officer (stage 9) stated that both defendants had agreed to be electronically tagged and that "H" agreed to attend an alcohol rehabilitation programme.

At this point, the duty solicitors for both defendants stated that their clients had not agreed to be electronically tagged because "the question asked [by probation] was unclear." One solicitor warned the court to "be careful" about imposing an order to tag because there was no evidence of an alcohol problem and in any event "drinking is a lifestyle decision." At this point, the court rose to consider its decision.

While the magistrates were considering their decision (stage 6) the defendants took a selfie of themselves in the witness box giving "the finger" to the court. When court resumed the magistrates announced (stage 9) that

[42] Mr "C" had previous, including a drink conviction in 2015.

[43] "H"'s previous included a conviction for assault and battery in 2015.

[44] The defendants used a racial epithet.

they would follow the recommendations made by probation and they imposed a community order that required both defendants to attend a twenty-day rehabilitation programme (a Rehabilitation Activity Requirement) and to be electronically tagged and fined. At this point, the defendants become verbally abusive. "H" said "I will breach the order," and both defendants stormed out of court. The prosecutor responded to their behaviour by asking the court to "uplift" their sentence by forty-five and sixty days, respectively. Eventually the defendants were persuaded to return to court and were sentenced: "C" was fined £270 and given a sixty-day unpaid community work order; "H" was fined £220. Both were to be electronically tagged and both were required to attend a DRR course to deal with alcohol problems. The hearing, which broke up three times over the course of the day, lasted seventy-four minutes.

In contrast to the behaviour of other defendants and members of the public attending court, these men could be clearly heard in the waiting area before their hearing, in the public gallery, and in the open dock (after the magistrates had withdrawn to consider their case). Their behaviour throughout was loud, their language was full of expletives, and they showed marked disrespect to the court and to other individuals who were present. While their behaviour was, in part, encouraged by their solicitors,[45] they clearly had no intention of cooperating with the court. In fact, "C" refused to provide a fixed address where he could be electronically tagged. Unlike other defendants, these individuals refused to recognise the authority of the court; indeed, they deliberately sought to disrupt it.

Sec. 5 is also used to prosecute individuals for their use of social media.[46] The charge that is usually laid against a defendant is "harassment" and, depending on the facts, "stalking." The cases examined below illustrate the discretionary way that Sec. 5 charges are used to prosecute "speech" acts. Thus, in case *R 219* an allegation was laid against a white male in his mid-thirties who pleaded not guilty to a charge of harassment. At the trial the Crown altered the charge to "stalking" because his activities were alleged to have caused "fear and alarm" to the victim over the course of five months. The victim was a news reporter who used her Twitter account to publicise her work.

The Crown alleged that the defendant initially responded to a tweet by the victim in which he asked for her assistance with a story he claimed

---

[45] After the bench rose to consider its decision the solicitors for the two men told their clients "next there will be a tag for smoking fags" and "this is a waste of a whole day. . . . Stop while you are ahead."

[46] For background information on the use of Sec. 5 to prosecute such cases, see House of Lords (2014).

to be working on. However, the defendant tweeted the victim repeatedly over a five-month period with requests to meet; he also sent flowers to her and tweeted that he was near her home, and so on. It was said that he disregarded the victim's request to stop contacting her. The defendant's solicitor noted that the CPS had failed to disclose evidence, as required by law, and she requested an adjournment to clarify the charge against his client. Instead the trial was put back seven weeks to allow time for all the evidence—that is, a printout of all the tweets, of unidentified "exhibits," and a statement from the victim—to be disclosed. However, while the PET form was being completed the prosecutor altered the charge from harassment to "stalking" (he inserted the initial charge "in the alternative"),[47] which was to be prosecuted "on the same facts." The defendant was released on bail and warned that a "no contact" order was in place; he was told that if he violated the order he would be arrested and could be detained until the trial. His hearing lasted forty-five minutes.

Case *R 168* illustrates a similar use of Sec. 5. In this case, a young black male was accused of harassment.[48] The court's legal adviser set out the charge against the defendant: "You used social media to make posts about 'M' on Facebook and you sent texts. How do you plead?" He pleaded not guilty. The LA then stated: "the Crown relies on admissions made in interview and an agreed summary. . . He denies that his conduct amounts to harassment and says his actions were lawful, justified, and in context do not amount to harassment." The defendant admitted to having been in a relationship with the victim but denied sending the messages because the account from which the messages were sent was not his. The defendant was released on conditional bail and told to attend his trial in four weeks. His hearing lasted eighteen minutes. The issue for the court was whether the defendant posted the alleged material.

It is worth pausing briefly to consider the way that the two social media cases were charged and the defence that is allowed for each charge. CPS guidelines (2018b) state that harassment involves:

> . . . causing alarm or distress . . . under section 2 of the Protection from Harassment Act 1997 as amended (PHA), and "putting people in fear of

[47] CPS (2018c) guidelines on drafting indictments state that "It may be necessary to consider whether to include a lesser or alternative count in the indictment. Such consideration will include whether a lesser or alternative count would be likely to attract a plea of guilty and, if so, whether such plea would be acceptable."

[48] While the defendant was charged with a Sec. 5 offence, he might just as well have been charged with an offence under the *Malicious Communications Act* (1988) or the *Protection from Harassment Act* (1997).

> violence" offences under section 4 of the PHA. The term can also include harassment by two or more defendants against an individual or harassment against more than one victim. Although harassment is not specifically defined in section 7(2) of the PHA, it can include *repeated attempts to impose unwanted communications and contact upon a victim in a manner that could be expected to cause distress or fear in any reasonable person.*

The guidance also notes that,

> A prosecution under section 2 or 4 requires proof of harassment. In addition, *there must be evidence to prove the conduct was targeted at an individual, was calculated to alarm or cause him/her distress and was oppressive and unreasonable.* Closely connected groups may also be subjected to "collective" harassment. The primary intention of this type of harassment is not generally directed at an individual but rather at members of a group. (My emphasis)

There are three defences available to individuals charged with this offence: "that the course of conduct was pursued for the purpose of preventing or detecting crime; that it was pursued under any enactment or rule of law or to comply with any condition or requirement imposed by any person under any enactment; or that in the particular circumstances the pursuit of the course of conduct was reasonable." In short, defendants are required to prove that their conduct was "reasonable."

In contrast, *the offence of "stalking" is not legally defined*, but CPS guidance provides a number of examples to guide prosecutors:

> The list is not an exhaustive one but gives an indication of the types of behaviour that may be displayed in a stalking offence. The listed behaviours are: (a) following a person, (b) contacting, or attempting to contact, a person by any means, (c) publishing any statement or other material relating or purporting to relate to a person, or purporting to originate from a person, (d) monitoring the use by a person of the internet, email or any other form of electronic communication, (e) loitering in any place (whether public or private), (f) interfering with any property in the possession of a person, (g) watching or spying on a person. Harassment that includes one or more of the above features is not automatically stalking. The course of conduct, assessed in the round, must fit the generally received interpretation of the word "stalking." Prosecutors should note that the list in s.2A(3) is not exhaustive and it will be open to courts to consider other acts by a defendant and conclude that those acts constitute stalking even if they are not on the s.2A(3) list . . .

Guidance also provides the defence available to a person charged with stalking, namely: "If the suspect is able to show that any of the defences to harassment under section 1(3) of the PHA are made out, he or she cannot be guilty of stalking as without harassment there can be no conviction for stalking." In short, defendants charged with this offence must prove that their alleged behaviour was "reasonable," which, logically, requires the judiciary to carefully consider the four inter-related aspects of all speech acts: action, speech, intention, and impact/meaning. In the following section I look at how the appellate courts have attempted to interpret criminal speech acts.

In contrast to remand hearings, trials provide a better opportunity to understand a case and hear the evidence. In case *T 23* the defendant, a thirty-five-year-old Asian male, was charged with three offences to which he pleaded not guilty. The defendant was arrested following an incident outside public housing (where he lived) for allegedly threatening a Housing Association officer. Before the hearing, the duty solicitor assigned to the defendant entered court and told the presiding District Judge: "I am in an awkward position. The defendant has mental health problems. He has refused to give me instructions. I can only ask questions on cross examination." Following a brief exchange, the DJ told the solicitor: "Given the nature of the charge, if there are mental health difficulties it might not be worth prosecuting such a person. It would be a matter for the Crown to decide. I don't have the file. Can you resolve it between you? If he has mental health problems I will adjourn to allow for a psychiatric report." However, the case was not adjourned, and a psychiatric report was not submitted.

At the start of the trial—which lasted one hour and twenty-four minutes—the defendant identified himself (stage 1), following which the DJ (stage 2) stated that the defendant was to be tried for three "matters": a public order offence, failure to attend a drug screening interview, and criminal damage to a police cell. The defendant confirmed his not guilty plea. The prosecutor then read out the indictment:

> "On [a date] the police were called to Woodhill House. Mr. K, who worked for the Housing Association, was assessing flats for fire hazard and was taking photos and making notes. The defendant threatened Mr K; he implied he had a handgun. The defendant failed to keep an appointment with the drugs team. The police were called, and the defendant was found not to be in possession of a firearm. He was arrested for a public order offence and taken to the station where he refused to attend an appointment following a positive drug test; while he was in the cells he spat on the floor."

A screen was erected in court to prevent the defendant from intimidating the victim, a male housing officer. The prosecutor led the victim through his evidence (stage 3) in which it was alleged that the defendant threatened him and implied that he was in possession of a handgun. The defendant's court-appointed duty solicitor cross-examined the witness (stage 4) who reiterated that he felt threatened by the defendant's behaviour. The DJ allowed the defendant to ask the victim one question: was the "weapon" that the victim perceived in his waistband a mobile phone or a handgun? The judge explored this issue further.

The prosecution then called a police officer to give evidence (back to stage 3) about the defendant's conduct after he was arrested and taken to the police station. Her evidence was that the defendant refused to come out of the cell for a drug appointment and that he spat on the floor and used abusive language toward her (which led her to caution him for his behaviour).[49] At this point the defendant was allowed out of the dock to question the officer (stage 4). His questions centred on why he had been kept in the cells for two days. In cross-examining the defendant the judge focused on the defendant's written admission of spitting on the cell floor. The DJ dismissed the charge that the defendant had failed to attend a drugs appointment (for lack of evidence) and she concluded that even though no CCTV footage of the alleged incident was made available, "a jury might accept the evidence" and therefore the charge of criminal damage (spitting) would be "continued."

In the remainder of the hearing the DJ assisted the defendant to give his evidence (stage 5) regarding the allegation that he had threatened the housing officer. The defendant admitted that he occasionally acted "loopy," however he denied that he had implied to the housing officer that he possessed a gun. He did, however, admit to fourteen minor drug offences. His final evidence was that he and his family of six were being evicted from their council flat because of the incident (stage 8). The DJ found him (stage 9) guilty of criminal damage and for the sec. 5 offence and fined him £582.[50] As he left court the defendant said: "This has been an expensive day . . . that's how the cookie crumbles."

Either the defendant had miscalculated his ability to defend his actions or he wasn't concerned about the consequences of his actions. DJs intervene regularly in trials to move the hearing along by pushing witnesses and defendants to give their evidence and by quickly deciding points of law. In this case the DJ "assisted" the defendant to give his evidence; however, in so doing the defendant contradicted himself, which provided the judge with sufficient reasons to convict him. Unlike remand hearings, trials

---

[49] The fine for criminal damage was £152.

[50] Fines against unemployed defendants are normally deducted from their benefits/income support payments.

undertake a more thorough exploration of the case by hearing evidence from all parties. Trials allow magistrates/DJs to assess the alleged actions/speech of defendants and, when necessary, to ascertain the possible intentions of the defendant and assess the impact of the defendant's actions on the victim, which are crucial to determining guilt/innocence. Why this defendant chose to represent himself was not clear, but the consequences of his decision proved to be costly.

vi. The "judicialisation" of criminal language

A small number of these cases have been appealed to decide whether specific forms of language constitute "threatening," "abusive," or "insulting" words. Appellate courts do not rehear a case: they consider a written summary of the evidence and the decision of the lower court. It is instructive to note that the wording of Sec. 5 in the PoA 1986 is taken from the case of *Brutus v Cousins [1973] AC 854*, when the House of Lords considered whether an individual charged initially with breach of the peace at a tennis match at Wimbledon should be charged under Sec. 5 of the POA 1936. Considering the fact that the alleged breach related to an anti-Apartheid protest, the House of Lords decided that,

> . . . distasteful or unmannerly speech or behaviour is permitted so long as it does not go beyond the bounds of any one of three limits. It must not be threatening. It must not be abusive. It must not be insulting. I see no reason why any of these should be construed as having a specially wide or narrow meaning. *They are all limits easily recognizable by the ordinary man.* (my emphasis)

As we have seen, prosecutions and convictions for sec. 5 offences rapidly escalated from the late 1980s (Broadbent 2013). The case of *DPP v Orum [1988] 3 A11 ER 449* focused on the question of whether a police officer could be caused harassment when confronted with language that is "threatening" and so on. In deciding the case, Lord Justice Glidewell stated,

> Very frequently, words and behaviour with which police officers will be wearily familiar will have little emotional impact save that of boredom. It may well be that, in appropriate circumstances, magistrates will decide . . . as a question of fact that the words and behaviour were not likely to cause harassment, alarm, or distress to . . . police officers. *That is a question of fact for the magistrates to decide having regard to all the circumstances*: the time, the nature of the words used, who the police officers are and so on. (my emphasis)

In short, the court decided that while offence to officers was possible, it was not inevitable, and that magistrates should decide whether certain words were offensive to police officers.

Southard v DPP [2006] EWCH 3449 Adm was the next appellate case to give guidance about how to interpret "abusive" language. The Lord Justices hearing this case stated that,

> . . . whether or not the person addressed is a police officer or a member of the public, the words "fuck you" or "fuck off" are potentially abusive. Frequently though they may be used these days, we have not yet reached the stage were a court is required to conclude that they no longer constitute abuse. *Questions of context and circumstance may affect the court's ultimate conclusion as to whether, in an individual case they are abusive . . . the decision* on an issue of this kind *will always be fact dependent.* (My emphasis)

In *Harvey v DPP [2011] EWHC 3993 Adm*, the High Court dealt with a case in which an individual was charged with swearing at a police officer. The police were searching for people in possession of cannabis when they came upon a group of men sitting outside a block of flats. When the men were searched, one of them told the police: "Fuck this man, I ain't been smoking nothing." The man was warned, and the subsequent search found nothing. At this point the man said: "Told you, you won't find fuck all." At this point the man was arrested and charged for a Sec. 5 offence and for assault against an officer. The defendant, H, was only convicted for the Sec. 5 offence. However, magistrates appealed the case[51] to clarify three issues: (i) Was the court entitled to conclude that the words used by the defendant amounted to threatening, abusive, or insulting words and/or behaviour or disorderly conduct? (ii) Was the court entitled to conclude that the police constables involved in the arrest were likely to have been caused harassment, alarm, or distress? (iii) Was the court entitled to conclude that bystanders were likely to have been caused harassment, alarm, or distress?

The judge found that the court was entitled to conclude that the use of expletives could amount to abusive or insulting words or behaviour; however, *in this case the officers provided no evidence to support this conclusion*. Second, no evidence was provided by other "witnesses" ("they have said nothing and were asked nothing" about the incident) and thus there was no basis for the court to conclude that they had been subjected to abuse and so on. Finally, the judge concluded that "it was not enough simply

[51] See https://www.casemine.com/judgement/uk/5a8ff72a60d03e7f57ea9017 (accessed 8 November 2019).

to say that . . . there were people around" who were/might have been frightened. For the above reasons the defendant's conviction was set aside/quashed. The key issue was the lack of evidence to support the charge.

The case of *R v Liam Stacey* heard in 2012 takes the issue of insulting language to the next logical step—its use in social media.[52] Following a number of "abusive" and "insulting" tweets on Twitter made in relation to a black football player, Stacey was identified and arrested for offences contrary to Sec. 31(1)(b) of the POA (these are offences connected with football). He pleaded guilty and was sentenced; however, he appealed against the length of the sentence imposed on him by magistrates (fifty-six days). The Crown court cited his messages and the strong responses they elicited from other Twitter users. The appeal did not hear legal argument about his words/comments, though it accepted that he was drunk.[53] In finding that he "had pleaded guilty to a crime of specific intent" and that "he intended to use words which were offensive, and he intended that the words should be racially offensive," the court dismissed his appeal.

The standard approach of the judiciary to sec. 4 and 4A offences, including the offence of "incitement to religious hatred" (Part 3A of the POA), is to ascertain the "intentions" of the defendant, whether distress or harm was caused and the colloquial/ordinary as distinct from the "legal"[54] meaning of the allegedly offensive words (a distinction that may have implications for freedom of speech).

In these cases, the courts infer "intention" by focusing on "the context" in which the actions took place. In *Harvey* the alleged Sec. 5 offence was construed as having occurred in a public place, whereas in *Stacey*, which was prosecuted under Sec. 31 of the POA, the court stepped back from the original definition of events (i.e., at or around football stadiums[55]) to define the "context" as the defendant watching a football match on TV at home in a state of drunkenness (and sending texts). The

---

[52] See https://www.judiciary.uk/wp-content/uploads/JCO/Documents/Judgments/appeal-judgment-r-v-stacey.pdf (accessed 7 November 2019). In 2003 the same form of words was adopted as Sec. 127 of the *Communications Act* as a serious offence. The number of prosecutions under Sec. 127 have increased from 143 in 2004 to 1500 in 2014; most charges end in a conviction/guilty plea. See http://Wiki.openrightsgroup.or.uk/wiki/Communications_Act_2003.Section_127.

[53] The courts do not accept that alcohol use is a mitigating factor.

[54] The "meaning that correctly conveys the legislative intention" (Goodall 2007, n69).

[55] Sec. 31 identifies threats of violence made towards another person or property while on a journey to attend a "prescribed" match or at the match, including a period two hours before and one hour after the match. See https://www.legislation.gov.uk/ukpga/1986/64/part/IV/enacted.

guidance of the appellate courts appears to be somewhat incoherent and has shifted from a focus on the mere utterance of a word (*Brutus v Cousins*), to a determination of the "facts" and circumstances (*DPP v Orum*), to the need for evidence to support a charge (*Harvey v DPP*) to a problematic conception of the context in which an alleged action occurred (*R v Liam Stacy*).

The decisions fail to resolve two other problems that hamper appellate court guidance to the lower courts, namely a poor understanding of colloquial uses of language that the police base their case on and a reliance on written evidence. The first issue is problematic because language and language-use constantly evolves whereas the language of judges and the courts is out of touch with common forms of speech. The second issue, reliance of the appellate courts on written texts, raises a key problem identified by Broadbent (2013, 98):

> The spoken word does not translate well into written prose. The words used, or allegedly used, by the defendants can be seen, but not heard. So much is lost. The exact way they were spoken, the volume and tone of voice, the context in which they were spoken, the emotional temperature at the time, the body language accompanying them and the environment in which they were spoken cannot be reproduced; the moment goes and it cannot be retrieved.

As Butler (1996) notes, while words can cause distress, a narrow focus on "injurious speech" seeks to attribute responsibility to a "singular subject," a person or defendant. However, the power of speech is "derivative": it occurs when a speaker adopts an identifiable, iterative model of speaking and acting based on past behaviour that is "cited" or "performed." Butler argues against a "theological construction" of performance adopted by the courts that postulates "the subject as the causal origin of the performative act when in fact the power of a performance, of specific words, is derived from 'linguistic conventions of authority, conventions that are themselves legacies of citation'" (ibid., 205). For instance, the use of "threatening" words may be a "ritualized practice" that derives its force from social interaction or in political contexts. Butler argues that the derivative power of certain words "establishes a permanent difficulty in locating accountability for that injury in a singular subject and its act" (ibid., 207). Indeed, the task of determining the "intention" of a speech act is fraught with interpretive difficulties that are not addressed by relying on the problematic assumption that there are no "unintended actions" (cf. Sidnell and Enfield 2017).

The difficulty of attributing intention for a (criminal) speech act is compounded by the shift in jurisprudence away from "the violence enacted by nation-states" to the idea that power is exercised by citizen-subjects, that is, an assumption that the state is a neutral instrument for enforcing legal rights. This ideological shift portrays the individual as a sovereign subject and invites the state to adjudicate claims made between citizens regarding criminal forms of speech and behaviour that may be inherently political if their referent is the state, the police, or the authorities. This shift is problematic for several reasons. First, the use of Sec. 5 by the police, Crown, and courts reflects political calculations by Parliament/the political establishment. It is also problematic because the appellate courts do not provide guidance to magistrates, who themselves are hardly representative of local communities, about how to interpret "insulting" language (Goodall 2007, 94). This situation leaves open the possibility that decisions as to what constitutes "insulting language" will be arbitrarily defined in a way that infringes on the right of free speech.[56]

Conclusion

From the date of its enactment into law in 1986 the POA has been used by the police and the CPS to prosecute large numbers of individuals for a diverse range of "criminal" behaviours. The criticisms levelled at the draft bill in 1986 have proved prescient in terms of predicting how the Act would be used. Quite apart from the regulation of public protest and picketing, the "legal language" in the POA together with the abandonment of a requirement to prove actual alarm, harassment, or distress provides a wide degree of discretion to the police and the CPS to arrest and prosecute individuals for a wide range of behaviours. Indeed, it could be said that the POA allows the police to arrest a person simply because of his or her demeanour or because officers want to discipline unruly individuals.

The PoA facilitates prosecutions because "of the relative ease of proof" but also because the broad language used in the Act provides the police and CPS with the power to use it to prosecute a very wide range of behaviours. Thus, depending on how the police construct a case—that is, the evidence/facts reported by an officer—an individual could just as well be charged with behaviour such as harassment/stalking or drunk and disorderly as with using threatening words or behaviour. The choice of

[56] The problems inherent in defining "threatening and insulting" speech are further compounded in British legislation prohibiting "hate speech" where there is even less agreement about key definitions; see "European Hate Speech Laws" at https://www.legal-project.org/issues/european-hate-speech-laws (accessed 5 November 2019).

which offense to lay against an individual rests on a calculation made by the police and the CPS, a decision which may loosely fit the facts in each case.

The cases examined in this chapter suggest that the number and range of behaviours that have been prosecuted for public order and related offences have substantially increased over time. Remand hearings convened to hear these offences are short and are presided over by magistrates with limited legal training to try defendants who, because they are placed in a glass dock, and are unable to hear or participate in their case. In these hearings many defendants plead guilty due to the pressure placed on them by the police and their lawyer, but also perhaps because their case is weak, because the language defining the offence is so general that they are unable to offer a valid defence, and/or because the CPS can alter the charges during the hearing. Furthermore, a successful defence is difficult to mount because public order offences are proved by the word/evidence of police officers. A defendant's ability to contest a PoA offence is subject to additional constraints, namely the courts' difficulties in assessing the words allegedly used by a defendant; the 'context' in which the alleged offence occurred; and the impact of the speech/behavior of the defendant on the public. The judiciary is also out of step with the colloquial, everyday language used by the public.

CHAPTER 4

THE PROSECUTION OF DOMESTIC VIOLENCE

In this chapter I look at how the police and CPS deal with allegations of domestic violence, and how magistrates' courts decide this type of offence. I begin by briefly looking at how domestic violence was considered by the law and the courts from the seventeenth to the twentieth century, a time when women were not considered to possess "rights" and when "a husband's physical correction of his wife" was not an issue that the courts addressed. I discuss how this situation slowly changed by the mid-twentieth century with the gradual recognition of formal equality before the law of men and women, except in the sphere of domestic, family life. Legal developments in the late twentieth and early twenty-first centuries addressing domestic violence are briefly described including an examination of how the police investigate and decide to prosecute domestic violence in London. In section (ii) I analyse remand hearings and in section (iii) I examine contested trials to show that an outdated approach to prosecuting incidents of domestic violence is pursued that results in a high attrition rate of reported incidents leading the police to drop many cases, the failure of the CPS to prosecute a large percentage of recorded cases, and court decisions that hand down the minimum sentence. The knock-on effects of this pattern of prosecution are two-fold: victims lack confidence in the police and the courts. and the level of domestic violence rises.

i. The law and domestic violence, circa 1700 to 2000

The British courts considered "domestic violence" as early as the seventeenth century. As Foyster (2005), among others, has shown, between the seventeenth and the mid-nineteenth century public attitudes slowly came to perceive that "a husband's physical correction of his wife" was something that the courts should deal with. A key problem throughout this period was to define the nature and significance of the "violence" used by husbands against their wives and whether it should be subject to legal sanction. Among the many "moral" issues that were linked to a consideration of domestic violence and that were slowly changing was the nature of the marital contract (and the right to civil divorce), reproductive rights (i.e., abortion), the age of consent, the right to corporal punishment (including rape in marriage), inheritance laws and, ultimately, gender equality.

Throughout this period there was an increasing acceptance of ideas about the social contract *and* "the person" (i.e., the concept of "the individual") as the bearer of "a unique and natural self" who is subject to the law (Collier et al. 1995, 5). For example, in addressing the demands of women for equality, the courts have been compelled to address and revise women's access to education, property, wages, the right to vote, and so on, all of which had previously been denied them on the basis that their difference from men was found "in nature." For this reason, women's claims failed to be addressed by the law. As women came to be perceived as rights-bearing individuals the privileges of men and of the political elite were redefined until a point was reached at which *formal equality* before the law between men and women was realised even though substantial socio-economic inequality prevents women from being protected from harm in private/domestic settings (Stark 2007, 208f). Over the past fifty years, the state has gradually assumed a growing role in regulating contemporary social life and individual liberty but not, as we will see, in the domain of private life.

The Home Office first issued guidance on domestic violence in 1986 that outlined the role and responsibility of the police to protect women and children from "violence in the home" (officers were supposed to be trained to recognise domestic violence [Police Foundation 2014, 3]). In 1990 the Home Office issued circular no. 60 that set out how the police should deal with "violence between intimates," though this policy did not translate into practice until the mid-1990s (Hoyle and Sanders 2000). The circular gave rise to a "pro-arrest" position aimed at increasing the number of prosecutions for domestic violence in the belief that arrest and prosecution was in the interests of victims and in the interest of justice. The pro-arrest policy called for the police to take a more active role by following up all reported incidents and liaising with other government agencies (Harne and Radford 2008, 127f).

However subsequent research showed major deficiencies in the implementation of this policy due in part to under-resourcing, the low priority given to the initiative and wide variations in how it was implemented. In the end it was found that mandatory arrest and prosecution of individuals for DV did not assist many victims because "criminal sanctions are unlikely to help to end the violence" (Hoyle and Sanders 2000, 14). Indeed, many victims of domestic violence want their partners to be "taught a lesson," but not prosecuted. While the reasons behind women's responses to this policy are complex, it is clear that victims need access to sustained support from police and social services. Without such support many victims withdraw their evidence or refuse to participate in criminal proceedings.

In 1996 the *Family Law Act* simplified and strengthened the availability of civil non-molestation orders and occupation orders. Even so criticism of ineffective policing of domestic violence continues (representations to government reinforced by litigation have changed the way in which the government funds and handles these offences).[1] The *Domestic Violence, Crime, and Criminal Act 2004*[2] introduced new "protections."[3] However, no definition of "domestic violence" was agreed upon or incorporated into the act because legislators believed that it "would be difficult for any statutory definition to reflect the breadth of domestic violence and to keep it up to date."[4] To date the government has not legislated a definition of domestic violence or domestic abuse, though a "cross-government" (working) definition was developed which is:

> any incident or pattern of incidents of controlling, coercive, threatening behaviour, violence or abuse between those aged 16 or over who are, or have been, intimate partners or family members regardless of gender or sexuality. (Home Office 2016)

Policy now recognises that domestic abuse may encompass, but is not limited to, psychological, physical, sexual, financial, and emotional elements. This understanding extends to "controlling" or "coercive behaviour"[5] and to forced marriage.[6] At the time of my fieldwork, individuals who were

---

[1] See "Legal aid shakeup hands lifeline to domestic violence victims" (*Guardian*, 23 February 2017).

[2] See http://www.legislation.gov.uk/ukpga/2004/28/contents.

[3] Specifically: (a) a new offence of "causing or allowing the death of a child or vulnerable adult"; (b) common assault was made an "arrestable offence"; (c) co-habiting same-sex couples and couples who have never co-habited or been married were eligible to seek non-molestation orders; (d) breaches of non-molestation orders were made a criminal offence; and (e) courts were allowed to impose restriction orders on those convicted of any offence.

[4] See Baroness Scotland, *Hansard*, 15 December 2003 column 1015.

[5] The work of Stark (2007) on "coercive control" seems to have pushed British legislators into action. For the legislation, see Sec. 76 of the *Serious Crime Act 2015* at http://www.legislation.gov.uk/ukpga/2015/9/section/76/enacted.

[6] In UK law, forced marriage is defined as being "forced to enter into marriage without their free and full consent." See Forced Marriage (Civil Protection) Act 2007 at https://www.legislation.gov.uk/ukpga/2007/20/contents.

accused of domestic violence/abuse (DV) could be prosecuted under any one of sixty-four different offences (UK 2015a). Indeed, the failure to agree a definition means that official statistics for this offence do not exist.[7] What is more, despite a 2011[8] government statement that it would draft appropriate legislation and fund support services for those affected by DV, very little has been achieved.[9] Instead it is widely accepted that the Criminal Justice System has failed to hold perpetrators of DV to account (AAPG 2014).[10] This situation was not helped by budget cuts to the police, the courts, local authorities, women's refuges, and prevention and treatment programmes (Towers and Walby 2012). Indeed, 23 Specialist Domestic Violence Courts (SPDC) were among the 142 courts designated to close in 2011 (UK Women's Budget Group 2018b).[11]

National statistics suggest that the number of victims of DV has stabilised at just over two million per year since 2008/9 (UK 2017b). Statistics on the incidence of DV in London taken from the Office of National Statistics for 2013–16 (2016) provide a disturbing picture not only of the number of DV-related offences but also of the failure of the police and the CPS to arrest, investigate, charge, and prosecute individuals accused of DV-related offences (Bowen, Qasim, and Tetenbaum 2013). Box 4.1 provides data on London for the year ending March 2016.

---

[7] Statistics reported in this chapter come from CPS reports. Statistics on reported DV incidents in England and Wales for 2017–18 indicate that 1.2 million incidents were reported to the police, but only 50 per cent were recorded as a crime (ONS 2018a, sec. 5).

[8] See https://www.gov.uk/government/speeches/theresa-may-consultation-on-the-cross-government-definition-of-domestic-violence (accessed 15 August 2019).

[9] A draft "Domestic Abuse Bill" was introduced in Parliament in early 2019. A Joint Committee published its initial view of the bill in June 2019, but as of September 2020 the bill has yet to be approved, see https://www.parliament.uk/business/committees/committees-a-z/joint-select/draft-domestic-abuse-bill/.

[10] This failure extends to other types of violence against women, including rape; see "Ministers urged to act as reports of rape rise but charges fall" (*Guardian*, 29 August 2019).

[11] See "Domestic violence courts to close" (*Law Society Gazette*, 6 May 2011).

Box 4.1. Police prosecution of domestic violence in London, 2016.[12]

i. The Metropolitan Police recorded a total of nearly 153,000 DV-related incidents (suggesting a rate of incidence of eighteen per thousand persons) whereas only just over 76,000 incidents were recorded as a criminal offence.
ii. 10 per cent of all recorded crimes in London during this period were DV-related offences.
iii. Sixty-nine domestic homicides occurred in London in which fifty were women and nineteen were men.
iv. The police referred about 18,800 DV cases to the CPS to prosecute (the lowest referral rate across England and Wales); however the CPS initiated prosecutions in just 10,464 cases (the lowest rate of prosecution in England and Wales).
v. In 2016 the CPS prosecuted just over 15,500 DV cases, which amounted to 14 per cent of its caseload (the eighth lowest rate across England and Wales) of which just over 9,300 (64 per cent) ended with a conviction (the lowest conviction rate for this offence across England and Wales).

The data in Box 4.1 raises many questions. Why do the police only record half of all DV-related incidents as crimes? [13] On what basis are individuals cautioned, reprimanded, or otherwise diverted away from the courts by the police? How many prosecutions were discontinued because the police failed to collect sufficient evidence to convict the accused? Why do the police refer only 25 per cent of recorded cases to the CPS for prosecution? Why is the conviction rate in London lower than elsewhere? While acknowledging the difficulty of the task that the police and CPS confront in dealing with DV, the problems involved are not new, they reflect a lack of trust in the police and a lack of training and resources to improve police and CPS performance (AAPG 2014, chaps. 2–3; Bishop and Bettinson 2018).

Recent data on domestic-abuse-related offences suggest further problems with the way the police handle this offence (Home Office 2018a). For the period 2017–18, the police experienced difficulties in collecting sufficient evidence to prosecute 48 per cent of reported offences (in part because victims refused to provide evidence).[14] The net effect of these

[12] Source: Source ONS 2017, various tables.

[13] Officers exercise considerable discretion as to how they handle reported incidents. Annex 1 of ONS (2016) sets out the stages of the criminal process.

[14] The most recent report by Her Majesty's Inspectorate of Constabulary & Fire and Rescue Services (2017a, 30), which looked at how Police forces investigate domestic abuse, found that: "In the cases reviewed, there was no evidence of body-worn video cameras having been used in sixty-three percent of applicable cases. . . .

problems, which have increased over time, is that in only 15 per cent of cases was a charge laid against a suspect.

CPS "Guidance" makes it clear that the police must collect "sufficient evidence for a realistic prospect of conviction *before* referring a case for a charging decision" (CPS 2015, 1). However, judging from the remand hearings and trials that I observed, the police restrict their investigations to taking statements from claimants/victims and defendants and they collect limited evidence in the form of photographs or the weapons used (as defined by sec. 76 of the *Serious Crime Act 2015* and by CPS prosecution guidelines, n.d. a).

To get a clearer picture of the legal process it is necessary to look at "The (CPS) Director's Guidance on Charging, 2013." First, the CPS reviews the evidence and decides whether to proceed by applying a "two-stage" evidential test. Cases that pass this test are sent to a magistrates' court to take the plea of the accused, assess the evidence, and decide the case.

Prior to May 2018, if a defendant pleaded guilty at "the first instance" or they were found guilty following a trial, perpetrators would be subject to a restraining order and a community sentence. However, in May 2018 new sentencing guidelines[15] were issued to ensure that perpetrators would be given harsher sentences. Thus for common assault, defendants would be fined and sentenced to up to twenty-six weeks' custody; for actual bodily harm (ABH), sentencing could include a community order to a maximum of five years' custody; for unlawful wounding (GBH s.20), a community order to a maximum of five years' custody; for wounding with intent (GBH s.18), three years' custody to a maximum of life imprisonment; for sexual assault, a community order to a maximum of ten years' custody; for harassment without violence, a fine and a maximum of six months' custody; and for harassment (putting people in fear of violence), a fine and a maximum of five years' custody.

Individuals convicted for "coercive and controlling behaviour" can be sentenced to a maximum of five years and fined; in addition, prosecution

---

However, this includes forces where body-worn video cameras are not available to all officers, or where the victim refused to allow body-worn video cameras to be used. Also, in over half of the cases reviewed, there was no evidence of photographing of injuries . . . or of gaining medical consent from the victim. . . ." Other important failures included a significant decline in the use of Domestic Violence Protection Orders (DVPOs [35-f]), a failure to respond when DVPOs were breached (38-f), and a tendency to warn offenders when sufficient evidence already existed to arrest him or her (41-f), and so on.

[15] See https://www.blasermills.co.uk/new-sentencing-guidelines-could-lead-to-harsher-punishments-for-domestic-abuse-crimes/ (accessed 11 September 2019).

under the *Protection from Harassment Act 1997* can lead to the imposition of restraining orders or convictions for stalking and the imposition of Domestic Violence Protection Orders. Remedies in civil law include occupation orders and non-molestation orders (banning contact with the victim for twenty-eight days). Statistics on the total number of prosecutions and convictions for domestic violence in England and Wales are in Table 4.1.

Table 4.1. Domestic abuse-related cases where a suspect was charged, year ending March 2010 to year ending March 2017.[16]

England and Wales								
	Apr '09 to Mar '10	**Apr '10 to Mar '11**	**Apr '11 to Mar '12**	**Apr '12 to Mar '13**	**Apr '13 to Mar '14**	**Apr '14 to Mar '15**	**Apr '15 to Mar '16**	**Apr '16 to Mar '17**
Number	62,087	68,927	66,184	60,189	72,905	84,711	82,157	79,413
Percentage	68.1	68.1	69.6	68.3	70.4	68.9	69.7	71.7

The large number of prosecutions that did *not* result in a conviction occurred because victims failed to attend court to give evidence or because a victims' evidence did not support a conviction, or for "other reasons" (ONS 2017, figure 14). As my analysis of cases reveals, two key reasons for the collapse of a prosecution are that the police failed to thoroughly investigate cases and the CPS failed to ensure that victims would attend the hearing to give evidence. ONS figures for 2017 indicate that the vast majority of defendants in domestic abuse-related prosecutions were men (92 per cent) and the majority of victims were female (65 per cent); 13 per cent of victims were male. It is also clear that many men found guilty of DV go on to breach a restraining order imposed on them and/or they assault another partner or family member.[17]

CPS data shows that between 2008/9 and 2015/16 the CPS only charged 70 per cent of the cases referred to them by the police, and that approximately 72 to 74 per cent of the cases that were prosecuted resulted in a conviction *because defendants pleaded guilty* (House of Commons

---

[16] Source: ONS 2017, table 3.

[17] I observed five cases where men who had been convicted of domestic violence re-offended against the same or a different woman (case numbers *R 76*, *R 100*, *R 116*, *R 121*, *R 144*) and two cases (nos. *R 49* and *R 220*) where, having been convicted, men failed to register with the police on the sex offender register or failed to meet their probation officer.

2019a). Once again official figures are somewhat misleading. In December 2018 an FOI request revealed that not only were there a relatively small number of arrests for "coercive and controlling behaviour" since the law was introduced in 2015, but also the majority of those arrested were not being prosecuted: in 2016/17 there were just over seven thousand arrests but in just over one thousand cases was someone charged.[18] The apparent reason for this failure relates to a tendency by the police to rely on "out of court resolutions" (Westmarland, Johnson, and McGlynn 2018) and to the "unique" evidential requirements that the police are failing to address because they see DV cases as isolated incidents and fail to investigate the wider context of repeated abuse and thus fail to see how abusers control a victim in the private, domestic context (Stark 2007).[19] This failure is also due to prosecution strategies that rely on evidence provided by victims in the full knowledge that many victims do not want to come to court (Harne and Radford 2008, 122f; Bishop and Bettinson 2018). My observations show that the ethnicity and the age of offenders varied considerably and that younger and older men and individuals of all ethnicities and social backgrounds were guilty of domestic violence.

Typically, remand hearings and trials are heard by a panel of two to three magistrates or by a District Judge; hearings can be very brief, whereas trials last between one and a half and three hours. DV cases are heard in a magistrates' court regardless of whether they have been designated as a Specialist Domestic Violence Court (SDVC).[20] SDVCs are tasked with a number of complex objectives (Cook, Burton, and Robinson 2006; Jackson 2007), which include: increasing the effectiveness of the court in providing protection and support to women and appropriate sanctions to perpetrators; enhancing the co-ordination of criminal justice with public and voluntary agencies working with victims of DV and with perpetrators; reducing delays in processing cases; and reducing rates of victimisation. In short, the courts are tasked with "narrowing the justice gap" for victims of DV, many of whom are reluctant to make a complaint or give evidence, and with dealing with the impact of DV on victims. The

---

[18] See "Domestic abuse: majority of controlling cases dropped" (Patrick Cowling, BBC, 4 December 2018), at https://www.bbc.co.uk/news/uk-46429520.

[19] Stark (2007) makes clear that the "gender strategy of coercive control" has a number of dimensions that need to be understood and that officers, prosecutors, and judges need to be better trained to grasp their own gender biases to investigate and prosecute this type of crime.

[20] In London, Specialist Domestic Violence Courts operated at Barnet, Brent, Croydon, Ealing, West London, Hillingdon, Hounslow, Stratford, Thames, and Haringey Magistrates' Courts.

ability of the courts to attain these objectives is undermined by budget cuts to all the agencies involved and by a very narrow focus on individual acts of violence. Independent evaluations of these courts show that each SDVC operated differently: case preparation appears to vary, as do conviction rates and the sanctions imposed on defendants (Cook et al. 2006).

ii. Remand hearings

I observed twenty-nine remand hearings in which an individual was charged with a domestic violence offence (15 per cent of all remand cases); all the defendants were male and twenty-eight of the victims were female. I also observed twelve criminal trials alleging domestic violence (49 per cent of all the trials I observed), two "breach" offences, and one case of harassment perpetrated by a man against his female partner (see table 4.2). My examination of remand hearings and trials illustrates the complex issues involved in determining guilt/innocence.

Table 4.2. Remand hearings and trials for domestic violence that I observed.

Defendants' gender	Breaching a domestic violence protection order	Remand hearings	Trial	Harassment/ stalking	Total
Male	2	29	12	1	42
Female	-	-	-	-	-
Total	2	29	12	1	42

Case analysis allows us to see behind the statistics on arrests and prosecutions and provides a much clearer understanding of the failure by the police to investigate DV offences, how the CPS and duty solicitors prosecute and defend cases, the varied kinds of "evidence" that victims bring to courts in support of their claims, and how judges decide between the competing accounts of witnesses.

In case *R 181* the defendant was charged with assault by beating in a "domestic context." The defendant was a white male in his forties (an immigrant). His solicitor had not seen the case file before the hearing, which lasted nineteen minutes. I have inserted bracketed numbers, e.g. (**1, 2,** etc.), to indicate the different stages of the hearing.

(1) Usher: "Mr M's representative is Ms C."
Defendant enters the [encased] dock.
Legal adviser to defendant: "Please confirm your name, date of birth and address."
Defendant: "A.M. 1 September 1972. 123 Somewhere Street."

(2) Legal adviser to court: "This is his first appearance. He is on bail and is charged with assault by beating."
Legal adviser to defendant: "Stand up. There is *one charge in relation to an event* between 12 February and 13 March 2017 when you assaulted your wife by beating. Do you plead guilty or not guilty?"
Defendant: "Guilty"

(3) Prosecutor: "The victim is his wife. They have a small child. On 3 June the police were called to the home but did not act on the incident. Subsequently the victim divulged a history of several assaults in February which caused bruising. She *described three other events for which he is not charged.* He was arrested and interviewed for all the incidents. He made a full and frank admission. He said the victim would 'not let it go' and that 'he was not providing for his family.' He is taking prescribed medication. He became so angry that he dashed her head against the dresser. He admitted other incidents but was not charged for them because they were time-barred. This is *not an isolated incident.* He is being charged for this one incident. He has no previous. This is his first appearance for DV. It was an aggravated assault in a domestic context. Marks of the abuse were visible. We seek costs of £85 and make an application for a restraining order."

(6) Solicitor: "I have been given access to very limited information. *We should not be speaking about previous incidents; they are not charged and do not come before the court.* Regarding the sentencing guidelines, I suggest the lowest in category 1. If you need a pre-sentence report, that's fine. Consider that the police could and should have issued a conditional discharge for this rather than charging him. He has made a full and frank disclosure. He has no previous. It would have been more appropriate to deal with this matter as a caution. The marriage is over; the event was five months ago. The victim's statement is nearly illegible. Are there photos (we haven't seen them)? He accepts that he pushed her down, but not that she was bruised. This was a low-level injury; he acted out of frustration. He admits he should have walked out. We can adjourn for a pre-sentence interview if you wish. "Given his time in custody, one-third will need to be taken off any sentence. The highest category for which he should be charged is . . . 'less serious.' He was holding her down; 'less harm' is my submission. "On culpability—he did not intend to hurt her. Maybe there are mental health issues. He takes medication and suffers from Attention Deficit Hyperactivity Disorder ADHT. The report suggests intermittent psychotic episodes. This is lower culpability and category 3 is the starting point, a fine. At most category 2, a community order. He has no previous. He missed out on a caution. He doesn't oppose a restraining order . . . Can we do the report today?" [Emphasis mine]

Following submissions by both parties, the bench—composed of three magistrates—rose (stage **7**) for two minutes to consider the arguments before returning to announce that the defendant was guilty but that before sentencing he should be interviewed by a probation officer. A pre-sentence report to consider "all options"[21] was to be submitted to the court in one week. At this point the legal adviser reminded the defendant that his bail conditions—a one-mile restriction order to stay away from the family home and a "no contact" order with his wife and child[22]—were renewed. The court remanded him on bail (stage **8**) with an order to return in one week to hear the report and be sentenced (I did not attend the sentencing hearing). The defendant now has a criminal conviction and he may also be fined and given a community order.

Among the issues that this case illustrates are the rapidity of the proceedings, the defendant's exclusion from the hearing following his plea (reinforced by being placed in an encased dock), and that his defence was potentially jeopardised because his solicitor had not been "served" all the evidence before the hearing. Arguments between the prosecutor and the solicitor about past offences illustrate the tactics of the prosecutor in attempting to secure a conviction; their comments draw attention to recent changes in legal aid aimed at assisting victims of DV to secure legal representation to prosecute cases extending back five years and a change in the rules allowing new forms of evidence to be submitted to support prosecution. The case also illustrates a decision by the CPS not to prosecute

[21] A pre-sentence report is prepared by the probation service and includes a detailed examination of the offender's background and behaviour to assist the court in determining the most suitable sentence. A Probation Officer is required to interview an offender and to gather information from a range of sources, for example, the family, employer, school, and police. The report is supposed to assess the risk that the person might re-offend and their suitability for a community sentence and rehabilitation programme. An "all-options" report requires the probation officer to set out a number of optional sentences—fines, community service, and a custodial sentence—for magistrates/DJs to consider. If an "all-options" report is requested, it means the bench probably anticipates imposing a custodial sentence. However, depending on the recommendations of the report, the court may accept mitigation and impose a fine, a drug/drink rehabilitation requirement (DRR) or unpaid community work. See http://www.correctiveservices.justice.nsw.gov.au/Documents/community-corrections/Policy%20and%20Procedures%20Manual/Section%20B/section-b-part-2.pdf (accessed 20 October 2017).

[22] Contact with his son would, for the time being, occur only through the family courts.

for "controlling or coercive behaviour,"[23] though it is not clear why he took this decision.

Case *R187* concerned a fifty-seven-year-old male who, from an encased dock, pleaded not guilty to a charge of assaulting his adult son. The remand hearing lasted twenty-two minutes and was taken up primarily with completing the PET form (stage 4) for trial. The incident occurred around midnight on a February evening when the defendant, who was said to be drunk, threatened to stab his son. The son's girlfriend phoned the police who arrested the defendant and took him to the station where he refused to be interviewed.

At his hearing the defendant refused to "instruct" the duty solicitor and expressed his intention to cross-examine his son and his son's girlfriend. It was pointed out to him that any cross-examination would have to be done by a solicitor. The three magistrates and their legal adviser identified the relevant information for trial—for example, a summons for the "no comment" police interview, a summons for the two police officers who attended the incident to give evidence—and they decided that the complainant/victim needed "special measures" (i.e., a screen) to allow him to give evidence. The magistrates decided that a two-and-a-half-hour trial would be required. They also imposed a restriction order preventing the defendant from entering his home (in which his son also resided) and a "no contact" order to prevent the defendant having any contact with his son and the son's girlfriend (who were now prosecution witnesses). The key point here is that the hearing was used to complete the PET form and that the magistrates accepted the police indictment containing the charge against the defendant (CPS 2018c).[24]

When the case (*T 12*) came to trial eight weeks later, the magistrates had to dismiss it because the Crown had failed to summon the claimant (the defendant's son) to give evidence and because the police officer scheduled to give evidence also failed to attend. During the proceedings it became apparent that the claimant had withdrawn his evidence against his father. The CPS asked for an adjournment to enable him to issue a summons on the claimant, and so on, which the bench refused. This trial highlights very poor case preparation by the CPS.

---

23 These changes are the result of a long and effective lobbying campaign by women's rights organisations.

24 At the defendant's trial, the prosecution's case collapsed when the Crown's witnesses failed to attend to give evidence (the CPS had not issued a summons to the plaintiff or his girlfriend). In DV cases victims, who are often related to the defendant, are reluctant to give evidence.

iii. Contested trials

Case *S 76* concerned a black male in his mid-fifties who breached a "no contact" order imposed on him six months earlier in a DV case in which he had been found guilty and given a suspended sentence. Standing in an enclosed dock, the defendant pleaded guilty to two offences, committed two hours apart, which occurred outside the victim's home. A DJ presided over the hearing, and the defendant was represented by his solicitor. The hearing lasted one hour and thirty-three minutes. I take up the case at stage (2) where the legal adviser read out a brief statement of the charges (the victim had called the police who initiated a prosecution on her behalf; during court proceedings the victims are referred to as "plaintiffs").

> Prosecutor: "The plaintiff says they have known each other since she was 19 and that she currently lives at 345 Somewhere Street. She was born in 1973."
>
> [The prosecutor and the solicitor quietly converse.]
>
> (**3**) Prosecutor: "The plaintiff says that the defendant groomed her as a prostitute between the ages of eighteen and twenty-two. This is disputed by the defendant. There is a gap in their relationship. In 2015, the defendant contacted the plaintiff and sought to prostitute her again. In January 2016, she was assaulted by the defendant. In January 2016, a restraining order was put in place to last until April 2019; there were conditions attached. On 11 July 2017, the defendant was seen outside her house in the excluded zone; she collected her son from school and went straight home and called the police. At this point, she began to take photos of him, and he approached her and told her to shut up. When another woman joined him, he drove away."
>
> DJ: "I have two charges . . ."
>
> Legal adviser: "They relate to the same date."
>
> DJ: "The facts are the same?"
>
> [The solicitor attempts to clarify the situation but is interrupted by the judge.]
>
> DJ: "On 3 March there was a breach of a suspended sentence?"
>
> Solicitor: "Yes."
>
> DJ to defendant: "Stand up please. On 17th March at Highbury Magistrates' Court you were convicted of assault and given a twelve-week sentence, suspended for eighteen months. This was for a breach of a conditional charge. Do you agree?"
>
> Defendant: "Yes, I was."

DJ: "You were convicted on 7 April 2016 for assault against another woman, a different partner, and given an eighteen-month conditional discharge to October 2017. It appears you are in breach of that order. Was no sentence imposed?"

The judge rose for five minutes while the clerk checked the records and confirmed that the defendant was in breach of a conditional bail direction and that he had been sentenced to thirty days custody. At this point the case resumed.

(**6**) Prosecutor: "I will read out the victim 'impact statement.' The victim has known the defendant for twenty years; he is the father of her four children. During their relationship he constantly abused and threatened her. She suffers from PTSD as a result and struggles to cope. She is worried by his presence near her home. On 17 July she saw him near her home . . . now she stays in the house except to get her child from school. Seeing him near her home has caused flashbacks and panic attacks. As a result, she has no social life; her friends come to her house, but she does not go out. He is frequently around her home despite a restraining order that he should stay one hundred meters away from the house. He breached the order on 20 September."

Solicitor: "That's the date of the trial!"

Prosecutor: "That is what the police have provided. In January 2017, he breached an order by attacking another ex-partner; that incident was treated as a domestic incident. That woman has trouble sleeping and has a damaged eye. In April 2016, he assaulted his sister-in-law and received a conditional discharge. In October 2016, he assaulted another ex-partner. His 'previous' demonstrates violence to all his ex-partners, not just to the plaintiff."

DJ to defendant: "Do you want to go to the Crown court?"

Solicitor: "The facts are incorrect. The 2015 assault was not against an ex-partner, it was a friend of the ex-partner."

DJ: "It violated a restraining order."

Solicitor: "This was someone he had known for thirty-two years. I submit that you have sufficient power to deal with this case. The restriction order was imposed fifteen months ago, and the July incident was the first breach and was of a minor nature. It occurred at four p.m. The defendant was at his car and she objected to his presence despite the distance, which was one to two hundred meters away from her house. She spoke to him first and he had a reasonable excuse for being there."

DJ: "The defendant's account [at his trial] was not accepted by the judge."

Solicitor: "The judge found that he responded to her taking pictures of him in the car. . . Regarding the second breach, this occurred two hours later when the plaintiff crossed the road and spoke to him. He replied: 'I am doing a job.' The judge accepted that he had a legitimate reason to be there. . . . The plaintiff had moved out of London, but later moved back near the defendant's residence. The incident was not a breach; he was not threatening. None of the earlier allegations count as they occurred prior to 2016. . .

"There are other issues. His behaviour is not an escalation; the attacks are on different people at different times and on different occasions. . . . He attended a 'building better relationships' class in July. I suggest that he be required to attend an additional class. He is willing to do unpaid work. I urge you to make a suspended sentence. . ."

At this point the DJ read aloud the statement of the judge who sentenced the defendant at his trial, which emphasised the defendant's "anger" and the impact of his behaviour on the victim. She then asked the parties to suggest an appropriate sentence for the defendant.

(7) DJ: ". . . I can see no reason why the suspended sentence can't be reactivated? You have committed violence against all your ex-partners. You could be imprisoned for the 2017 conviction. I haven't taken representations about sentencing but then there are the breaches of suspended sentences. You are looking at a twelve-month sentence. . . . In mitigation you are caring for your mother, but your behaviour has put those arrangements in jeopardy. The sentence is in excess of this court's jurisdiction. I am committing you to the Crown court for sentencing for two convictions and the breach. Take him into custody for sentencing by the Crown court."

Solicitor: "I want to make a bail application for the period prior to sentencing" [he hands forward a completed form].

[The solicitor and the defendant speak briefly.]

DJ: "I will hear you."

Solicitor: "I ask for bail. Mr X is no risk; he is too well aware of his situation. There is every incentive for him to comply. He attended the trial. At that trial he believed that my firm would represent him, but we only had ten minutes to prepare a defence. There is no danger that he will fail to surrender. There are conditions which could be made. He could live and sleep at his address."

DJ: "I have heard your application for bail . . . I am not prepared to grant bail. Take him into custody."

The details set out during the hearing provide a clear picture of the nature of domestic violence that, in this case, might more appropriately have been prosecuted on the more serious charge of "controlling behaviour" rather than for breaching a suspended sentence. The DJ's interventions caused the proceedings to be moved forward by assertion and counter-assertion rather than via the more formulaic role-play that occurs when magistrates preside. There were no witnesses for the defendant, and the prosecution's evidence was in the form of a police interview with the plaintiff. The police are required to obtain an "impact statement" from the victim, and prosecutors are obligated to read out the statement during the hearing (CPS, n.d.). These statements are intended to give "victims an opportunity to describe the wider effects of the crime upon them, express their concerns and indicate whether or not they require any support." Prosecutors use these statements to drive home a key message to the court about the serious nature of the offence and its long-term consequences for the victim. Note how the argument about the seriousness and relevance of the defendant's previous convictions led the DJ to read aloud part of the sentencing judge's comments about his previous offence.

On two occasions during the hearing, the DJ asked whether the defendant wanted the case to be heard in the Crown court, a question his solicitor refused to answer because he knew that the magistrates' court had limited sentencing powers. In the end, the DJ made it clear that the minimum sentence for having twice breached a court order was twelve months imprisonment. Since she only had the power to sentence a defendant to a maximum of six months, she remitted the case to the Crown court for sentencing. She also refused to grant the defendant bail (though she failed to provide specific reasons for her decision).

It is important to note that, as with case *S 76* above, some male defendants are repeat offenders. This pattern of behaviour is apparent in case *B 153*, which concerned a man who was awaiting trial for assault against his partner. A "no contact" restraining order was imposed on him at his remand hearing and he was released on bail, following which he confronted his partner on the street and broke into her home to threaten her. The man was later arrested and placed in custody for breaching a restraining order. At the breach hearing, the CPS applied for a "bad character reference" to be made against him. He cited Sec. 101 of the *Criminal Justice Act 2003*,[25] which, if granted by the court, would have "substantial probative value" in relation to his forthcoming trial; that is, it would be useful in proving the defendant's guilt. The bench took fifty minutes to hear the

[25] See https://www.legislation.gov.uk/ukpga/2003/44/section/101.

application and, despite a robust argument between the parties, agreed that the incident did provide evidence of a "propensity to commit further [criminal] acts." In short, the defendant's action in breaching bail provided additional evidence that would be used against him at his trial.[26]

When an individual pleads "not guilty" at their remand hearing the court schedules a trial (usually within eight weeks). During the interim period the two parties are required to disclose their case[27] to each other. The Crown must provide witness statements, data from the Police National Computer (PNC)[28] about the incident, the defendant's police interview, and all unused evidence to the defence; and the defence must disclose its case to the Crown. Ideally, both parties agree the evidence and ensure that their witnesses attend. As will be seen, however, and regardless of the time spent filling in the PET form to ensure an "effective" trial, trials are beset with problems. While disclosure requirements were usually met in advance of the trial, from time to time this did not happen. I observed two case management reviews where the defence argued that the Crown had failed to meet its obligations to disclose (in both cases the male defendant was charged with domestic violence).

In *CM 240* the defence argued that the Crown had failed to disclose its case (the trial was two days away). Defence argued that it wanted a number of items from the Crown—the police interview tape, the custody record, police statements, the 999 tape, the PNC, CCTV seized by the police, and the CAD report[29]—failing which it would submit a "wasted costs"[30] or an "abuse of process" application[31] against the Crown. At the end of the forty-three-minute hearing, the magistrates ruled that all the required evidence should be submitted to the defence no later than the morning of the trial. In *T 11*, involving an allegation of domestic violence against the defendant's partner, the failure of the Crown to disclose its case resulted in the original trial date being vacated; a new date was fixed to allow disclosure to take place.

---

[26] This was the only case I observed in which the CPS attempted to secure a "bad character" reference against a defendant.

[27] See http://www.cps.gov.uk/legal/s_to_u/streamlined_summary_disclosure/.

[28] Data on defendants is held on the Police National Computer, see https://www.acro.police.uk/subject_access.aspx.

[29] CAD is the computer-aided dispatches system that records 999 calls.

[30] For the most recent guidance, see "*[2015] EWCA Crim 1568*" [Practice Direction (Costs in Criminal Proceedings) 2015] at https://www.judiciary.gov.uk/wp-content/uploads/2015/09/pd-costs-in-crim-proc-2015.pdf.

[31] See http://www.hse.gov.uk/enforce/enforcementguide/court/abuse-abuseprocess.htm (accessed on 4 May 2019).

Judicial decisions hinge upon an assessment of the competing stories of victims and defendants that is a difficult task because usually there is no independent evidence about the incident in question. Such was the situation in *T 1*, a trial presided over by a DJ that lasted two hours and twenty-five minutes and that concerned an incident between a young Asian man and woman married according to Muslim custom.[32] During the trial, the defendant sat in the encased dock and the plaintiff gave her evidence via a video link from another court.[33] The plaintiff was assisted by Witness Protection; and the police officer in charge came to court to hand the CPS a CD containing the evidence.

> **(6)** Prosecutor: "You have heard from Ms. Y. It was difficult to elicit her evidence.[34] She alleged assault. She was physically threatened and violently treated; a blanket was held over her head. She delayed in speaking to the police because she didn't have the courage. She made a covert recording which Mr X has had an opportunity to refute; but he ignored it. He denied at his police interview that anything happened. There are the photos of the plaintiff's injuries and there is the transcript of the recording.[35] The Crown's case is that despite her difficulties in giving evidence, Mr X was angry and upset. Her evidence should be believed."
>
> Solicitor: "You must be sure [i.e., about the evidence]. The claimant has not disproved the defendant's claim of self-defence. In her evidence, she didn't mention that he had put her in a headlock, which was in her police statement. She has contradicted her evidence because she said nothing to the police when they came to the flat. This goes against her credibility because she did not tell the police when they arrived. She tried to obtain a confession the next day. Be careful about giving weight to this evidence [the recording]. It merely shows that the defendant did not take part in the conversation. She only reported the incident five weeks later: Why? Why still live with him? I ask you to find the defendant not guilty."

---

[32] They were married according to the Muslim ritual of *Nikah*, which is not recognised in civil law as constituting a marriage (Malik 2012).
[33] The legal adviser proved inept at setting up the video link, which caused the trial to be delayed.
[34] Despite giving evidence via a video-link, she broke down several times, which led to several lengthy adjournments to allow her to compose herself.
[35] After the incident, the claimant went to a support worker who advised her to collect evidence. She subsequently approached her partner and, surreptitiously using her phone, interviewed him about what happened. The recording was later submitted in evidence against him.

(7/8) DJ to the defendant: "The Crown has brought this case, and it must prove the case. If there is any doubt, I must find in your favour. This is a factual dispute about what happened. You have given evidence which contradicts her evidence. She sustained injuries, as shown in the photos. These were clearly caused by a third party that evening. Neither of you spoke to the police (when they arrived). In refuting her evidence, you said that you didn't push her to the floor. Both accounts cannot be true. In the recording made the next day, she said you used a knife and you didn't respond to that. You were silent. She also said that you were holding a knife over her, and in the recording you were silent. I have assessed her evidence to be credible; it was clearly difficult for her to give evidence. She did express it clearly; her evidence was credible, clear, and plausible.

"The delay in reporting the incident to the police is not unusual. It doesn't undermine her case. I don't accept your explanation. . . . Her responses, the photos and her evidence [are] credible. The incident as described did occur. I reject your evidence. You are guilty of assault by beating."

Solicitor: "I haven't got the PNC form."

Legal adviser: "Sentencing will be in three weeks. He is barred from entering the claimants' home; no contact is allowed with her of any kind."

DJ to defendant: "Stand up. I have found you guilty. In three weeks there will be a probation assessment; there is a real possibility of custody. I will take the probation report into consideration. While the level of violence is not serious, the custody threshold has been crossed. . . . You must return to this court at 9:30 a.m. The same conditional bail applies as before. There is to be no contact with the claimant. You can't ask anyone to contact her. If you breach bail, you may end up waiting in prison for sentencing. I don't know whether you will be legally represented at sentencing. You must apply for legal aid or secure representation privately. If you do not have a representative, the court won't delay sentencing."

There are numerous aspects of this case worth noting. The evidence submitted to the court took the form of written statements (from the claimant, the defendant and from three police officers who attended the incident when neither party spoke to the police) as well as a transcript of the claimant's forty-two minute recorded "interview" of her partner and several photos she took of her wounds. It is also important to note that increasingly complainants are documenting their claims using phones, recordings, and photographs, which the court accepts as evidence. The second notable aspect of this case was that the court appointed Sec. 38 legal representation for the defendant[36] to cross-examine the plaintiff. However, the solicitor also led the defendant in his evidence and made final submissions on his behalf (though he was not paid to do this).[37] Finally, victims/claimants can be assisted to give their evidence by the Witness Protection Programme which includes being present while they give evidence and providing evidence with the use of protective screens or video links, which are intended to prevent the defendant from intimidating the victim while they give their evidence.

Case *T 10* provides a different angle from which to understand the importance of issuing a summons to plaintiffs requiring them to give evidence at a hearing, and how magistrates/DJs assess conflicting evidence. This case concerned an allegation made by a woman against her husband: that he threatened and intimidated her and their children. The trial, which was presided over by three magistrates, lasted two hours and fifty-five minutes. Though the plaintiff and her husband were immigrants whose first language was Arabic, the proceedings were in English. The alleged incident occurred when the defendant came home late and began to argue with his wife about his relationship with another woman. The defendant was in his mid-forties; his wife was thirty-nine; the couple had been married for fifteen years.

Neither the plaintiff nor her daughter wanted to give evidence, but the Crown had issued a summons requiring them to attend. Their evidence was heard first; both women spoke from behind a curtain (a "screen"). The witnesses confirmed that an incident occurred in the stepdaughter's bedroom where they were sitting when Mr. D arrived (during the argument they were joined by the couple's younger children). Cross-examination of the stepdaughter revealed that although a virulent argument occurred during which the defendant spat at his wife—the spit hit the stepdaughter instead—she did not see her stepfather kick her mother. The defendant also spat at his two younger children. I take up the case at the point where the prosecutor read the statements (stage 3) provided by the police officers who attended the incident.

---

[36] If a defendant is not legally represented in court, Part 23 of the *Criminal Procedure Rules* prohibits him/her from cross-examining the plaintiff. In this situation the court must appoint a legal representative to undertake the cross-examination. See https://www.justice.gov.uk/courts/procedure-rules/criminal/docs/ 2015/crim-proc-rules-2015-part-23.pdf (accessed 29 October 2017).

[37] I frequently saw duty solicitors appointed on a Sec. 36/38 order who represented their clients beyond what was required by the law.

Prosecutor: "I refer to the statement by PC "A." He was on duty with a colleague when the 999 call came through and they attended the scene: 'When we arrived at the door we heard screaming. We attended with blue lights, we knocked, and the door was opened, and we were invited in. We spoke to a young woman (later identified as the defendant's stepdaughter) who was scared. The wife was prompted by her daughter to speak to us. There had been an argument and the husband had left the address. He had been rude and had been asked to leave the house. He had been rude again and had spat and kicked the wife. She showed me her lower-right leg which had three-inch red marks on the calf; it was swollen. She didn't require an ambulance. It was 11:45 p.m. There was no camera[38] available. Children were present; we checked on their welfare. We asked A to phone Dad and to ask him to return to the address. When he returned, he was arrested and taken to custody. We took statements separately from each person so that their accounts were independent of each other."

Police Constable "B" also attended the residence: "We called at the address at 22:49 p.m. I couldn't hear noise. A young Asian female answered and invited us in. Her father had left; her mother was upstairs. Her mother joined us and said that he had shouted, spat, and kicked her. She showed me two marks three inches long on her leg. The girl confirmed the spitting. I had them phone Dad and left the other PC to complete the interviews. There were two boys who were very upset. They explained the incident. Their father had come home; there had been shouting; he kicked her and tried to push the daughter away. He spat at them. I told them they needn't be afraid as their father would be going to the police station . . . The dad enters and is arrested for ABH for kicking and spitting on three persons and to prevent any harm to the wife and children. He was cautioned and did not reply. At 23:28 he was handcuffed and transported to the station.

"Regarding the 999 call, the statement of PC 'M' stated that he spoke to the mum and dad. The parties did not want to go to court or for the father to be prosecuted. The mother said she had not been pressured to change her evidence but did not want prosecution to proceed. . . . The daughter was the caller to the police, and she did not want to assist us further.

"Regarding the 999 transcript, the caller was not able to be understood and the question had to be repeated. A male voice came on that was angry. In the background I could hear a woman's voice raised. The woman said 'I need you' to the police operator. She told us of a problem, the address, that the husband was the problem, and named the husband.

"I refer to the transcript summary [of the defendant's interview] which has been agreed [by both parties]. The Dad declined a representative. The wife, daughter, and sons provided evidence. [The Dad] had been jailed in 2003 for violence but was released. The wife is very jealous; he is much

---

[38] The reference is to police body cameras that have been provided to some Metropolitan police officers.

more Westernised. The wife wants to get a divorce; the husband is very disrespectful to her and the children. She turned the children against him. They use comments about him from his wife. He can't understand her attitude. She shouted at him. He never went to his daughter's bedroom. He denied the spitting incidents. He became emotional at the end of the interview. That's the Crown's case."

The defendant, who was sitting in an encased dock, was called to the witness box (stage 5) and the duty solicitor led him through his evidence. Cross-examination (stage 6) by the prosecutor confirmed many elements of the allegation, for example, that it occurred late at night, that he had gone into his stepdaughter's "very small" bedroom where he argued with his wife in front of their children, and that he had been spending considerable time with another woman. His admission of entering the bedroom contradicted the evidence he had given to the police. However, he denied spitting on his wife and children and that he kicked his wife.

At this point both parties summed up their arguments (stage 6) and pointed out how the oral evidence provided by all the witnesses contradicted the statements that they had given to the police after the incident. The magistrates rose to consider their verdict and asked the legal advisor about the relevant law; they returned to court one hour and thirteen minutes later to announce the verdict (stage 7):

Magistrate: "We have listened carefully to the parties, the evidence, and the witness statements. There is significant variation in the evidence of all three witnesses.[39] We place greater weight on the witness statements and the Sec. 9 reports by the PCs . . . We find all matters proved."

Prosecutor: "Thanks. We ask for £620 in costs. There are the 'previous' matters and we are minded to ask for a pre-sentence report."

Legal advisor: "We have to wait three weeks for a probation report."

Magistrate: "What are your observations on the bail position?"

Prosecutor: "We continue with existing conditions."

---

[39] The magistrates relied on Sec. 119 of the *Criminal Justice Act 2003*, which allows them to decide that when a person provides oral evidence that contradicts the evidence s/he gave to the police, they can rule that his/her evidence is not admissible. See https://www.legislation.gov.uk/ukpga/2003/44/section/119.

> Legal advisor: "These are, not to enter the residence and no contact—direct or indirect—with the two witnesses. Sentencing is set for the 29th at Hammersmith Magistrates' Court."

> Magistrate to defendant: "We are requiring a pre-sentence report to assist 'the other bench'[40] in sentencing. We order you to come back here at 9:30 a.m. on the 29th for an interview. The bail and bond conditions continue" [she repeats what the legal advisor said earlier].

I did not attend the sentencing hearing but, since the incident involved limited violence, the sentence was probably a restriction, a community order, and/or a fine. At the heart of this case was the fact that the defendant, the plaintiff, and their daughter provided oral evidence that conflicted with the written statements they had given to the police. The contradictions emerged because of effective cross-examination by the Crown and the DS. It is worth reiterating that, unlike *R 187* (discussed above), the trial would have collapsed if the CPS had not issued a summons requiring the plaintiff and her daughter to attend court to give evidence. The evidence—in the form of police statements, statements given by the parties to the police, the 999-emergency phone call and the parties oral evidence—was critical in allowing the magistrates to arrive at a decision. The magistrates relied on Sec. 119 of the *Criminal Justice Act 2003*, which allowed them to attach greater weight to the evidence of the plaintiff. The role played by the duty solicitor is also worth noting. Before the proceedings began, he told the legal advisor that, in accordance with a Sec. 39 application made by the court, he would only cross-examine the plaintiff. Instead, he led the defendant in his evidence and summed up the defendant's case before the magistrates.

Conclusion

As the cases analysed in this chapter illustrate, whereas there are a high percentage of guilty pleas in remand hearings, the outcome of a trial is less predictable. The reasons for acquittals and/or the collapse of a trial arise from the failure of the police to adequately investigate allegations before passing the case to the CPS, a failure to persuade the victim that prosecution is in her/his interests, a failure by the CPS to assess whether a successful

[40] The "other court" referred to is the bench that will hear the probation report and sentence the defendant. It is rare for magistrates who hear and decide a case to sentence the defendant (probably because most magistrates sit part-time).

prosecution can be mounted, and a failure to issue a summons to ensure that claimants and their witnesses attend court to give evidence.

There is, however, a further problem. Limited police investigation and a poor review of a case by the CPS may result in the prosecution of cases that should have been dropped or discontinued. Difficulties in reaching a just decision may be compounded because magistrates/DJs only admit evidence that they deem relevant to an alleged offence; they exclude a history of the relation between the defendant and the victim/claimant, which might help explain events leading up to the alleged offence. This narrow judicial focus is reinforced by the court's concern to identify individual *culpability for a single act*—the act of hitting, holding, or making a threat—in proceedings that are short (Campbell 2018). In the absence of an adequate investigation into an offence, the narrow focus by the police and CPS on a specific act may result in a failure to gather historical evidence[41] of controlling and/or coercive behaviour as set out in sec. 76 of the *Serious Crime Act 2015* [42] as opposed to collecting witness statements and compelling victims to testify in court.

While official statistics show that the police exercise considerable discretion in deciding which incidents will be recorded as a crime (they refer about 25 per cent of recorded DV offences to the CPS to prosecute), and the CPS only prosecute 70 per cent of the cases passed to them by the police (there has been a significant decrease in the number of DV cases finalised, prosecuted, and convicted [CPS 2018/19]). Why does the CPS fail to prosecute the remaining cases? From the vantage point of the court, it is clear that the police do not investigate these crimes and that prosecutions collapse because there is insufficient evidence to convict a defendant and because victims often do not want their partner to be prosecuted.

The result of this ineffective approach to prosecuting domestic violence results in a high attrition rate of reported incidents, which leads the police to drop many cases, to the CPS failing to prosecute a large percentage of recorded cases, and to court decisions that hand down the minimum sentence. The knock-on effects of this pattern of prosecution are two-fold: victims lack confidence in the police and the courts, and the level of

---

[41] Researchers have consistently pointed out that the police require better training and awareness to investigate these crimes and that in addition to adopting special measures enabling victims to give their evidence in court, the police and CPS could rely on a number of "innovative" techniques to gather data including making admissible hearsay evidence (999 calls, emergency service calls, photos, e.g., from body worn cameras, etc., CCTV footage) and *res gestae* statements (Bishop and Bettinson 2018).

[42] See http://www.legislation.gov.uk/ukpga/2015/9/contents/enacted.

domestic violence rises.[43] The situation lends credence to calls by campaign groups that the CJS is failing to protect victims. In view of the fact that prosecuting and sentencing offenders has no effect on repeat offending (Garner and Maxwell 2011),[44] perhaps it is time to consider other ways to deal with rising levels of domestic violence including providing adequate support for specialist DV units but also re-examining the school curriculum to better educate and prepare young people for adult life. If the law provides limited solutions to deal with domestic violence, it is time to reconceptualise the problem and identify different and hopefully more effective solutions.

---

[43] The latest reports indicate that the number of DV offences in London increased by two-thirds between 2011 and 2018 and that recorded rape offences have risen 134 per cent in 2018 compared to the same time in 2017 (Sarah Marsh, "Domestic abuse offences in London rise sixty-three percent in seven years," *Guardian*, 27 February 2019).

[44] The Government has announced a review of the way that rape cases are heard in an apparent effort to stop trial by jury (Charles Hymas, "Rape case jury trials could be scrapped in justice review," *Daily Telegraph*, 6 March 2019). However, as the above discussion and published research clearly shows, the principle problem is not with jury trials but the failure of the police and the CPS to secure better evidence.

CHAPTER 5

THE PROSECUTION OF DRUG OFFENCES

Public concern about the sale and consumption of illegal drugs has, over the years, been shaped by official statements about the extent and cost of crime (Garland 2002) and by conflicting "expert discourses" about deviance and whether incarceration or therapy are effective forms of intervention. The dominant view is that "hard drugs" such as cocaine and heroin are linked to "acquisitive crimes," that is, crimes aimed at securing money to pay for a drug habit, which should be punished/sanctioned. This view is also prevalent in magistrates' courts, but it is tempered by a belief that some individuals can be helped to change their behaviour and address their addiction. The *Misuse of Drugs Act (1971)* identifies the sanctions for possessing, supplying, the intent to supply, or the production of illegal drugs, which are set out in Box 5.1.

The therapeutic "turn" in dealing with addiction persists for two reasons. First, over the past several decades, the consumption of nearly all types of drugs has declined and levelled out; currently just over 4 per cent of adults and 9.5 per cent of young people consume illegal drugs (Home Office 2018c). Indeed, cannabis has become the most commonly consumed drug with 7 per cent of the population currently thought to be consuming it. Second, there is a commonly held view that if substance abuse/addiction is a "disease,"[1] then it is capable of being "cured" or at least controlled by learning "new technologies of the self" that leave open the possibility of individual reform/redemption (Garriott and Raikhel 2015). Conflicting views about addiction as something that should be dealt with via sanctions/imprisonment or via therapy are visible in magistrates' courts when magistrates decide whether to imprison a defendant or to impose a Drug Rehabilitation Requirement (DRR). This chapter illustrates the selective nature of policing *and* a general failure to investigate many crimes

---

[1] Garriott and Raikhel (2015) look at the plurality of explanations for addiction, each of which tends to be linked to a specific type of intervention. They argue that "expert models of addiction" exhibit an ambivalence about the underlying causes of addiction, which is reflected in equally ambivalent and contradictory understandings about the effectiveness of therapeutic as opposed to punitive interventions.

in an apparent focus on arresting and prosecuting individuals for "simple possession" of drugs, which is easy to prove. The cases examined in this chapter show that magistrates/DJs often fail to question the CPS about the classification of a specific drug and therefore about appropriate sentencing guidelines and that magistrates/DJs do not sentence defendants in a consistent manner. Worryingly, the causative factors behind offending are

Box 5.1. Penalties for possessing drugs, supplying, intent to supply, or producing drugs.[2]

Class	Examples of drugs covered	Mode of prosecution	Possession	Supply, intent to supply, and production
A	Crack cocaine, powder cocaine, LSD, MDMA, methadone, methamphetamine, psilocybin-containing mushrooms, U-47,700	Indictment	Up to seven years in prison, an unlimited fine, or both	Up to life in prison, an unlimited fine, or both
		Summary	Up to six months in prison, a fine of £5,000, or both	Up to six months in prison, a fine of £5,000, or both
B	Amphetamines, barbiturates, cannabis, codeine, ketamine, methylphenidate (and related compounds), synthetic cannabinoids, synthetic cathinones, methiopropamine	Indictment	Up to five years in prison, an unlimited fine, or both	Up to fourteen years in prison, an unlimited fine, or both
		Summary	Up to three months in prison, a £2400 fine, or both	Up to six months in prison, a £5000 fine, or both
C	Anabolic steroids, benzodiazepines (including designer benzodiacepines such as etizolam), GHB, GBL, khat, and piperazines	Indictment	Up to two years in prison, an unlimited fine, or both	Up to fourteen years in prison, an unlimited fine, or both
		Summary	Up to three months in prison, a £1000 fine, or both	Up to three months in prison, a £2,500 fine, or both

2 Source https://www.gov.uk/penalties-drug-possession-dealing (accessed 11 February 2020).

Temporary class drug order	No substances currently controlled by TCDO	Indictment	None, but police can take away a suspected temporary class drug	Up to fourteen years in prison, an unlimited fine, or both
		Summary	None, but the police can take away a suspected temporary class drug	Up to six months in prison, a £5000 fine, or both
Public Service Agreements (PSA)	All psychoactive substances not covered by the *Misuse of Drugs Act 1971* or otherwise exempt	Indictment	None	Up to seven years in prison, an unlimited fine, or both
		Summary	None	Up to 12 months in prison, an unlimited fine, or both

not taken into account by the legal process, which results in imprisoning defendants and in turn increases the likelihood of repeat offending.

Home Office reports (2018c) indicate that in 2017/2018 the police made 37,000 arrests in London for drug related offences.[3] The boroughs with the highest rate of drug-related arrests are in central London (Newham, Westminster, Southwark, Lambeth, and Brent); these boroughs overlap with the epicentre of the 2011 riots and are areas of economic deprivation.[4] Data on police "sanction rates" for drug offences (see Table 5.1), which provide very different statistics on the number of arrests, clearly show that sanction detection rates are falling (the Home Office does not publish statistics on crime "clear-up" rates).

---

[3] The Metropolitan police made over 35,000 arrests, 269 arrests were made by the City of London Police, and the British Transport Police made 1,500 arrests. See "Recorded crime data at police force area level" (including pivot table) at https://www.ons.gov.uk/peoplepopulationandcommunity/crimeandjustice/datasets/recordedcrimedataatpoliceforcearealevelincludingpivottable.

[4] See https://www.met.police.uk/sd/stats-and-data/met/crime-data-dashboard/ (accessed 12 October 2019).

Official statistics indicate that there has been a continuous decline in the number of recorded offences from 2011 onwards for drugs (UK 2017d, 164–66, Table 5.1). Unsurprisingly, the number of arrests and prosecutions for drug offences has also fallen (UK 2018c, 4). Declining arrests and prosecutions undoubtedly reflect a decline in the number of officers on the streets (due to budget cuts) but it also reflects the "discretion" exercised by officers in deciding whether to ignore, warn, fine, or arrest the individuals who come to their attention.

Table 5.1. Police sanction detection rates for drug offences in London, 2016–18.[5]

Offence type	Offences 2016–17	2017-18	Sanction detection 2016–17	2017–18	Change 2016–17	2017–18
Drug trafficking	3,864	2,835	3,253	2,820	-26.3%	-13.31%
Other drugs	317	243	275	196	-23.34%	-28.73%
Possession	34,855	32,630	32,118	28,933	-6.38%	-9.2%
Total	39,036	35,708	35,646	31,949	-8.53%	-10.37

Fieldwork allowed me to observe how minor drug offences are prosecuted (see Table 5.2) and while my observations are not representative of how the courts handle all drug offences,[6] my data shows the role played by all parties in court proceedings and how these cases are decided. Fieldwork, informed by published reports, establishes key links between policing, prosecution, and sentencing.

Table 5.2. Drug-related prosecutions I observed.

Number of cases	Offence
14	Possession of cannabis (and related cases)
1	Possession of ecstasy
1	Possession of MDMA
2	Possession of spice
2	Possession of cocaine
2	Possession of heroin
22	Total (percentage of all cases: 9%)

While drug-related offences constituted 4 per cent of all arrests in London between 2016 and 18, they constituted 9 per cent of the remand

[5] Source https://www.met.police.uk/sd/stats-and-data/met/year-end-crime-statistics/ (accessed on 1 September 2018).

[6] The prosecution of individuals who sought to import/distribute large amounts of drugs into the UK involves lengthy trials at a Crown court.

cases I observed. In this chapter, I discuss how the offences of "possession" and "intent to supply" the principal drugs sold on London's streets were prosecuted.

Cannabis

Cannabis is a class B drug[7] in which the main active chemical is tetrahydrocannabinol (THC). THC can make you feel chilled out, happy, and relaxed; but it can also cause hallucinations. Cannabis affects the brain. It can make a person anxious and paranoid; it can make it difficult to concentrate, it can also affect one's memory and make you feel less motivated. Smoking cannabis is linked to tuberculosis and lung cancer.

The cannabis market in the UK is estimated to be worth £2.6 billion per year; that is, about 255 tons of cannabis is sold every year (IEA 2018). Most of what is consumed is produced in Afghanistan and Morocco and secondarily in southern Africa, the Caribbean, and the Netherlands. It is shipped into ports and taken to larger cities such as London for onward distribution and sale. Judging by the amount seized by police, domestic production of cannabis—said to be reliant on modern slave labour—stabilised at an estimated value of £62 million in 2013 (NPCC 2014, 7). Curiously, despite a ban on its consumption, the UK is the largest exporter of legal cannabis in the world.[8] While cannabis, along with most other illegal drugs, was initially brought in by "foreign criminals," many British nationals are now involved in importing, distributing, and selling it.

In recent years there has been an ongoing debate about whether cannabis should be reclassified from a class B to a class C drug, or indeed whether it should be decriminalised.[9] The debate over legalising cannabis has been given an impetus by recent statistics that suggest a sharp decline in the number of police cautions and arrests for possession, which has been seized upon as an indication that the police are *de facto* "decriminalising" the drug.[10] While conviction for "possession" or "intent to supply" can

[7] See https://www.talktofrank.com/drug/cannabis (accessed 9 September 2019).

[8] See "UK world's largest producer of legal cannabis, finds UN body" (*Independent*, 7 March 2018).

[9] See Pudney (2002); "Official report triggers Home Office row over decriminalization of drugs" (*Telegraph*, 30 October 2014); "Is it time for the UK to decriminalize drugs?" (*Week*, 18 July 2018), at http://www.theweek.co.uk/86841/is-it-time-the-uk-decriminalised-drugs.

[10] See "Police 'decriminalizing' cannabis as prosecutions fall away" (*Guardian*, 14 July 2018). In reality a declining level of arrests is reflected across all categories of crime.

result in imprisonment for between three months and two years, plus a fine (see Box 5.1), fieldwork indicates that the CPS and magistrates adopt very different strategies in prosecuting this offence. The first three cases arose fortuitously, whereas the "three-hander" was the result of officers using their authority to stop and search youth. While the CPS was willing to alter the charge against defendant *R 19*, a first-time offender, and reduce it to a fixed penalty notice, it is clear that regardless of whether a defendant had legal representation, each defendant received a different sentence.

In February 2016, Mr B, a young white male (case *R 17*), was arraigned in a seven-minute hearing for possession of cannabis; he pleaded guilty and chose not to be legally represented. The CPS read out the charge (stage 2):

> "He attempted to enter a venue which was being watched by the police. He was searched and a small amount of cannabis for personal use was found on his person. He has a previous conviction for the same offence. . . . He was bailed until 15 February. There is a previous conviction in 2015 and in 2014 for fraud. He has apologized. . . ."
>
> Magistrate: "Are his previous convictions serious?"[11]
>
> CPS: "Which ones?"
>
> Magistrate: "Robbery, shoplifting, obstructing a constable, fraud."
>
> CPS: "Yes. The Crown suggests a cost application of £85, a fine of £100, and a victim surcharge of £20."
>
> Magistrate to defendant (stage 3): "What do you want to say?"
>
> Defendant: "It is not who I am. I am not a constant user. I have had a lot of stress and use it for relaxation."
>
> Magistrate: "How are you supported?"
>
> Defendant: "I am receiving housing benefits from which is deducted money for prior loans."

The magistrates conferred briefly on the bench (stage 7/8) before stating:

> Magistrate: "We will give you credit for an early guilty plea, otherwise the penalty would have been higher. We fine you £100 for possession of a class

[11] The bench did not have access to the case file.

B drug, £85 court costs, and £20 for the court surcharge. That is a total of £205. We also make an order to forfeit and destroy the drugs. . . . You are offering to pay £30 every two weeks? . . . We will accept that offer. We are imposing a fines collection order; you must pay £30 on 12 February and £30 every fortnight. If you fail to meet the payments a bailiff will come to your home and seize property to the remaining value plus property to meet his costs."

Case *R 19* concerned a black male in his early twenties who was arraigned for possession. However, unlike the previous case, he was represented by a duty solicitor who pre-empted the CPS by making an application to the court.

"On arrest the officers smelled herbal cannabis. He was not represented at the police station. He had been stopped in the park and he made a full confession. He is of good character. The police could have given him a fixed penalty notice for possession, but instead they charged him. I ask for a three-week adjournment to obtain a report."

When the CPS stated that he would not oppose the application,[12] the bench agreed that the defendant would be released on unconditional bail while the CPS discussed the case with the police. A further hearing was scheduled in three weeks. His hearing lasted five minutes.

In case *R 82* the defendant was a middle-aged white male. The CPS read out the charge (stage 2):

"The defendant was stopped while driving a white Fiat. Without prompting, he pleaded guilty to smoking cannabis. He underwent a roadside test and was found to be positive; he also provided officers with a small bag of cannabis. His blood was tested and found to have six milligrams. He said it was for his own use. We apply for forfeiture and destruction of the drugs and for costs."

The defendant pleaded guilty to the charge (stage 3) and the duty solicitor set out the defendant's situation (stage 6):

"This is an unfortunate case. Mr X works for an international company. He is a family man with a wife and child. His salary is £56,000 per year. In

[12] This could lead the police to drop the charge and issue a "warning" (which does not form part of a person's criminal record), a penalty notice (i.e., a fine issued for a second offence of possessing a small amount of cannabis), or a caution (reflecting an admission of guilt that creates a criminal record).

> effect he handles two jobs which makes it very stressful; work causes sleeplessness and depression. . . . He is not a herbal cannabis user. He went online and discovered that cannabis can relieve pain symptoms. He has several testimonials. If he is disqualified from driving, he might lose his job . . . He has no previous relevant convictions and he is remorseful for his actions and is of good character. There are no signs of mental disorder and he is the sole carer. I invite you to impose a penalty at the lowest end of the scale."

After looking at the PET form and reading the defendant's testimonials the magistrates asked the defendant to stand (stage 8/9):

> "We have heard about the offence and what was said on your behalf. We have no discretion but to disqualify you from driving. We note your early guilty plea and your good record. The minimum period of disqualification is twelve months . . . This is a serious offence and if you re-offend again the court could further disqualify you from driving. Do you understand? You will have to apply for a new license. We fine you £600 plus court costs and a victim surcharge of £95, this totals £811. Can you pay the fines?"

After agreeing a payment schedule, the defendant was released. His hearing lasted twenty-five minutes.

The defendants in cases *R121*, *R 133*, and *R 135* were arrested in a local park when police stopped and searched a group of young (white, black, and Asian) men.[13] The police refer to this type of arrest as a "three-hander." *R 121* was found in possession of cannabis and he pleaded guilty. After stating the charge, the CPS read out his "priors":

> "In May 2015 while a youth, he was arrested for possession of drugs. In July 2015, he was given a community order. In March 2016, he was arrested for possession of cannabis and was given a youth rehabilitation order. In February 2017, he was arrested for cannabis and fined £8. In March 2017, he was given a conditional discharge for twelve months for possession of a class B drug. We need to put these breaches to him."

The magistrates suggested that a probation officer should interview the defendant and prepare a report. The duty solicitor agreed and told the court that the defendant was in college three days a week.

---

[13] No family members were present in court.

> Magistrate: "We are sentencing you for three matters. You are to attend the drug rehabilitation centre for twenty-four hours.[14] This is concurrent for all three sentences. They will help you. You must attend. If you fail to attend, they will breach you and you will be summoned to court and possibly sentenced to custody. We also impose fines of £170."

After agreeing to pay the fine within one month, the defendant was released. His hearing lasted seven minutes.

Some cases raise additional issues.[15] Thus, in case *R 87* the defendant, a black male in his late twenties, was charged with "simple possession" but he had attempted to flee from police officers. After catching him, the police searched his car and found "four wraps of a substance." At the hearing it emerged that the defendant, who was on a jobseeker's allowance, had "priors" including a Crown court conviction for possession of "a bladed instrument." The defendant pleaded guilty to possession and, in a fifteen-minute hearing, he was fined £200 (to be deducted from his jobseeker's allowance).

Spice

Spice[16] is a synthetic cannabinoid that is also known as "fake weed," "bliss," "Black Mamba," "skunk," or "Bombay Blue." It is a mixture of herbs and artificial chemicals that simulates marijuana, but it is often much stronger. Problems associated with spice include agitation, nausea, and an abnormally fast, racing heartbeat through to serious "events" such as stroke, seizure, heart attack, breakdown of muscle tissue, kidney damage, psychosis, and severe or prolonged vomiting. Death linked to the consumption of spice is less common. A striking feature of spice products is their ability to cause outbreaks of mass poisonings over a short period. Consumption can create "spice zombies," a phenomenon that is increasingly visible in towns.[17] From mid-2016 all forms of spice were placed on the Home Office *Psychoactive*

---

[14] The calculation is for twenty-four contact hours spread out over a defined period, which the defendant is required to attend; s/he is also required to control his/her consumption of drugs.

[15] See case *S 57*, discussed in chapter 1, which involved an allegation of assault and the possession of class B drugs.

[16] See https://www.talktofrank.com/drug/synthetic-cannabinoids (accessed 15 September 2019).

17 See: "Outcry over drug abuse after photo shows 'spice zombies' slumped on bench in town centre" (*Independent*, 16 June 2018); "Vapers tricked into smoking spice" (*Observer*, 23 September 2018).

Substances Act list.[18] Spice is illegal to produce, supply, or import for human consumption. It is a class B drug and conviction carries heavy fines and long periods of imprisonment.

Most of the synthetic cannabinoids used in "legal high" products are manufactured by chemical companies in China and are shipped in bulk powder form to Europe (EMCDDA 2016a, 2). Once in Europe, the powder is mixed with or sprayed onto the plant material, typically on an industrial scale using solvents such as acetone or methanol to dissolve the powder; equipment like cement mixers are then used to mix the ingredients. The mixture is dried, packaged, and sold on the internet by "legal high" retailers and in "head shops." Each kilogram of bulk powder may produce thousands of packets of "legal highs." The discovery of processing and packaging facilities and large quantities of synthetic cannabinoids in the Netherlands and Belgium suggests the involvement of organised crime.

The three prosecutions discussed below indicate that the CPS did not prosecute defendants for "intent to supply," presumably because it is more difficult to secure a conviction, but rather for "simple possession." It is also clear that the CPS has argued that magistrates should treat possession of spice as a class A rather than as a class B offence, which would attract a higher sentence.

In case *R 48* the defendant, a white male in his mid-20s, was initially charged with "intent to supply" spice and with "possession," though the defendant only pleaded guilty to "possession." The CPS (stage 2) stated:

> "On 25th August officers followed an old Skoda [car] which took a number of U-turns to try and loose the police. When the car was stopped the police spoke to the driver, Mr M. They found snap bags full of powder. There were two other individuals in the car and all three were detained for a search. The defendant attempted to move away from the officers but was stopped, searched, and found to have a packet of cannabis he claimed was a "legal high." He was handcuffed and searched and found to have a nine-inch knife in his belt. When the car was searched, he had lots of bags of herbal cannabis, many empty snap bags, and a driving license in the name of an unknown person. A quantity of drugs was seized together with a bag containing £225. The drugs were later confirmed as spice. He has denied possession with 'intent to supply.' There are antecedents . . . There are no sentencing guidelines for this substance.[19] Courts, in my experience, have treated this

[18] See "A simple(ish) guide to the Psychoactive Substances Act (PSA)," at http://www.sdf.org.uk/wp-content/uploads/2017/11/Psychoactive-Substances-Act-2016.pdf (accessed 27 September 2018).

[19] While his statement was technically correct in the sense that spice was not specifically mentioned in the sentencing guidelines (see Sentencing Council 2012),

as a class C substance. You may feel it is more appropriate to treat it as a class A or B substance. A standard sentence would be twenty-six weeks. It is aggravated by the possession of a knife. You can refer it to the Crown court or hear it yourself. If it is considered a class B substance, sentence is for one year. It would not then be suitable to be heard in a magistrates' court. If you consider it a class A substance, then it must go to the Crown court."

The duty solicitor (stage 6) suggested that the case should be sent to the Crown court; the defendant, naturally enough, wanted his case to be heard by magistrates. The District Judge decided to hear it and invited both parties to address him about the appropriate sentence. The judge completed the PET form, ensured that the analysis of the drugs would be made available at the trial, noted that the defendant had a "bad character reference" and scheduled a one-hour trial. In considering whether to bail the defendant, the CPS noted that he had sixteen offences and that on two occasions he had failed to attend court. The CPS argued: "He has continued to offend and had breached an order in June. He is wanted in Glasgow on other related matters. He would fail to attend and should be remanded into custody."

While recognising his priors, the duty solicitor asked that the defendant be bailed to his Glasgow address; however, the court could not verify the address he provided. At the end of the nineteen-minute hearing the District Judge remanded him into custody to await trial in London.

In case *R 45*, a white male in his mid-30s was charged with "intent to supply," to which he pleaded guilty. The CPS read out the charge:

"On 1st March officers who were on patrol were flagged by the public about a man with a crowbar chasing another man down the street. They responded to the call and found the defendant holding a crowbar. The defendant turned towards the officer and threatened him. He was detained. He was found to be in possession of nine snap bags of drugs, a further two snap bags, several empty snap bags, a bag of suspected pills, weighing scales, and SIM cards. He was charged with threatening officers and possessing a weapon. He is on the "warned list" for the Crown court[20] on a separate matter.[21] He was bailed but now he is charged with possession of a class B drug, spice. He made a 'no comment' interview with the police. He also has twelve previous offences for drugs between 2014 and 2017; in two cases he was sentenced. Since then he was at City of London Magistrates' Court for possession of drugs on three offences and failure to pay a train ticket. We ask £85 costs."

---

nevertheless the first step of the court should have been to determine his culpability and role in using spice; mere possession would normally be a class B offence.

[20] This means that a case against the defendant was already listed for trial.

[21] The defendant told the court that he had previously pled guilty to possession of a bladed instrument and had been sentenced to twenty-six weeks.

In a five-minute hearing the defendant confirmed that he could not remember the incident; however, he asked for all the matters to be considered by the magistrates. The CPS informed the court that the police had dropped the charge of "intent to supply" against the defendant, but his possession of "drug paraphernalia" indicated he was a user of spice.[22] He was represented by a duty solicitor who did little more than confirm the details of his criminal record. The magistrates swiftly reached a verdict:

> "Stand up Mr C. You were caught red-handed in possession of a class A drug; you have twelve simple offences of possession. Various attempts have been made to assist you, but here we are again. The sentencing guidelines indicate that this is a class A substance with a minimum of a fifty-one-week custodial sentence. In my view, with all your previous convictions and the aggravated offence of the weapon, I am sending you to the Crown court for sentencing. You will be remanded into custody because you would fail to attend court and you will continue to commit offences. No date has been set for your sentencing. I adjourn this case to the Crown court."

Cases *R 45* and *R 48* were heard in the same court by the same DJ. It is noticeable that the CPS encouraged the court to conclude that spice is a class A substance when in fact it is listed as a class B substance. His ability to convince the judge to treat spice as a more serious drug allowed him to argue for a heavier sentence. Questions also arose regarding why the police and the CPS failed to charge *R 45* with "intent to supply" given the amount of drugs found on the defendant and his possession of "drug paraphernalia." For their part, magistrates and District Judges fail to question the Crown about the classification of the drug and thus its argument regarding the minimum sentence that should be applied following conviction.

Ecstasy/MDMA

Ecstasy is a class A synthetic designer drug, sometimes referred to as MDMA.[23] It is often seen as the original designer drug because of its high-profile link to dance music culture in the 1980s and 1990s. Clubbers took ecstasy to feel energised, feel happy, stay awake, and dance. The main effects of ecstasy are an energy buzz and temporary feelings of love and affection for the people one is with. Short-term risks can include feeling anxious or getting panic attacks, and developing confused episodes,

---

[22] Normally the possession of drug paraphernalia is taken to indicate "intent to supply."

[23] See https://www.talktofrank.com/drug/ecstasy (accessed 20 September 2019).

paranoia, or psychosis. Ecstasy is usually adulterated with other substances. Defendants found guilty of possession of ecstasy can face a sentence of six months (plus a fine of up to £5000) or up to seven years imprisonment (with an unlimited fine, or both).

Most MDMA is produced by organised criminal gangs (OCGs) in Europe who cooperate to produce and distribute synthetic drugs across Europe and globally (EU 2016). In most cases, OCGs have diversified their activities to include other drugs such as cocaine and cannabis, and to a lesser extent heroin. With respect to synthetic drugs, Europe is evolving from a producer and consumer region to one of transit and export facilitated by the EU's logistical infrastructure. Expansion in the consumption of ecstasy is driven by the high profits that accrue from its sale (it may be gifted to friends and is sold on the street or in parks). The offences discussed below were committed by young, unemployed men who were arrested following the use of stop and search powers; they were charged with possessing small amounts of MDMA. Both defendants had a small number of prior arrests/convictions, both pleaded guilty, both were fined but one was given a conditional discharge.

Case *R 61* concerns an allegation against a young black male of "possession," to which he pleaded guilty. He was not legally represented. The charge was read out by the CPS:

> "On 1 August at 8:45 am the police entered Olympic Park, which is commonly used by drug dealers. They observed a number of men sitting in the park and executed a Sec. 23 search[24] of the defendant and found him to be in possession of a small bag of white crystals. He was cautioned and arrested. A test revealed that the substance was MDMA. At his interview, he admitted that the drugs had been in his pocket and that they were for his personal use. He has three previous convictions, but the most recent was seven years ago."

After confirming that the defendant was unemployed and was not supporting anyone, the magistrates fined him a total of two £265. He was released after agreeing a payment schedule. His hearing lasted nine minutes.

In an eight-minute hearing (*R 135*) a young black male was charged with possession of cannabis and MDMA, to which he pleaded guilty. He was part of a large crowd attending an impromptu music event and was arrested after being stopped and searched. Officers found cannabis in one sock, more cannabis in a tracksuit pocket, and a "pot" of fifteen pills

---

[24] The reference is to section 23 of the *Misuse of Drugs Act 1971*, see https://www.legislation.gov.uk/ukpga/1971/38/section/23.

in his shorts.[25] He was arrested and made a full admission saying that the drugs were for his personal use. The previous month he had been cautioned for possession of amphetamines (a class B drug). The duty solicitor's only comment was: "He is not working. . . . He does not rely on public funds. He is aware that the conviction will not go away. He has zero means, but there is no dark history here. Unless I can help you further. . . ." Following an eight-minute hearing, the magistrates gave him a conditional discharge for one year and imposed a £100 fine.

Heroin and cocaine

Heroin and cocaine are class A drugs.[26] Heroin is made from morphine, which is extracted from the opium poppy. Opium was originally used to treat pain, sleeplessness, and diarrhoea. "Street" heroin, sold as "brown," is sometimes used by clubbers as a "chill out" drug. The main effects and risks of heroin are: (i) a small dose gives the user a feeling of warmth and well-being, bigger doses can make you sleepy and very relaxed; (ii) heroin is highly addictive and people can quickly become hooked; and (iii) injecting heroin and sharing injecting equipment can be very risky.

Powder cocaine[27] (also called "coke"), "freebase," and "crack" are forms of cocaine. They are all powerful stimulants with short-lived effects. Both "freebase" cocaine (powder cocaine that's been prepared for smoking) and "crack" (a "rock"-like form of cocaine) can be smoked. This means that they reach the brain very quickly, while snorted powder cocaine gets to the brain more slowly. All types of cocaine are addictive, but by reaching the brain quickly, freebase and crack tend to have a much stronger effect and are more addictive than snorting. Injecting cocaine reaches the brain quickly but has serious additional risks, including damaging veins and spreading HIV and hepatitis C. The main effects and risks of taking cocaine are: (i) it can make you feel on top of the world, very confident, alert and awake, but some people can get over-confident, arrogant, and aggressive and end up taking careless risks; (ii) when the effects start to wear off, people experience a long "comedown" or "crash" when they feel depressed and run down, which can last for days. The cases discussed below show the inability of the courts to deal with persistent users of cocaine, many of whom are addicted. The cases also show linkages between addiction and crime.

---

[25] He must have been strip-searched in the park or at the station; strip-searching is frequently used and can be very humiliating.

[26] See https://www.talktofrank.com/drug/heroin (accessed 20 September 2019).

[27] See https://www.talktofrank.com/drug/cocaine (accessed 22 September 2019).

Heroin is produced in South America by cartels that use armed groups to control the area where coca is grown and the routes along which it is transported for export.[28] The bulk of cocaine is processed in Bolivia, Columbia, and Peru though processing laboratories have been detected globally (EMCDDA 2016b). Cocaine is shipped to Europe in vessels departing from Brazil, Ecuador, and Venezuela and via the Caribbean and West Africa, primarily into southern European and the Netherlands. The market for cocaine in Europe is estimated at €5.7 billion a year. In addition to individual couriers, small boats and increasingly containers, airfreight on commercial flights, and private aircraft are all used to ship cocaine.

During a forty-minute hearing, magistrates heard case *R 100*, which concerned an allegation of "possession" against a thirty-year-old white male who pleaded guilty. The arrest occurred in a suburban neighbourhood when police spotted the defendant crouched behind a wall with a "crack pipe." He was searched and found to be in possession of six wraps of cocaine. At the police station he made a "no comment" interview. Some months earlier he was convicted at Crown court for possession of a class B drug and was sentenced to two months community work. The duty solicitor told the court: "He wants help. This could be done on license."

After confirming that the amount of cocaine found on Mr H was small (valued at £30 to £40) the magistrates asked for a probation report before sentencing him. After a brief adjournment, probation reported that the defendant had been using drugs for twenty years but that he wanted to stop. He was single and lived with an uncle. He was learning a trade but was currently unemployed; he was willing to do unpaid work and would abide by a curfew. The magistrates addressed the defendant as follows:

> "Please stand up. Thank you for cooperating with probation and agreeing to find a solution to your drug problem. We will try to help you. We impose a community order of forty hours of unpaid work; probation will direct you. Probation will also support you to deal with drugs. We impose costs of £85, but we waive the court and victim surcharge of £115 as time spent in custody. I hope we don't see you again."

The defendant in *S 55* was a tall, poorly dressed black male of indeterminate age who had been asleep on the benches outside the courtroom while waiting for his case to be called. He had already been convicted of "possession" and appeared before the court to be sentenced. In

[28] To understand Columbian cartels and their effect on the local economy and population, see "'Without the cocaine traffickers, we'd have peace': Columbia villagers flee new killings" (*Observer*, 23 September 2018).

a fifteen-minute hearing the court was informed that Mr H had attempted to run from police in central London. When they chased him down, he stuffed a wrap into his mouth, which officers made him spit out. It was tested and found to be cocaine. He had two prior arrests for possession of cocaine, and ten previous convictions. The previous year he had been convicted for possession of a class A drug and was fined £120. Probation reported that he had been subject to a DRR[29]; however, after interviewing him it was clear that:

> Probation Officer: "He doesn't want help. He will continue to use heroin. He uses between £10 and £20 a day and does not commit crimes to pay for the drugs. He is of no fixed abode. There is an appointee responsible for his finances. He kept falling asleep during the interview. Frankly he is more alert today than during the interview."

The duty solicitor asked the court to

> "... listen to probation. He turned up for the court hearings and he has turned up for his assessments in the past. His lifestyle is chaotic. He attends meetings at Charring Cross Hospital to receive medication. He cooperated with the officers when he was arrested. This is a low-level criminal offender."

Following a very brief recess, the magistrates dealt with the offence by imposing fines of £220 that were to be deducted from his benefits.

While the above cases set out the standard approach that the CPS, lawyers, and the court adopts to deal with class A drug offences, magistrates decisions for this offence can vary.[30] For instance, *R 139* concerned a young Asian male who admitted possessing cocaine. In a seven-minute hearing, he was convicted and fined £130 because it was his "first drug matter." In

---

[29] A Drug Rehabilitation Requirement. Sec. 209 of the *Criminal Justice Act 2003* created a DRR, which comprises structured treatment and regular drug testing. It is available to courts as a sentencing option for offences committed on or after 4 April 2005. A DRR can be made as part of a community order (CO) or a suspended sentence order (SSO). The *Legal Aid, Sentencing, and Punishment of Offenders Act 2012* removed the restriction for a DRR to have a minimum length of six months (National Offender Management Services 2014).

[30] In *R 88*, a young white male was convicted for six offences of theft. His previous convictions included one for possession of cocaine; he admitted to smoking heroin and that he offended to pay for his drug habit. After hearing the evidence, the magistrates noted that they were considering imposing a community order but delayed sentencing to hear from probation regarding the defendant's suitability for DRR (which required them to impose a suspended sentence).

passing sentence, the bench stated: "You have accepted that you have a [drug] problem, but this court can't deal with that. We can only sentence you. You need to speak to probation for assistance." In *R 166*, a young white male was accused of being in "possession" of cocaine. Following a ten-minute hearing his case was referred to the Crown court for trial (the specific charge was unclear, but he must have been in "possession" of a substantial amount of cocaine and/or he was charged with "intent to supply"). In *R 222* the defendant, a young black male, pleaded guilty to possessing nine wraps. His priors, which included a breach of an earlier sentence for assault, led the court to deal with the offence by fining him £315. His hearing lasted nine minutes.

The above cases illustrate that many of the individuals convicted for serious drug offences are repeat offenders who have not been assisted by the court or prison service to deal with their addiction. *B 49* concerned a forty-year-old white male who appeared before the court because he had failed to comply with reporting conditions (imposed in 2003 for a sex offence). During the thirty-four-minute hearing it emerged that he owed the court £2000 in outstanding fines and that he had repeatedly failed to comply with court orders. His situation was linked to the fact that he was an addict who lived rough on the streets without any state "support." The court sentenced him to thirty-eight weeks imprisonment (he was to serve twenty-four weeks). He was also fined £115 and was to be brought back to court to "discuss his debt." There is little chance that he will receive support for his addiction in prison due to a relatively short sentence and because of cuts to, and the reorganisation of, addiction services.[31]

Finally, *S 155* concerned a white female in her forties who appeared before a District Judge for sentencing (the precise charge was not clear) in a hearing that lasted twelve minutes. Probation set out her history:

> "She has been taking drugs since the age of fourteen and is a frequent user of heroin and crack cocaine. She has never worked and had a very tragic life. She is currently living in a hostel, but she is in serious financial difficulties. Her food is limited, and her benefits have been cut from £240 a month to £30 a month. She is on universal credit, but no payments have been made to her for some time. I recommend a community order and a RAH[32] but I am concerned that a DRR would set her up to fail. She needs to deal with the drugs first before being referred for DRR. The probation officer feared that

---

[31] See "Colin Drummond: cuts to addiction services are a false economy" (25 May 2017), at https://blogs.bmj.com/bmj/2017/05/25/colin-drummond-cuts-to-addiction-services-in-england-are-a-false-economy/.

[32] RAH is a rehabilitation requirement regulation, which stipulates a twenty-day treatment.

> if she were given a suspended sentence to attend a DRR, she would not attend and would find herself in breach and back before the court."

After reading the probation report, the DJ addressed the defendant as follows:

> "Stand up. For the offence for which you are charged I sentence you to a community order of nine months, including the Rehabilitation Act Requirement of twenty days and a DRR for nine months. I think you can meet the requirements, but it is up to you. I am fixing a review date for the DRR here in two months. The victim surcharge of £85 is deemed served for one day in custody. There is no court cost awarded. Speak to your representative and the drug worker! Do you understand?"

In the above cases all the defendants were arrested fortuitously, not as part of a police sweep/operation. The defendants were older than those convicted for using other illegal substances, and all had prior convictions and a history of substance abuse. As discussed earlier, defendants who "co-operate" with the court and with probation, or who are being charged with a first offence, tend to be let off with a fine and may be given a DRR requirement. This situation seems to arise because magistrates assume that these defendants want to beat their addiction, even in the face of a lack of evidence that DRR and treatment programmes are effective. However, as cases *R 49* and *S 155* indicate, many defendants are addicted to heroin or cocaine and the imposition of a DRR may only "set up a defendant to fail." To qualify for a DRR, a defendant must be given a suspended sentence and must not be imprisoned; during a DRR they are required to confront and deal with their addiction. If they fail to deal with their addiction, they are sentenced to prison.

A contested trial for drug offences

Contested trials provide insight into the nature of drug offences, addiction, and links between drug use and other types of crime. As discussed in chapter 3, the cases of *R 91* and *R 92* involved two brothers who were charged with knifing and killing a man in a fight over drugs. The link between drugs and violence was also clear in a "five-hander" case concerning *R 93*, *R 94*, *R 95*, *R 96*, and *R 97*. These men—of varying ages, some with extensive previous convictions and some with no priors—were caught in a bungled attempt to raid a cannabis factory in south London. They were charged with "attempted theft" but appeared before magistrates only to make an application for bail while awaiting trial at Crown court. Magistrates denied all five defendants bail claiming they would fail to surrender to the police/attend court. Below I examine a trial for "intent to supply" drugs heard at a magistrates' court that provides insight into the nature of drug offences and about how judges try this type of case, hear evidence, and decide guilt.

In a one-hour-and-thirteen-minute trial the defendant, *T 21*, a Middle-Eastern male aged twenty-six, was charged with four drug offences and with breaching an anti-social behaviour order (ASBO).[33] The defendant pleaded guilty to four charges of possessing class B and class C drugs, but not guilty to breaching an ASBO and to the charge of "possession" with "intent to supply."[34] The CPS read out the charges (stage 2) against the defendant that, in brief, was that he had been arrested following a brief car chase. He was searched and found to be in possession of ten "dealer bags"

[33] According to CPS guidance: "ASBOs are civil orders to protect the public from behaviour that causes or is likely to cause harassment, alarm or distress. An order contains conditions prohibiting an individual from carrying out specific anti-social acts or (for example) from entering defined areas. The orders are not criminal sanctions and are not intended to punish the individual. They are designed to be preventative. . . ." (CPS 2018e; Home Office 2019).

[34] The CPS charging guidelines state: "An intention to supply may be proved by direct evidence in the form of admissions or witness testimony, for example, surveillance evidence. Another method of proving an intention to supply is by inference. Evidence from which intent to supply may be inferred will include at least one or, more usually, a combination of the following factors: Possession of a quantity inconsistent with personal use. Possession of uncut drugs or drugs in an unusually pure state suggesting proximity to their manufacturer or importer. Possession of a variety of drugs may indicate sale rather than consumption. Evidence that the drug has been prepared for sale[:] If a drug has been cut into small portions and those portions are wrapped in foil or film, then there is a clear inference that sale is the object; Drug related equipment in the care and/or control of the suspect, such as weighing scales, cutting agents, bags or wraps of foil (provided their presence is not consistent with normal domestic use). Diaries or other documents containing information tending to confirm drug dealing, which are supportive of a future intent to supply, for example, records of customers' telephone numbers together with quantities or descriptions of drugs. Money found on the defendant was considered in *R v Batt (1994) Crim. LR 592*. It is not necessarily evidence of future supply. It may be evidence of supply in the past but on its own the money is not evidence of a future intent to supply. Evidence of large amounts of money in the possession of the defendant, or an extravagant lifestyle which is only *prima facie* explicable if derived from drug dealing, is admissible in cases of possession with intent to supply if it is of probative significance to an issue in the case *R v Morris (1995) 2 Cr. App. R. 69*." See: CPS 2019b.

of cannabis resin, two bags of sixteen (Xanax)[35] pills, and £500 cash. When he was strip-searched at the police station "a large wrap of cannabis resin" was found "under his scrotum." Officers checked his record and found that he had been arrested inside an "exclusion zone" imposed on him at an earlier trial.

The Crown read out the statements of two police officers (stage 3) involved in arresting, searching, and charging the defendant. Their statements included a map indicating that the arrest occurred inside an area from which the defendant was excluded as a result of an ASBO. The defendant had made a "no comment interview" at the police station at which his legal representative was present; he subsequently submitted a statement prepared by his solicitor that read: "I had cannabis in my pocket, it was for personal use. I had no intention to supply drugs to others . . . Xanax is for my own personal use. The cash found on me was given to me by my fiancé to pay debts."

When the defendant gave evidence (stage 5) from the witness box, he confirmed that he was subject to an ASBO at an earlier trial and that a map of the area he was prohibited from entering had been given to him at his previous trial. The defendant confirmed the details of his arrest and his possession of the drugs and the cash. He also confirmed that he was self-employed, that his car payment was £900 and that he regularly purchased £400 of cannabis a month for personal use. He said that he was unaware of the drugs in his coat. At this point, the defendant's solicitor quietly spoke to the defendant and to his witness/fiancé; he then stated that the defendant would not be calling his partner to give evidence (at stage 5).

The Crown summed up its (stage 6) case by stating that while

> ". . . there is no direct evidence of dealing, we invite the court to draw inferences from the evidence. He intended to supply drugs. . . . The question is, why hide the drugs if they were for personal use. He concealed them. . . . What about the cash? He said he consumes £200 of cannabis every two weeks. The inference must be that he is supplying. We say the cash was a product of dealing. There is not much to say about the ASBO. We ask for a verdict of guilty."

---

[35] Xanax, also known as alprazolam, is an anti-anxiety medicine in the benzodiazepine family; it is similar to diazepam (Valium) but is twenty times stronger and takes effect more quickly. Alprazolam can quickly make you feel relaxed, tired, and sleepy. Long-term use could make you dependent on it and you could get withdrawal symptoms if you stop using it. Alprazolam can cause blackouts and put you at greater risk of being taken advantage of sexually. If you mix it with alcohol, you're at risk of overdose caused by heart and breathing problems. See https://www.talktofrank.com/news/dangers-xanax-misuse (accessed 2 November 2019).

Neither the defendant nor his solicitor were able to convince the court that Mr. C could afford, or personally consume, £400 of cannabis per month[36] or that he wasn't attempting to mislead the police by hiding drugs on his body.

The DJ summed up his decision (stage 7/9) by noting:

> ". . . possession of the drugs is not in dispute. You have pled guilty to "simple possession." With respect to possession of sixteen tablets of Xanax, I find you not guilty. I am entirely satisfied and sure that Mr C. was carrying "dealing bags" and other drugs. He was operating a mobile shop to sell cannabis. . . . The defendant's evidence is that he forgot about the drugs in his pockets and the fact that he only showed two bags to officers indicated that he was attempting to deceive them. . . . He had them to sell. In relation to the specific charges: possession of the class B drugs (resin), guilty with "intent to supply"; possession of forty-eight grams of cannabis, guilty with "intent to supply." I am satisfied that you were fully aware of the ASBO order and that you breached it. The excuse that you were allowed to drive through the exclusion zone is not accepted. . . . Because of your criminal record and a suspended sentence, I am remitting the case to Southwark Crown Court for sentencing. Take him to the cells."

It is clear that the CPS and the DJ made good use of the charging guidelines to elicit evidence from the defendant that would, alongside the defendant's attempt to lie about the drugs in his possession, convict him. The resulting sentence exceeded the DJ's power to sentence and he was thus referred to the Crown court to be sentenced.

Conclusion

This chapter raises important questions about "state-illegality relations" (discussed in the prologue; Schneider and Schneider 2008) that reflect the social construction of crime that labels and targets specific social groups and/or behaviours as "illegal" while ignoring the socio-economic factors that give rise to crime or indeed that ignore "white-collar" crime. The cases discussed in this chapter illustrate how crimes are constructed by the state that define specific groups and/or actions as "criminal." First, and with the partial exception of heroin/cocaine offences, nearly all the defendants are young, unemployed males—members of the precariat—who were not arrested in co-ordinated drug operations.

Because many young unemployed males socialise in public spaces in London, they are subject to police "stop and search" procedures that result

[36] A drug test failed to find evidence of drug use.

in the arrest (but not necessarily the prosecution or conviction) of disproportionate numbers of individuals from ethnic minority groups. Research by Release (2011, 11) concluded that "Enforcement of drug laws is unfairly focused on Black and Asian communities, despite their rates of drug use being lower than the white majority." In their 2018 report, Release found that "Black people were stopped and searched for drugs at almost nine times the rate of white people, while Asian people and those in the 'mixed' group were stop-searched for drugs at almost three times the rate of white people." Tellingly, "The 'find' rate for drugs is lower for black than white people, suggesting that such searches are carried out on the basis of weaker 'grounds' for black people." In line with findings elsewhere in this book regarding the use of the Public Order Act, Release also found that "Forces vary sharply in their overall use of stop and search as well as their rates of disproportionality. Such differences are evident between forces with similar crime-relevant profiles, suggesting they are largely a function of police policy and decision-making" and that "High rates of stop and search in London are an important driver of ethnic disproportionality because a large proportion of the black and minority ethnic population live in the capital" (ibid., iii). Indeed, all the cannabis (*R 17*, *R 19*, *R 121*, *R 133*, *R 135*) and ecstasy prosecutions (*R 61*, *R 135*) I observed were the result of stop and search operations.

In London the search rate is thirty-four per one thousand of the population for white people, but sixty-six per one thousand for black people. The number of stop and searches conducted by the Metropolitan Police (approximately thirty-three thousand between 2009 and 2019) is nearly double the number used by other police forces, and there are significant differences in the way the police use this power in London. The boroughs with the highest levels of deprivation also experience the largest number of stop and searches. Tellingly, the *arrest rate* varies from 4 to 9 per cent of those who are stopped and searched (Release 2011, 29). This means that more than 90 per cent of all stop and searches fail to find drugs, weapons, and so on. The discrepancy between the number of persons who are stopped and searched and those who are arrested indicate that police powers are exercised arbitrarily, which supports claims made by Release (2011, 30f; MoJ 2016b).

With respect to the use of stop and search in London, Release (2018, 25) found that:

1. Overall rates of stop and search are higher among inner than outer London boroughs.

2. Variations between boroughs are strongly linked to levels of deprivation. Overall rates of stop and search tend to be highest in areas of deprivation and inequality.
3. The concentration of stop and search activity in deprived boroughs cannot be explained by the prevalence of drug use or specifically cannabis use.
4. "Race" confounds the general relationship between stop-and-search and deprivation. Rates of stop and search for black people do not vary according to levels of deprivation. And,
5. Affluent boroughs are characterised by very low rates of stop and search for white people and high rates of black/white disproportionality. This pattern is consistent with ethnic profiling because it indicates that black people are singled out for suspicion.

My analysis supports arguments about the selective nature of policing *and* a general failure to investigate many crimes in an apparent focus on arresting and prosecuting individuals for "simple possession" of drugs. In short, the police fail to investigate whether a defendant was involved in selling/distributing drugs (e.g., *R 48*, *R 45*, *R 49*, *R 155*, *R 91*, *R 92*, and *T 21*). The situation strongly suggests that the police focus their efforts on securing a conviction for "possession," which is easy to prove.

The cases examined in this chapter raise two further issues. First, magistrates/DJs often fail to question the CPS about the classification of a specific drug and therefore about appropriate sentencing guidelines. Finally, the cases in this chapter show that magistrates/DJs do not sentence defendants in a consistent manner. Some defendants are required to attend DRR, some are not; most defendants are fined, even though many have consistently been unable to pay their fines; some are given custody, whereas others are given a conditional discharge. Worryingly, the causative factors behind offending—that is, poverty, the absence of reasonably paid work, homelessness, poor educational/job skills, or addiction—are not taken into account by the legal process, which results in imprisoning defendants and in turn increases the likelihood of repeat offending because offenders are not given help to deal with their problems or with addiction.

CHAPTER 6

THE PROSECUTION OF FRAUD (AND ORGANISED CRIME)

While fraud became a crime in England and Wales in 1275 in the First Statute of Westminster, it was not until the nineteenth century that fraud was actively prosecuted, first via private prosecutions and, from the 1880s onwards, increasingly by a public prosecutor in the criminal courts (specifically the Old Bailey [Griffiths 2017]). As Taylor (2018, 351) has remarked,

> by 1880 there was a statute criminalising misappropriation and misrepresentation, and a public official tasked with prosecuting frauds. But significant barriers to the effective punishment of fraud remained. For one thing, the new office was not generously resourced, with the DPP given just one assistant and three clerks. Moreover, the DPP's role was envisaged as limited: to supplement, rather than supplant, private prosecution.

It remains the case today that allegations of fraud are still not systematically investigated or prosecuted by the state because: (i) of the difficulty of gathering evidence, (ii) many crimes are not reported, (iii) of problems involved in multi-agency and cross-border co-operation, and, (iv) the government has failed to commit adequate resources to the police to investigate fraud and to the CPS to prosecute fraud. While statistics on fraud have been recorded for some time, a systematic effort to record fraud only began in 2011, which means that reliable long-term data does not exist (ONS 2018b, sec. 3).

In this chapter I analyse prosecutions of "lower-level" fraud *and* extradition cases to explore two inter-related issues. First, I want to question conventional ideas about, and legal definitions of, fraud that see it as a scam or trick in which one person takes advantage of another (alternatively fraud is seen as a "victimless" crime in the sense of individuals defrauding business). Second, I argue that prosecutions of "minor" fraud and extradition hearings reveal that defendants are linked to hierarchically organised criminal networks and that these cases are not adequately investigated and pursued by the authorities.

I begin by briefly setting out how the government defines fraud and note the growth in reported cases; I then examine the cases I observed to show how fraud is prosecuted. While the cases I examine are not representative of the full range of fraud offences, they provide insight into the nature and scale of fraud and how it is prosecuted. I argue that the narrow focus of criminal prosecutions in magistrates' courts on individual culpability fails to identify links to organised crime and that if the police, CPS, and judiciary took a wider view of these cases, they could do more than convict the odd low-level perpetrator. In section (ii) I examine extradition bail applications and extradition hearings at Westminster Magistrates' Court. From the perspective of international law, extradition is a key tool in international cooperation against organised criminal groups (OCG). Most countries enter into special agreements[1] to facilitate extradition, and extradition hearings provide insight into complex "layers of associations" and global connections that characterise OCG/transnational crime.

Following Nordstrom (2008), I argue that OCGs—which involve money laundering, drug and people trafficking, cyber-crime, the exploitation of children, and fraud, and so on—create "global fractures"[2] or fracture lines that radiate out internationally from a specific crime. To understand the nature of these crimes, we need to look beyond individual culprits to grasp the complex linkages between crime, legitimate business, and the state (i.e., the networks through which fraud is organised and conducted). Nordstrom argues against "reducing any question to a single causal equation" or factor; instead she suggests that a careful examination of "individual" crimes can reveal broader "layers of association" or linkages that need to be thoroughly investigated. As Nordstrom (ibid., 75) observed,

[1] For the *UN Convention against Transnational Organized Crime*, see https://www.unodc.org/documents/treaties/UNTOC/Publications/TOC%20Convention/TOCebook-e.pdf; for the *UN Convention against Illicit Traffic in Narcotic Drugs and Psychotropic Substances*, 1988, see https://www.unodc.org/pdf/convention_1988_en.pdf.

[2] While Nordstrom (2008, 72) focuses on war as a type of crisis that creates instability and "vulnerabilities in trade networks, financial systems, economic enterprises, and socio-political services," I argue that the actions undertaken by OCGs/transnational crime in perpetuating fraud provide good examples of "a fracture zone" that only becomes apparent by looking "at the big picture" as opposed to focusing on specific incidents.

> Virtually all extra-legal activities intersect with state institutions and practices: in laundering profits to legitimacy; in using state systems of transport, communications, and industry; and in wresting political authority in these processes.

Her arguments challenge normal intuitive approaches that focus on local incidents and the actions of individual criminals—those that are pursued in standard police investigations and court prosecutions, fail to investigate the majority of frauds. This problem arises out of a cognitive failure to see the wider picture *and* the administrative division of labour between magistrates' and Crown courts and between the work of the police[3] and the Serious Fraud Office/National Crime Agency. I argue that many of the crimes that are not investigated fall between the remit of the different public and private institutions responsible for investigating fraud. I spell out this argument below, which is supported by Ryder's (2018, 10) review of criminal prosecutions by the SFO in which he concluded that "The UK's efforts to tackle financial crime concentrated on targeting individuals as opposed to corporations."

i. Defining and prosecuting fraud

In law, fraud involves a person dishonestly and deliberately deceiving a victim for personal gain, property, or money or by causing loss or risk of loss to another. Most "low-level" incidents fall under the definition of "fraud by false representation," which occurs when a person makes a representation that they know to be untrue or misleading. The majority of fraud cases are prosecuted under the *Fraud Act (2006)*,[4] which applies to individuals and small companies. The most prevalent forms of recorded fraud are banking and payment card fraud, which involves individuals falsely obtaining or using personal bank or payment card details to carry out fraudulent transactions.

Sec. 1 of the *Theft Act (1968)*[5] defines fraud as:

---

[3] A good example is the extent to which organised crime operates in the City of London property market (see "The dark side of Britain's gold rush: how corruption crept into our suburbs" (*Observer*, 14 January 2017; and Transparency International, n.d.).

[4] See http://www.legislation.gov.uk/ukpga/2006/35. However, some cases may also be prosecuted using other legislation, for further information see, Fraud Advisory Panel, n.d.

[5] See: https://www.legislation.gov.uk/ukpga/1968/60

> 1. A person is guilty of theft if he dishonestly appropriates property belonging to another with the intention of permanently depriving the other of it; and "thief" and "steal" shall be construed accordingly.
> 2. It is immaterial whether the appropriation is made with a view to gain or is made for the thief's own benefit.

The meaning of the terms used in the act have been developed in case law (and in subsequent legislation) and clarify the actions that constitute fraud. The act also sets out the minimum sentence for various types of fraud, which range from a fine and a short period of imprisonment to fourteen years imprisonment.

A second type of fraud is computer misuse crime, which includes offences such as spreading viruses and malicious software, hacking and "denial of service" (DDoS) attacks (the flooding of internet servers to take down network infrastructure or websites), and unauthorised access to computer material to carry out an act of fraud. This type of fraud is set out in the *Computer Misuse Act (1990)*.[6] One key feature of contemporary, organised crime is the important role played by rapid changes in technology and communications that has meant that an increasing number of crimes are committed using the internet. Many of these crimes are perpetrated by individuals and organisations with links to persons residing outside the UK, and the money gained from these crimes is transferred out of the UK.[7] As Albanese (2012) and others have noted, this type of fraud requires organisation and cannot effectively be carried out by "lone offenders"; this type of fraud should be understood, and prosecuted, as part of a larger criminal enterprise.

The Home Office's attempt to set out "the scale and nature of fraud" reflects a narrow focus on individual criminal acts, the growing scale of reported fraud, and the failure of the police and regulatory bodies to prosecute fraud. Between 2011 and 2014, when a shift to centralised reporting of incidents occurred, the number of reported incidents of fraud escalated from just over 72,000 in 2010 to nearly 650,000 in 2017 (at this

---

[6] See https://www.legislation.gov.uk/ukpga/1990/18/contents. Doig (2006, 102) has argued that the crimes dealt with by this act could just as easily have been addressed by using existing legislation.

[7] A recent example of a complex form of fraud is provided by the ongoing prosecution against Cambridge Analytica, and threats of massive fines against and greater regulation of Facebook (see "Facebook hit by 'explosive' new allegations as criminal prosecutions loom," *Forbes*, 16 March 2019).

time fraud constituted 31 per cent of all reported crime [Home Office 2017c]).[8]

However, better reporting has not been accompanied by an increase in prosecution. In 2016/2017 the outcome of investigations into reported fraud showed that: *in only 14 per cent of cases was a suspect identified and prosecuted*; *in 33 per cent of cases the police faced "evidential difficulties"*; *in 41 per cent of cases the case was closed without identifying a suspect* (Home Office 2017c). A somewhat clearer picture of the failure to prosecute fraud is provided in Table 6.1 (in the table, the term "dissemination" refers to the "outcome" of police investigations into reported crimes). The table shows that many more crimes are reported than are investigated by the police, and that a very small number of cases are prosecuted.

Table 6.1. Number of fraud offences and disseminations in England and Wales, 2017 and 2018.[9]

	2017	2018	Percentage change
Total number of fraud offences	652,362	638,882	-2%
Number reported by Action Fraud	261,943	277,561	6%
Number recorded by CIFAS and FFA	390,419	361,321	-7%
Total offences with dissemination	64,501	49,861	-23%
Number of disseminations	16,781	11,094	-34%

The Home Office (2018c) recognises three types of "victim" and multiple types of fraud (see box 6.1). However, as the analysis of cases in this chapter will show, the police and CPS tend to prosecute individual perpetrators operating at the lowest tier of criminal activity.

---

[8] Confidence in official reports of fraud have declined following the revelation that the Home Office has been manipulating figures by telling Action Fraud to drop tens of thousands of cases ("Home Office manipulates crime figures by telling Action Fraud to dismiss identity theft," *Times*, 18 September 2019.

[9] Source: Home Office (2017b). Action Fraud is the national organisation tasked with recording and reporting all forms of fraud; CIFAS is a fraud prevention service that maintains a national database on all forms of crime, it reports to the police; Financial Fraud Action (UK; FFA) deals with fraud in the UK payments industry. Its membership includes the major banks, credit, debit, and charge-card issuers, and card payment acquirers.

Box 6.1. Victim types and types of fraud in the UK.[10]

Type of victim	Type of fraud
Individuals	(1) Investment; (2) pension; (3) bank and credit account; (4) other scams; (5) advance fee; (6) consumer/retail.
The financial sector	(1) First party fraud; (2) Third party fraud; (3) fraud by employees and others.
Businesses	(1) Fraud by employees and others; (2) fraud by customers.

To understand why so few cases of fraud are investigated and prosecuted, it is necessary to step back and look at the national "fraud-scape"/situation. First, unlike in Scotland, in England and Wales a myriad of state and private institutions record, investigate, and "prosecute" different types of fraud. While the CPS is the largest prosecuting authority, "there is no definitive list of organizations that institute prosecutions" in England and Wales (House of Commons 2009, ¶116). A recommendation that the CPS should be made solely responsible for prosecuting all crime was rejected by the government in favour of an assurance by the CPS of enhanced cooperation and consultation between existing agencies. This undertaking is set out in "The Prosecutors Convention" (2009), which is intended "to ensure that cases are conducted in a way that is just and which best serves the overall public interest, so that the public can have confidence in the outcome." The distinction drawn between minor and serious crime, and between the fuzzy remit/work of different agencies involved in investigating and prosecuting fraud, may be partly responsible for the overwhelming focus by the police and CPS on individual acts of fraud.

As I have demonstrated with other types of crime, since the 1980s the state has increasingly devolved responsibility for fraud prevention and prosecution to non-state actors through "partnerships," "multi-agency groups," and "community initiatives" with the result that today the vast majority of fraud cases are dealt with outside the CJS, to the extent that they are dealt with at all (Garland 2002; Button and Brooks 2016, 211). This situation arises from the continued failure of government to set out a national policy on fraud in combination with pressure on the police for continued efficiencies, demands to meet targets, and cuts to police budgets (by 19 per cent in real terms between 2010/11 and 2018/19).[11] As Doig and Levi (2013, 149) have observed, the demands placed on the police by "populist" government agendas favouring "front-line policing" come at the expense of local force priorities, including their ability to investigate fraud.

---

[10] Source: Home Office (2018, 2).

[11] See https://fullfact.org/crime/police-funding-england-and-wales/ (accessed 15 November 2019).

Responsibility for investigating and prosecuting fraud is divided between different agencies/organisations. Whereas local police forces are responsible for investigating and prosecuting "low-level" fraud; large-scale, complex forms of fraud, bribery, and corruption are dealt with by the City of London Police, the Serious Fraud Office (SFO), or the National Crime Agency[12] who pursue a small number of "high-value," complex cases including corporate fraud and cases with an element of corruption requiring "specialist knowledge." When allegations of fraud are reported to the police via the national "Action Fraud line" a decision is made regarding whether the case is worth prosecuting, for example, whether it is sufficiently high value and there is a likelihood of securing a conviction.[13] If it is decided to pursue a case it is allocated to a specific force to deal with (though a majority of cases are not investigated). In view of police disinterest in dealing with fraud, insurance companies have found it necessary to pursue fraudsters through a combination of private, civil, and criminal prosecutions (see below; Cifas 2018; Doig 2006; Doig and Levi 2013; Button and Brooks 2016).

The prosecution of "organised crime" complicates and adds to the work of the SFO/NCA. Organised crime is defined by the Council of Europe as: (a) a collaboration of three or more people, (b) for a prolonged period of time, (c) suspected or convicted of committing serious criminal offences, and (d) with the objective of pursuing profit and/power (cited in May and Bhardwa 2018, 14). This type of crime is planned, coordinated, and conducted by people, through various forms of organisation or via individual networks, who work primarily, but not exclusively, for financial gain. There are at least sixty-two different types of recognised fraud in the UK. It is estimated that there are 4,629 OCGs active in the UK, made up of 37,000 individuals. One study that examined the impact of fraud on local communities in two police force areas in England found that between 31 per cent and 45 per cent of frauds committed locally were linked to OCGs (Garner et al. 2016).[14]

---

[12] Between 2012 and 2018 the SFO successfully prosecuted thirty-nine of the forty-seven cases it investigated (about ten to twelve cases per year; SFO 2017/18). Schneider (2013) provides an overview of the profits that accrue to organised crime.

[13] The decision to investigate a specific case appears to be triggered by the availability of reliable "intelligence" and/or evidence provided, for instance, by banks regarding the actions of junior employees. The decision is the result of a trade-off between the potential "harm" to the public caused by an alleged fraud, the "cost" of investigating the crime(s), and the likelihood of securing a conviction.

[14] Garner et al. (2016) estimated the average fraud perpetrated against local people at £10,000 per offence, though many cases exceeded this amount.

The average value of reported losses to an individual from fraud is between £50 and £250, whereas the annual estimated loss due to payment card fraud was £618 million in 2016. Retail fraud was estimated at £183 million in 2015; there are no estimates for the cost of cyber/DDoS attacks. It has been estimated that *the total cost of fraud in the UK in 2016 was £193 billion* (comprising private sector fraud valued at £144 billion; public sector fraud at £37.5 billion; individuals at £10 billion, and charity sector fraud valued at nearly £2 billion [May and Bhardwa 2018, 16–17]).[15] The growth in fraud and the amount of money involved strongly suggests that police/official investigations need to pay much greater attention to how crimes in the UK are linked to OCGs and transnational crime.[16]

Table 6.2 sets out the number of fraud prosecutions, extradition bail applications, and extradition cases that I observed.

Table 6.2. Fraud and extradition cases I observed.

Fraud prosecutions	Extradition bail applications	Extradition hearings
7	17	6

As a proportion of the total remand hearings (N = 239) I observed, fraud constituted just under 3 per cent of all cases. With respect to trials (N = 23), extradition hearings constituted 20 per cent of all the trials I observed. It was noticeable that the same procedures used to prosecute crime that I set out in the introduction are used in fraud and extradition hearings (though extradition bail applications were far more chaotic). All types of fraud can be prosecuted in England and Wales provided that some part of the offence occurred in the country. If the alleged defendant is overseas, it is possible to seek his/her extradition to stand trial in a British court. The decision to extradite a defendant, assuming s/he can be identified and arrested, will depend on the seriousness of the offence and whether there are extradition arrangements between the UK and the country where the defendant resides.

ii. The prosecution of fraud in magistrates' courts

I begin by examining relatively straightforward cases of fraud before turning to more complex cases involving larger sums of money and clear

[15] A depressing account of the government's failure to detect, much less prosecute, public sector fraud can be found in Home Office (2018d) where it is estimated that in 2016–17 total losses from fraud were between £2.7 billion and £20.3 billion.
[16] Channing May (2017) has estimated that the revenue accruing to transnational crime is between US $1.6 and $2.2 trillion a year.

links to OCGs. The complex nature of "low-level" frauds prosecuted in magistrates' courts, which requires considerable time and investigatory skill, is evident in the applications made by the police to the court for additional time to investigate individuals. As the magistrates observed in these cases, all the police need to justify their investigations is "suspicion."

Case *R 64* concerned an allegation of fraud against a thirty-five-year-old Asian male who pleaded guilty to seven counts of making false representations. As the CPS argued, the defendant made numerous attempts to falsify his car registration with the ridesharing company Uber[17] by uploading false documents to its website. He also used documents issued to another person in an attempt to register as a driver with Uber, entered into a finance arrangement to purchase a car (for £22,000), and used a stolen credit card to access an ATM. The duty solicitor argued that he was of "previous good character" and that the actual financial loss only amounted to £100 for using the stolen credit card. The case was briefly adjourned to allow probation to interview the defendant.

When the case resumed, the probation officer noted that the defendant had been working as a taxi driver since 2012, but when Uber began he experienced a significant decline in his work. At that point the defendant decided to register with Uber but, once registered, had to use a hire car. He carried on working but was reported for not driving a registered car in 2015, with the result that Uber suspended his registration and dropped him. It was at this point that he attempted to use someone else's identity to falsely register with Uber as a driver. Probation argued that "he was a desperate man who made a bad decision" to support his family. He was "unlikely to reoffend" and the court was advised to give him a community order and a suspended sentence. After a brief deliberation, the magistrates imposed a sixteen-week sentence, suspended for twelve months, and a fine of £315. It was agreed that payment of the fine would be deducted from his benefits. The hearing took twenty-four minutes.

Case *R 69* concerned an allegation of fraud against a black female in her early twenties who was charged with "acquiring criminal proceeds" as a result of fraudulently removing £48,000 pounds from the victim's bank account.[18] The defendant accepted responsibility for her actions at the police station, but she hesitated to enter a plea at court where she was represented by a duty solicitor. The details, as set out by the CPS, indicate that the

---

[17] For information about Uber, see https://www.uber.com/gb/en/. For a discussion of recent "scandals" involving Uber in London, see "Uber London ban: The scandals that brought down the ride-hailing app" (*Independent*, 22 September 2017).

[18] See "Banks close thousands of 'money mule' accounts, MPs told" (*Guardian*, 13 February 2019).

defendant had attempted to enrol the victim in an "advance fee" scam in which, for a fee, money would be temporarily transferred into her account.[19] The defendant's meeting with the victim was caught on CCTV and the evidence indicated that the victim refused to allow the funds that had been transferred into her account to be withdrawn from it. At this point, the defendant went to the victim's bank and attempted to withdraw money from her account, which set off the alarms and the bank was locked down: she was caught. Her house was searched, and £18,000 was returned to the victim. The defendant claimed she had been set up to transfer money between accounts (an act that she believed would provide her with money to send to her mother). She reportedly had no idea where the money originated from. While the duty solicitor attempted to argue that the case was unlikely to go to trial, the CPS disagreed stating: "The issue is not whether she knew the victim. She took the money. There are no other charges." The defendant elected to be tried at magistrates' court and was looking at a minimum sentence of nineteen months in custody. A trial date was set, and the defendant was released on unconditional bail. The Crown did not intend to investigate the defendant's links to the "gang" that encouraged her to enrol the victim in the scam.[20] The hearing lasted fifteen minutes.

Case *R 54* concerned an allegation of fraud against a thirty-year-old Indian national. He pleaded not guilty to two counts of fraud involving the selling of shares to an elderly woman worth £20,000 and making false representations to the same victim for a further £29,200 (an investment scam). The CPS argued that the case was not suitable for a summary trial because of the amount of the fraud and because it was a "complex" fraud that would need to be investigated. The magistrates scheduled the case for trial at a Crown court and then heard the defendant's bail application.

The CPS objected to bail claiming that, as a foreign national, he would fail to attend his trial. The defendant had previously left the country and had been refused an entry visa to the UK. He was arrested in transit at Heathrow and was currently on conditional bail. "He has no link to the UK; all his links are to India. He has large debts and faces a court order for £800, which he is due to pay. Given the amount of money and the vulnerability of the victim, he is facing custody for three years." Indeed, the Home Office was also proceeding against the defendant for illegally entering the UK and had seized his passport.

---

[19] See https://www.actionfraud.police.uk/fraud-az-advance-fee-fraud (accessed 10 November 2019).

[20] The scam could easily have been part of a larger scheme of money laundering (see May and Bhardwa 2018, 49–50).

The duty solicitor struck a different tone:

> "The defendant has no previous. He is of good character. There is no reason to refuse bail, and he denies the accusation. . . . He was to fly to Paris and was arrested in transit. . . . Regarding conditions for bail, the defendant can offer a surety of £10,000. He is a respected businessman. This is a mistake; it didn't take place. . . ."

At this point, a police officer was called to give evidence and he set out the Crown's evidence:

> ". . . we have her [the victim's] supplementary bank records, email, and phone records and there is a witness statement from the victim's cleaner who was present at some of the discussions. In relation to the defendant's account, it is not credible. The companies do not exist. He made representations about 'Excellent Company,' a company that is non-existent. The victim was duped by the defendant. There is a fictitious website for the company. This is a fairly complex fraud trial."

Following a ten-minute adjournment, the bench returned and refused the defendant bail. At this point, a police officer entered the dock to make an application to the court to seize money taken from the defendant. The officer repeated the Crown's case against the defendant and stated that he was arrested in possession of traveller's cheques worth €2000 and 500 Australian dollars in cash. She concluded: "We need time to investigate and to make further checks regarding where the money is."

Speaking for the defendant, his solicitor stated that the money seized was legitimate and came from his business. At this point, the bench asked the defendant to stand: "You have followed the proceedings? A trial has been set for 19 September at Crown court. Thank you. You may take him away" (his bail application was refused, and he was to be held in custody until his trial). The prosecution focused on the defendant; it was unclear whether "Excellent Company" was to be investigated. The hearing took fifty-three minutes.

Box 6.2. IFED—a private investigatory agency involved in criminal prosecutions[21]

In 2012, due to longstanding police disinterest in investigating and prosecuting insurance fraud, the insurance industry funded and established the Insurance Fraud Enforcement Department, which is hosted at the City of London Police. The Department employ forty-plus full-time detectives and financial investigators and its operations are funded by grants from its members. In its first year of operation it investigated "crash-for-cash" and other types of fraud worth £11 million and achieved 260 arrests, 76 cautions, and 12 convictions. The IFED targets all kinds of insurance fraud from organised gangs operating "'crash-for-cash" rings through to individuals making fraudulent claims on personal injury, motor vehicle, or home and contents policies. The IFED conducts intelligence-led investigations and prosecutions of those who perpetrate and facilitate insurance fraud, and it also seizes and recovers assets on behalf of the industry. Additionally, the IFED supports proceedings against corrupt professionals who enable fraud, acting to bar or otherwise restrict their ability to practise in the future. The team takes up a range of insurance frauds, from high-volume, low-value fraud committed by individuals, through to more organised, systematic criminal attacks against the insurance industry.

Case *R 85* concerned allegations against seven Asian men ranging in age from nineteen to thirty-five (six of whom appeared at the hearing) from Manchester and Oldham who were allegedly involved in a "crash-for-cash" scam.[22] This type of fraud involves individuals who deliberately crash into the vehicle of innocent motorists in order to submit a false insurance claim.[23] The case was brought to the City of London magistrates' court because City of London Police is the principle police force investigating large insurance scams; it was very likely that the scam was initially investigated by a private organisation called "IFED" (see box 6.2).[24] The

[21] Source: Button and Brooks (2016, 219) and https://www.cityoflondon.police.uk/advice-and-support/fraud-and-economic-crime/ifed/Pages/About-IFED.aspx.

[22] "Crash-for-cash" insurance fraud costs are estimated to cost £340 million per year; see https://insurancefraudbureau.org/insurance-fraud/crash-for-cash/ (accessed 10 October 2019).

[23] The intention is to make as much money as possible from the exaggerated claim, with proceeds used to fund other accidents or more serious crimes. The scam goes well beyond the initial accident. Car insurance fraud adds an estimated £50 to the annual insurance bill of every UK policyholder and it endangers drivers and passengers.

[24] See https://www.cityoflondon.police.uk/advice-and-support/fraud-and-economic-crime/Pages/default.aspx (accessed 2 October 2019). IFED is one of a number of

defendants were represented by three solicitors and a Queen's Counsel (a senior barrister).

The bench rose while the court's legal adviser processed the paperwork. The defendants were called to the dock one at a time to identify themselves and give their date of birth and address. When this phase of the hearing was complete, the bench returned to court and the case resumed. All the defendants were arrested in relation to a fraud committed eleven months before the hearing; they pleaded not guilty and were released on unconditional bail. The magistrate addressed the defendants, who were sitting in the dock, in the following terms:

> "Since you are all accused of the same crime, I will not repeat this for each individual. It is the same decision for all of you. This offence will be dealt with in the Crown court. Trial is scheduled for October 9th at Crown court X at 9:30 am. There will be no discussion of the allegations today. You are released on unconditional bail; you must turn up for the trial. If you fail to attend, you will be fined and imprisoned. Is that clear?"

The defendants, who did not appear to be particularly concerned about their situation, said "Yes." They were advised to pick up a bail form on the way out. The defendants appeared to consist of two different groups of individuals who were allegedly recruited to operate at the "chaotic lower tier" of an OCG; the "principal" involved in organising the scam[25] was not in the dock (May and Bhardwa 2018, 65f). The hearing took forty-two minutes.

In *R 3* the defendant, a white, middle-aged, well-dressed male, was accused of misusing £600,000 belonging to another person for his personal advantage. The Crown asked that the case be referred to the Crown court for trial, and the DJ agreed. The defendant was bailed to his home address to await his trial. However, in *R 212* the police had already been granted twelve months to investigate a "pansy fraud" alleged to have been perpetrated by a thirty-one-year-old white businessman. The police justified their request for a further six months to investigate the case by stating that the defendant had not co-operated by providing the information they requested

---

privately funded and run investigatory agencies that conduct their own investigations, undertake surveillance of suspects, operate "semi-public" databases, and pursue private, quasi-criminal, and/or criminal sanctions against suspects (Button, Brooks, and Blackbourne 2016).

[25] Police investigations into serious fraud rarely investigate a case in its entirety; it is also rare for individuals operating at the top tier of the OCG and for "professional enablers" (solicitors, bank clerks, officials, etc.) to be successfully prosecuted and convicted (May and Bhardwa 2018, chaps. 4 and 5).

about his firm and payments from sixty different bank accounts. For his part the defendant stated that his firm provided marketing services and that the sum in question—variously stated to be £123,000 or £134,000—concerned payments made by his customers. Furthermore, the defendant stated that the ongoing investigations, which had provided no evidence of criminality, had "decimated my life and finished the business." The bench concluded the hearing by stating: "We are concerned that the investigation is taking so long. Though Ponzi[26] cases are complex, it would be helpful to see some progress in this case. We grant you [the police] a three-month extension. We hope that Mr. X will satisfy you at the next interview. Then you can charge him or refund him." The hearing lasted fifteen minutes.

In *R 216*, a twenty-four-year-old black male was accused of failing to assist the police during a four-month investigation of a phone-text scam. In a thirteen-minute hearing, it transpired that the police were seeking an additional four months to investigate him for an "HMRC text scam." According to Her Majesty's Revenue and Customs, "fraudsters alleging to be from HMRC send text messages to unsuspecting members of the public which falsely state that an individual is due a tax rebate. These messages usually include links to websites that harvest personal information or spread malware. This can in turn lead to identity fraud and the theft of people's personal savings."[27] The defendant claimed that his case had been delayed because he was not notified of the original hearing date. He also claimed that the police had come to his home and taken money from his bedroom (which included £3000 to be loaned to a cousin, and £600 to pay his rent). "They entered my house for no reason!" To which the magistrate replied: "All they need is suspicion." The police argued that the defendant had failed to provide acceptable evidence about the money they had seized. The bench gave the police a further four months to complete their investigations.

Proving that a financial transaction is fraudulent requires time and forensic skill to find the evidence. In case *R 64*, finding evidence of the crime required gaining access to documents lodged on the website of a UK business. However, *R 69* raised more difficult issues. Despite the very clear statement that the defendant was only being prosecuted because "she took the money," it is clear that some kind of network/organisation was involved in illegally transferring substantial funds between bank accounts that merited further investigation. The investment scam highlighted in *R 54*

---

26 For a discussion of these schemes, see https://www.thebalance.com/what-is-a-ponzi-scheme-history-examples-vs-pyramid-scheme-3305877 (accessed 10 October 2019).

27 See https://www.gov.uk/government/news/hmrc-halts-thousands-of-scam-text-messages (accessed 3 September 2019).

clearly had an international dimension in that the defendant was an Indian national and the money allegedly conned from the elderly lady had disappeared overseas (where it was feared that the defendant would also disappear if he were granted bail). Case *R 85* fits a well-known pattern of large-scale, multi-million-pound insurance frauds in which local people are paid to set up accidents and make fake insurance claims; these schemes are often coordinated from abroad. Finally, cases *R 3*, *R 212*, and *R 216* involved different types of fraud including scams of varying levels of complexity, which require varying amounts of investigatory skill, time, and resources to prove.

Critically, the CPS focused on specific incidents of fraud and investigated and prosecuted individuals rather than the transnational network/organisation in which the defendant was embedded (Albanese 2012, 5). Taken together, and seen in the wider context of fraud prosecutions (tables 6.1 and 6.4), it is clear that the number of incidents of fraud are growing, that losses from fraud are immense, and that the public prosecution of individuals offers little hope of recovering funds or dealing effectively with the criminal organisations involved in fraud.

iii. What do extradition cases reveal about organised crime?

Extradition law and practice began with an 1842 treaty of extradition linking the UK and the US and an 1843 treaty linking the UK and France (Baker, Perry, and Doobay 2010). All extradition treaties incorporate key legal principles.[28] The "founding principles" are that: (i) extradition is based on comity and cooperation between states (this requires countries to accept and cooperate, within limits, with the criminal justice systems of other countries); (ii) although cooperation is a founding assumption, it is not absolute (for example, the UK has a responsibility under the European Human Rights Act to protect those it extradites from foreseeable human rights abuses); (iii) extradition is not a process concerned with determining the innocence or guilt of a person, guilt is a matter for trial in the state that issued the arrest warrant; and (iv) while the fundamental purpose of

[28] Specifically the rule of double/dual criminality; the principle of specialty; the rule against the surrender of persons wanted in connection with the commission of offences of a political character; the requirement (in "accusation" cases) that a *prima facie* case must be made before a magistrate to support the application for extradition; the ability to challenge the magistrate's order for committal by application for a *writ of habeas corpus*; and the Secretary of State's discretion to decline to issue an order to proceed and to decline to order the fugitive's return to the foreign state.

extradition is to bring criminals to justice, the interests of the victims of crimes must also be considered (cited in House of Lords 2014–15, 7).

UK extradition law and practice has been shaped by official concerns of efficiency and cost, the need for international cooperation (particularly in the European Union), and requirements of fair treatment reflecting rights guaranteed under the European Convention on Human Rights (Baker et al. 2010; Joshi and Gibbins 2003). These concerns strongly influenced the *Extradition Act (2003)*,[29] which sets out how extradition requests should be processed. In brief, the extradition process involves six steps: (i) an arrest warrant is submitted electronically to the British Judicial Authority (JA)[30] at the National Crime Agency via the Schengen Information System; (ii) the JA assesses whether the warrant meets the UK's "proportionality standard"[31] and, if it does, it issues a certificate; (iii) the police arrest the wanted person; (iv) there is an initial bail hearing, (v) followed by an extradition hearing; finally, (vi) if extradition is refused, the wanted person is released whereas if extradition is granted, the person is handed over to the authorities from the requesting state where s/he will either stand trial or be incarcerated (if they are found guilty of a serious offence by the requesting state).

Implementing the act has given rise to numerous difficulties. District judges, who preside over extradition hearings, and defence lawyers have encountered problems and made recommendations to government concerning how to reform the act and handle litigation. Judges have uniformly been concerned to expedite hearings and complain that defendants "have no incentive to cooperate with the extradition process" and that they make use of their "unfettered right to appeal which is frequently invoked regardless of merit" (Extradition Judges Review

---

[29] See https://www.legislation.gov.uk/ukpga/2003/41/contents.

[30] The Judicial Authority is the CPS, it represents foreign governments in extradition proceedings and prosecutes extradition warrants on behalf of the Home Office/NCA. The starting position of the JA is always that a prosecution should proceed, and the warrant should be executed in line with the obligations of the UK under the Extradition Act.

[31] The "proportionality test" relates solely to "accusation" warrants and seeks to ensure that requests are for "serious" offences (see sec. 3 of the House of Lords 2014–15 report for a discussion of this test and an assessment of the evidence). For instance, between 2009 and 2014, Poland issued over nine thousand EAW warrants for its nationals resident in the UK (about 40 per cent of all EAWs), many of which were for trivial and dated offences.

2010).[32] In contrast, lawyers[33] have expressed concerns about the "lack of rigorous safeguards" for defendants in countries that fail to ensure that a suspect has access to legal counsel and to an interpreter.

I begin by looking at statistics on bail applications made by individuals detained under a European Arrest Warrant (EAW) while awaiting an extradition hearing from member states of the European Union.[34] Table 6.3 provides basic statistics on the number of requests, arrests and individuals surrendered by the UK to other EU countries. It is noticeable that while the number of warrants/requests has risen rapidly over the last decade, on average only about 12 per cent of all extradition requests made to the UK were granted.

The reason why a relatively small proportion of requests are granted is primarily due to the "proportionality test" that is intended to ensure that individuals are not returned to face "trivial" crimes. In addition, and as the cases discussed below illustrate, extradition bail applications present considerable difficulties to District Judges because some warrants are not certified, some are not proven, and some cases revolve around the disputed identity of the wanted person. Indeed, some requests face delays because of poor prison conditions in the requesting country, which potentially violates a defendant's Art. 3 rights under the European Convention on Human Rights.[35] Despite this winnowing down in the number of extradition requests that are granted, the cases provide insight into the nature and extent of organised crime.

---

[32] District judges were primarily concerned to reduce delays and "the time from arrest to final hearing" and the "time taken for each hearing" (¶12). Towards this end they have argued that legal aid should be made available at a defendant's first appearance in court to ensure legal representation and to stop the right of appeal to the administrative court.

[33] D. Cronin, "No justice in EU extradition system" (*Guardian*, 5 August 2009).

[34] Under the Extradition Act (2003), these are Part I applications that revolve around the submission of a European Arrest Warrant. Extradition requests from non-EU countries follow a different procedure.

[35] Art. 3 states that "No one shall be subjected to torture or to inhuman or degrading treatment or punishment." In 2017 imprisonment in sub-standard and crowded conditions in Albania was found to violate this right and delayed the return of numerous individuals from the UK.

Table 6.3. European arrest warrants dealt with in the UK, 2009–17.[36]

Part 1 EAWs	2009	2010	2011	2012	2013	2014	2015	2016	2017	Total
Requests	2,842	4,369	6,512	6,290	5,522	13,460	12,613	13,797	16,837	**82,242**
Arrests	732	1,307	1,332	1,331	1,775	1,519	2,041	1,843	1,510	**13,390**
Surrenders	537	1,038	1,079	1,025	1,126	1,097	1,149	1,431	1,164	**9,646**

The ability to convene a bail application hearing[37] depends upon the availability of adequate "paperwork" from both parties, which includes the completed bail form, details of the bail/extradition request, and, in the case of individuals detained in prison, a video-link to the prison. A bail hearing was convened at Westminster Magistrates' Court to hear the bail application of *EB 17* who is a serving foreign national prisoner. However, the prison where he was detained did not "produce" him for the video-link, which meant that his bail application was refused. It was very likely that the case paperwork wrongly identified the prison he was being held at. The bail hearing for *EB 5* concerned an arrest warrant issued by Norway, which is not a member state of the EU; however, the defendant was not produced at court. Nevertheless, the DJ remanded him into custody to attend a hearing in two weeks. The hearing for *EB 7* concerned a Polish man who was held at Wormwood Scrubs Prison who was not "produced" for his bail application; the DJ issued an order to produce him via a video-link the following day. Case *EB 8* concerned a Belgian woman whose bail application had been heard the previous day and who had already been released on conditional bail. Finally, case *EB 1* concerned a request by the Spanish authorities for a British national for an undisclosed crime. During an eleven-minute hearing the defendant, who had been detained in prison, agreed to be extradited without a hearing.

Indeed, most bail applications on the court's list that day had already been dealt with. Of the remaining cases some were bail applications for individuals being prosecuted for a criminal offence in the UK and some individuals were detained under a European Arrest Warrant (EAW). Among the latter was case *EB 13*, a British national wanted in France on a money laundering charge (for €118 million). His solicitor claimed that he had been convicted in 2008 for money laundering and had recently been released. In

---

[36] Source: "European Arrest Warrants, wanted from the UK, Part. 1, 2009-2017; National Crime Agency, at: http://www.nationalcrimeagency.gov.uk/publications (downloaded 2 October 2018).

[37] A summary of the current bail policy can be found at https://www.inbrief.co.uk/court-proceedings/bail/ (accessed 3 November 2018).

short, the claim was that this was a case of "double jeopardy," that is, the defendant had already been tried and convicted on the same facts.[38] The judicial authority—who was almost always a junior legal counsel—argued that this "was a substantial offence" and that the defendant had failed to surrender. She argued: "It is a very large sum for a robbery in 2008/9. He has previous convictions in this court." His solicitor argued that he was imprisoned for money laundering in 2015 and his passport had been seized. It was at this point that the video-link to the defendant, who was in prison, was activated and he was told by the DJ that his "full hearing" was scheduled in six weeks and that he was being remanded back into prison because "there are substantial reasons to think that you will not surrender to the court." The video-link hearing took six minutes.

Case *EB 7* concerned a fraud committed in Poland by a Polish national. The defendant had allegedly forged a surety to purchase a car (valued at £1250) and had been given a suspended sentence. However, he had allegedly fled the country and been tracked to the UK where he evaded the British police several times before being apprehended. In explanation for having evaded the police, his solicitor claimed that the defendant had not understood why the police wanted to speak with him, and that putting an electronic tag on the defendant and allowing him to live at his home address would be more appropriate then custody. The JA outlined the defendant's criminal history and argued that a suspended sentence had been activated and that he was a fugitive wanted on a recognised warrant who should not be granted bail. Noting that a full hearing was scheduled in three weeks, the DJ refused to grant bail and remanded him back into custody to await a hearing. The bail application took nine minutes.

Finally, two bail applications illustrate potential links between individuals arrested on an EAW and organized crime. Case *EB 15* concerned a Polish man sought on an extradition warrant by Poland who had been arrested and detained. When the video-link opened, the defendant's solicitor stated that she had not had time to take instructions from her client. A visibly upset DJ asked whether a surety has been offered, noting that £1000 was "too scanty" to grant bail. The JA argued that the defendant was wanted on an "accusatory" EAW warrant for violent robbery committed twelve years ago when he used violence to obtain a credit card, a pin number, and the victim's phone. Conviction for this offence could result in up to twelve years imprisonment. His solicitor countered by saying that he had been extradited for a previous matter and released: "He is not a

[38] Part I, sec. 12 of the *Extradition Act 2003* sets out the rule prohibiting double jeopardy; see https://www.legislation.gov.uk/ukpga/2003/41/section/12.

fugitive." At the end of a thirty-seven-minute hearing, the DJ asked about the defendant's current residence and work and decided to bail him to his address; the DJ also imposed a daytime curfew (he worked nights) and he accepted the £1000 surety. He told the defendant that he must attend his full hearing in one month and that he must not travel out of the UK.[39]

Case *EB 16* concerned a Hungarian national who was detained in prison. The hearing, which lasted seventeen minutes, was conducted via a video-link (his wife and two friends were in the public gallery at Westminster Magistrates' Court). The JA made her "observations on bail":

> "A warrant was issued, but he failed to surrender. This is a conviction warrant from Hungary for two offences for a period [a sentence] of two years and nine months. The entire sentence remains to be served. Around 2000 he was a member of an organised criminal group involved in drug cultivation, storage, and the distribution of drugs. . . . In September 2004 he was stopped and searched and was found in possession of amphetamines and five to six ounces of ecstasy and speed. On arrest his passport was seized. He has no previous convictions 'in this jurisdiction' [i.e., in the UK]. However, as this is a conviction warrant, there is no presumption of bail. He is a fugitive."

The defendant's solicitor offered mitigation, which focused on his family responsibilities, his father's rapidly declining health, and the offer of a surety of £8000. Speaking through an interpreter, the defendant stated: "I didn't commit the offence, it was fourteen years ago. I was sentenced for the use of drugs. I was never a member of a conspiracy of organised criminal activity." After confirming the date of the full hearing, the DJ stated:

> "You do not enjoy a presumption of bail. The warrant says you were a member of an organised criminal group involved in the distribution of drugs and that at the trial you ran away. The bail suggested does not allay my fears. You will remain in custody. I am concerned that you wouldn't surrender yourself. You will be brought before the court in four weeks. That's all for today."

There are numerous obstacles facing individuals who apply for bail while waiting for an extradition hearing. While legal aid is usually granted at the first hearing, lawyers are unable to take instructions from their clients who may be held anywhere in England and Wales (a fact that disrupts and slows down proceedings). Furthermore, a defendant's case file—which relies on

---

[39] It is standard practice for the police to seize travel documents from individuals wanted under an EAW when they are arrested; however, foreign nationals may possess multiple ID/documents that they can use to leave the UK.

paper files because the courts electronic filing system did not extend to extradition cases—often provides incorrect information about where defendants are detained, which means that when they are not "produced" for their video-link bail application, their application for bail is refused. Case *EB 13* illustrates poor communication between the JA and her counterpart in the requesting country: has the defendant already served time for bank robbery/money laundering or did he fail to surrender to the French authorities? Cases *EB 7* and *EB 15* suggest that EU nationals flee to the UK to avoid the consequences of their criminal behaviour, though some of the crimes that individuals are accused of committing are "trivial" and dated. Finally, "conviction warrants" carry a presumption that the defendant should not be bailed and should be extradited; at the initial hearing this presumption is acted upon and defendants are remanded into custody to await a hearing to decide whether their extradition will be granted.

iv. Extradition hearings

While bail applications provide limited insight into organised crime, extradition hearings can provide more detailed information about criminal organisations, about threats and intimidation against potential witnesses, and about how different countries issue warrants (which requires British judges to carefully scrutinise the arrest warrant). The cases discussed below begin with a relatively straightforward case and move on to cases that raise more complex issues. My intention is to demonstrate the complex issues that arise in extradition cases and to infer from these cases possible evidence about a defendant's involvement in organised crime.

Case *E 5* (see case *EB 5*, above) involved an individual who had been remanded into custody for four weeks to await his hearing. On the day of his hearing he was transferred from Wandsworth Prison to court and was brought up from the cells in handcuffs. Asked to confirm his name and date of birth (stage 1), he gave a different name to the name on the indictment. The JA stated: "he has an alias, sir. Take a seat." In a fifty-four-minute hearing in which the sole issue was the defendant's identity—was he the person named on the indictment?—his legal counsel and the JA argued about the validity of the "Interpol Red Note"[40] that authorized his arrest, and about the finger print evidence provided by the Norwegian police and by

---

[40] For an overview of red notices, see https://www.interpol.int/INTERPOL-expertise/Notices/Red-Notices (accessed 23 October 2019). For a discussion of possible injustices arising from these notices, see Heard and Tinsley 2012.

British Immigration.[41] Three issues were disputed that the DJ was required to address. First, was the evidence cited in the Interpol Red Note reliable?[42] Second, if the information was not reliable, was the judge allowed to "identify" the defendant as the person wanted in the warrant? Third, in the absence of DNA and supporting evidence from the Norwegian Police, was the fingerprint evidence supplied by the Norwegians reliable (because the prints did not appear to have come from the crime scene)? After hearing the evidence, the DJ retired to consider his decision (stage 7). I was unable to hear his decision. However, since there was case law on all the key issues, it seemed highly likely that the defendant would be extradited to Norway to stand trial.

The case of *E 1* illustrates why extradition hearings encounter so many delays. This case concerned an "accusatory" EAW for a British national who was said to have fled Spain prior to her trial (the precise details of the alleged offence were not stated). Legal argument arose because the Spanish EAW was not available and could not be seen by the judge. Counsel for the defendant argued that she had not fled Spain; rather, she had been in a hospital and had missed the flight to Spain and that in the absence of the warrant the case should not proceed. In contrast the JA argued that the defendant deliberately chose not to attend the trial and that the warrant existed but was not immediately available. A key issue turned on arguments about whether, if the defendant were returned, she would be given a retrial or whether she would be sentenced and imprisoned. After three minutes the DJ adjourned the hearing, part heard, for three weeks to allow all the evidence to be made available. In the meantime, the defendant was granted unconditional bail (I was unable to attend the resumed hearing and do not know the decision).

---

[41] Ten years after the alleged offence, the defendant was fingerprinted in an immigration detention centre and the system flagged up an arrest warrant for him, which triggered the current proceedings.

[42] For a summary of the case, see http://www.corkerbinning.com/interpol-got-the-wrong-man-edward-granges-comments-published-in-new-law-journal-2/ (accessed 24 October 2019). "At appeal, in *Leke Prendi aka Aleks Kola v Government of Albania [2015] EWHC 1809 (Admin)*, Kola's lawyers argued that the red notice was not duly authenticated, and the fingerprint evidence was third or remoter hearsay and therefore neither of these should have been admissible evidence. The circumstances in which Prendi's fingerprints had been obtained remained unexplained, and the local prosecutor had twice stated that no photos or fingerprints of Prendi were available. Lord Justice Aikens held that 'whoever made up the red notice could not speak to the truth of any of the facts directly' since they all came from sources other than Interpol Tirana. Aleks Kola was free to go."

Case *E 2* concerned an extradition request from Lithuania for a fifty-one-year-old British national to assist with police investigations (it was an accusatory warrant). The defendant, through his legal counsel, sought to argue that "Lithuania was the most corrupt country in the world." He sought to support this with his testimony and testimony from family members regarding his experience as a director of a company operating in Vilnius, which the Lithuanian authorities claimed to be investigating. At the outset both parties asked for an adjournment, but the DJ decided to hear the evidence and, if necessary, adjourn the case part heard.

The first issue raised was whether the 2015 EAW had been certified by the JA. Both parties agreed that, to resolve this issue and proceed with the case, the defendant would be re-arrested and issued with a new arrest warrant. The court briefly adjourned to permit him to be re-arrested. When court resumed, the JA read out the charge (stage 2):

> "This is a two-step investigation: In March 2014 an arrest warrant was issued for the defendant to investigate 'Stone Co.' for fraud, which the defendant was a director of; however, the defendant failed to attend an interview and was listed as wanted in June 2015, and the EAW was issued in July 2015."

The Lithuanian authorities thought that the defendant was in Malta. However, the defendant's evidence (stage 5) was that he had left Lithuania in 2011—well before police investigations—because he feared a Lithuanian co-director of the company who had connections to the mafia and who had threatened him and his family. A key issue in the case concerned the threats made against the defendant.[43] The defendant and his wife[44] provided the court with statements and gave oral evidence about events in Lithuania to the effect that armed thugs had threatened the defendant and that the police repeatedly arrested him to secure bribes from his firm.[45] The defendant also alleged that threats had been made against him in the UK by the Lithuanian co-director of the company. At the end of two hours, counsel for the

---

[43] The defendant sought to raise a human rights claim under the *European Convention on Human Rights*. However, as Arnell (2018) has argued, the European Court of Human Rights has held that extradition hearings do not consider a defendant's civil rights, nor do they consider the criminal charge against him/her. However, as pointed out by Davidson et al. (2015, 510), under Article 1(1) of the Framework Decision on the EAW as implemented in s.2(3)(b) and (5)(b) of the 2003 act, it is no longer legitimate for an EAW to be used to surrender an individual to investigate a crime; it can only be used "for the purpose of being prosecuted for the offence."

[44] She provided evidence about the impact that extradition would have on the family.

[45] It was for this reason that the defendant had employed bodyguards.

defendant sought a further three hours to present evidence. The DJ agreed to schedule a two-hour hearing in two weeks at which the defendant was required to provide proof of a complaint made to the UK police about threats and intimidation by the Lithuanian company director. After three hours seventeen minutes the case was adjourned part heard (I was not able to attend the second hearing and I do not know the judge's decision).

As with the extradition bail-hearings discussed above, extradition hearings (e.g., *E 3*) indicated poor communication between the judicial authorities in both countries and they raised a number of legal issues, for example, how to determine the identity of the defendant, the legal status of Interpol Red Notices, the validity of arrest warrants and evidential issues, including (in *E 1* and *E 2*) the defendant's ability to provide the court with objective evidence regarding admission to hospital or a record of a complaint made to the police. The latter two cases also raised, in different ways, potential human rights issues. However, since extradition hearings are not criminal trials, the likelihood is that both *E 1* and *E 2* would be extradited. The cases also illustrate potential links with organised crime as well as allegations of corruption.

Conclusion

As the cases discussed in this chapter show, the prosecution of fraud in magistrates' courts is narrowly focused on determining individual culpability; this situation arises from the language used in legislation, which in turn shapes how the police investigate and how the CPS prosecute these cases. Unlike other types of criminal offences, there are a number of government agencies—local police forces, the SFO, the National Crime Agency, and the City of London Police—involved in assessing, gathering information/intelligence, and deciding whether and how to prosecute allegations of fraud. Unfortunately, very little information is publicly available about how most of these agencies work or about the extent to which they cooperate to investigate and prosecute offences. Even so, given the predominant focus of the CPS on prosecuting individuals, taken together with pressure on the CPS to secure a conviction and budget cuts, the British authorities are unable to protect the public from fraud because they lack the ability and resources to investigate and prosecute most allegations, much less the organised criminal networks responsible for fraud. This occurs despite a careful analysis of "minor offences" and extradition cases which reveals clearly evidence of important links between individual defendants and organised crime, which remain invisible to the police and the courts in their search for individuals who can be held accountable for a singular, reported crime.

The Criminal Justice System is relatively slow in dealing with fraud because the cost of prosecuting these cases is high and because of budget cuts, which means that the chance of recovering lost money is limited. In response to the inability/unwillingness of the police and CPS to investigate/prosecute fraud, an increasing number of private organisations have been created by insurance companies to investigate and prosecute fraud. It is estimated that private organisations investigate and "prosecute" 70 per cent of all reported allegations of fraud (see Table 6.4).

Table 6.4. Fraud offenders sanctioned by enforcement category, 2014–15.[46]

Enforcement type	Justice route	Number of offenders	Per cent	Per cent
Criminal	Criminal (excluding tv)	15,696	1.5	17.1
	Criminal tv licensing	162,869	15.6	
Contempt of court (criminal)	Civil court[47]	12	0.0	
Regulatory	NHS	606,063	57.9	70.0
	DWP	10,155	1.0	
	HMRC	14,760	1.4	
	Insolvency Service	1,122	0.1	
	Transport for London	100,113	9.6	
Regulatory - professions	Professions regulators	395	0.03	0.03
Database record	Cifas	135,485	12.9	12.9
Total		1,046,670	100%	100%

As noted earlier, there is a proliferation of quasi-public and private organisations that use diverse methods to investigate and prosecute allegations

---

[46] Source: Button et al. 2016, table 1, p. 3. Home Office (2018, table 5.2). Information on the outcome of fraud cases indicates that fifty-two thousand cases were dealt with in 2017–18. CIFAs is a not-for-profit fraud prevention membership organisation that holds a database of instances of fraudulent conduct.

[47] Civil cases are private actions undertaken by individuals against an individual or company; the claimant must prove the case they allege to secure a judgement in their favour. There are different legal procedures available depending on the amount of money/damages being claimed. In cases that go to trial, the claimant meets the costs and, if they are successful, the defendant must pay their legal costs. Civil suits can last many years.

of fraud. Government agencies investigating fraud include the National Health Service,[48] the Department for Pensions and Work,[49] and Her Majesty's Revenue and Customs.[50] The majority of private organisations that exist are not legally regulated and they attempt to deal with fraud[51] in very different ways, in part because they lack the resources and training to investigate claims and they operate with a lower standard of proof than required in criminal law. Some organisations impose penalties[52] on offenders and are cost effective (because they are informal). However, many private organisations do not hold hearings or engage in an independent assessment of the evidence; if a person is found guilty, they may not be informed, nor will they necessarily have a right to appeal against the decision. In short, many private organisations fail to respect due process in the way they assess and decide allegations of fraud and, as with the CJS, they focus on individuals and specific types of fraud that the police show little interest in investigating.

In conclusion, the vast majority of cases of fraud are not reported to the police, and those that are reported tend to be addressed by organisations that lack the capacity to fully investigate and fairly decide allegations. In the meantime, limited efforts are made by the police and CPS to investigate and prosecute allegations of "white-collar" and organised crime and the "professional enablers" involved in organised crime (May and Bhardwa 2018).

As my analysis of the prosecution of domestic violence (in chapter 4) and drug offences (chapter 5) found, the number and type of fraud cases that are prosecuted is limited. While the reason for this situation varies, the inability of the government to address such offences points to a pressing need to rethink prevention strategies, provide better public education, and promote awareness about these crimes (and the cost to the public). Indeed, the government needs to prioritise fraud prevention and prosecution by investing in local police force capabilities, and it must provide much better training and support for the police, the CPS, and the SFO to enable them to investigate and prosecute a broader range and greater number of fraud offences.

---

48 To investigate fraud by opticians and pharmacists, doctors' lists, patient prescriptions, dental work, procurement fraud, and so on.

49 For falsely claiming benefits, and so on.

50 For failure to pay taxes or repay student loans, or when businesses avoid tax liabilities, and so on.

51 Some organisations deal exclusively with falsified qualifications, employee fraud, disguising poor work performance (e.g., exams, plagiarism), and so on.

52 Some organisations are restricted to publicly shaming individuals: they may issue a warning, suspend or revoke a license, and impose financial penalties or make cost orders against individuals.

CONCLUSION

I began by noting that public interest in the courts and in the administration of justice surfaced briefly in the aftermath of the 2011 riots in English cities before sinking back into indifference. This situation is in sharp contrast to the past, when the courts and public trials played an important role in educating citizens about what constitutes a fair trial and how the law determines criminal guilt. Indeed, the relationship between law, the state, and justice in England and Wales was extensively debated by Adam Smith, Thomas Hobbes, Jeremy Bentham, and many others at a time when the courts were gradually becoming independent of the Church. In London, public interest in justice arguably began in the eighteenth century with the creation of Bow Street Magistrates' Court (Beattie 2007) and continued well into the mid-twentieth century as demonstrated by widespread public interest in censorship trials such as *Lady Chatterley's Lover* (Bedford 1959) and the prosecution of individuals charged under the *Official Secrets Act* (Grant 2016).

However, judging by the limited amount of academic work and press coverage today, there appears to be little interest in the courts or in knowing whether prosecutions and judicial decisions produce justice or injustice—a situation that may change if the Black Lives Matter movement catalyses political and legal change. How have we reached this state of affairs? Is it due to complacency or a perception that the police and the courts no longer play an important role in defining moral standards or controlling crime? Perhaps this lack of interest is due to populist political discourse on crime control with its emphasis on "front-line policing"? Given the policy drift towards virtual pleading[1] and the closure of growing numbers of courts,[2] we seem to be witnessing a significant shift away from the public reckoning of justice in a court of law. If this is the case, the

---

[1] See P. Gibbs, "Court hearings on demand—a triumph for openness or an invasion of privacy?" on the Senior Judiciary's adoption of virtual courts and the nature of public access (25 January 2019) at http://www.transformjustice.org.uk/2811-2/.

[2] See "Half of all magistrates' courts in England and Wales closed since 2010" (162 out of 323) (*Guardian*, 27 January 2019); "Court closures: sale of one hundred twenty six premises raised just thirty four million pounds, figures show" (*Guardian*, 8 March 2018); NAO (2018).

situation raises serious questions in view of the diverse population of England and Wales, widespread evidence of wrong-doing[3] (including racial inequities related to police "stop and search" operations), and growing levels of hate crime.[4] Is a shift away from a public reckoning of wrongdoing advisable?

My examination of London's magistrates' courts has revealed serious concerns about the CJS, which requires consideration and quite possibly major reform. Specifically, I have found four inter-related factors that seriously question the "overriding objective" of the criminal procedure rules, which is to acquit the innocent and convict the guilty, deal with the prosecution and the defence fairly, and recognise the rights of defendants, and so on. In sharp contrast to the rhetoric of the rule of law, in magistrates' courts the vast majority of criminal defendants waive their right to a trial by pleading guilty and/or are found guilty, including some who are innocent, some "vulnerable" defendants who should have been diverted out of the court, and others who may have been poorly defended. These are long-standing problems that require serious attention (Ashworth 1988; Sainsbury 2009; Sanders et al. 2010).

The first set of factors concerns the role of legal actors in the CJS whose work ensures a high level of prosecutions and convictions. The police play a dual role in this process. On the one hand, the police arrest over one million people every year, many of whom are arrested via the discriminatory use of police "stop and search" powers. At the same time, however, and for reasons that remain unclear, the police fail to record a large percentage of reported incidents, they divert many cases away from court (by issuing cautions, penalty notices, and warnings), and a large percentage of cases are dropped[5] prior to prosecution (see Box 1.3 and 4.1). In addition, the vast

---

[3] The number of criminal offences recorded by the police in England and Wales has, until recently, been falling from an estimated one in five persons affected by crime compared to two in five persons twenty years ago. However, the quality and coverage of official crime statistics is problematic. See https://fullfact.org/crime/crime-england-and-wales/ (accessed 11 October 2019).

[4] The number of reported incidents of hate crime has steadily increased since 2013 with big spikes occurring in 2016 (at the time of the EU referendum) and again in 2017 (following major terrorist incidents). However, the number of hate crimes actually prosecuted by the police and CPS is small. See https://fullfact.org/crime/hate-crime-england-and-wales/ (accessed 12 October 2019).

[5] A decision not to prosecute may arise from budget cuts and/or a decision not to prosecute "minor crimes" or indeed from a decision to drop prosecutions (see "Met police dropped thirty thousand criminal investigations in first twenty four hours of last year" (*Guardian*, 9 September 2018); and "Police chief admits 'cultural problem' with evidence disclosure" (*Guardian*, 24 January 2018).

majority of offences that are prosecuted in magistrates' courts are not investigated by the police or, as with prosecutions under the Public Order Act 1984, prosecutions succeed on the word of a police officer without independent corroboration. As argued in this book and in other research, the way that the police exercise their powers, and indeed the primary purpose of policing, urgently needs to be reviewed.

The work of the Crown Prosecution Service also needs to be reviewed. As noted by Sanders (2002, 2016), the cases that the Crown prosecutes are the ones that the police "construct" and that they want prosecuted. It appears that the CPS lacks the resources to open police files/cases for further investigation and that it does not adequately screen cases before prosecuting them.[6] Viewing its work from the court, I found that in 94 per cent (181 of 193) of the remand cases which I observed, the evidence relied upon by the CPS came only from statements provided by police officers. It is important to ask whether cases can be fairly tried if the police limit their investigation to taking statements from victims and defendants (and sometimes submitting footage from police body cameras)? Finally, it appears that the Police and CPS prosecute cases that are easy to prove, namely those that rely on an admission of guilt, public order offences (i.e., the word of police officers), cases alleging "simple possession" of drugs and cases in which defendants have mental health problems and/or are absent from court. This situation cannot be right.

The ability of magistrates to decide a case fairly is seriously undermined by the speed at which cases are heard, their limited legal training, and their reliance on the advice of the courts' legal advisor and the Crown. This situation tends to result in a failure to question police evidence and prosecutor decisions.[7] In 45 per cent (92 of 204) of the cases for which I have information, defendants pleaded guilty; in 45 per cent of cases, defendants pleaded not guilty; and in 9 per cent of cases, no plea was taken.[8]

---

[6] Sanders (2016, 4) notes that "ten percent of CPS charge decisions are incorrect," that frequently the information provided to the CPS by the police is inadequate and that 61 per cent of cases forwarded to the CPS are not subject to a proportionate review. Her Majesty's Inspectorate of the Constabulary (2017b) also notes that police files are often incomplete.

[7] Reiner (2010, 223) has observed that the CPS fails to regulate police conduct by prosecuting officers for crimes, by failing to take civil actions against officers, or failing to judicially review policy decisions. He also notes that the courts seldom exclude police evidence or question whether it was legally obtained.

[8] The reasons why no plea was taken in a case included: three case management hearings; nine summonses were issued for a failure to attend court; one defendant was sent for a "paragraph-five" assessment; one hearing was transformed into a "Newton hearing"; there were fourteen statutory directions granted; four legal

Just as importantly, in 28 per cent of the remand cases I observed (49 out of 173), a defendant was not legally represented. Since magistrates and DJs do not assist unrepresented defendants to give their evidence it is highly likely that a number of judicial decisions against unrepresented defendants may have given rise to an injustice.

In total, thirty defendants were sent to a Crown court for a jury trial, and eighty-two defendants who pleaded not guilty were listed for a trial at magistrates' court.[9] With respect to the twenty-three criminal trials I observed, the majority of trials did not result in a conviction (see table C.1). While this may be a small number of cases to draw conclusions from, my observations appear to confirm Ministry of Justice statistics on the large number of "cracked" and ineffective trials (at approximately 45 per cent; MoJ 2018c, figure 3). Interestingly, the Ministry of Justice does not report statistics on the number of cases that were dismissed/not proven or when a conviction was reached in the defendants' absence.

---

applications were made to the court; one "closure order" was granted; in one case, the charge (drunk and disorderly) against the defendant was dropped; in two cases, defendants were sentenced following a guilty plea/decision; two adjournments were granted; there were twenty-three breach hearings; in one case a defendant pleaded not guilty to one charge and guilty to a second charge; finally in one case the charge (simple possession of marijuana) was to be reconsidered by the police.

[9] Three defendants scheduled for trial were absent and were convicted in their absence, a number were summoned to appear at a future hearing, and a smaller number were returned to magistrates' court as a result of having filed a "statutory direction."

Table C.1. The outcome of the criminal trials I observed

Found guilty	Dismissed/ unproven	Trial vacated	Trial adjourned	Case management hearing	Convicted in defendant's absence	Case adjourned because CPS failed to disclose evidence	Total
7	2	4	3	2	3	2	23

Table C.2. Ethnicity, guilty plea, and legal representation.

Ethnicity	Defendants by ethnicity	Legally represented	Not legally represented
Black	46 (25%)	38 (82%)	8 (17%)
Asian	42 (23%)	36 (85%)	6 (14%)
White	81 (45%)	66 (81%)	13 (16%)
Other	12 (6 %)	8 (66%)	4 (25%)
Total	181	148 (82%)	31 (16%)

Table C.3. Defendants by ethnicity and ethnicity in London (2011 Census).

Ethnicity	Defendants ethnicity	Ethnicity in London
Black (and mixed race)	46 (25%)	18.3%
Asian	42 (23%)	18.5 %
White (and white other)	90 (50%)	59.8%
Other	3 (1%)	3.4%
Total	181	100%

Turning to the work of legal representatives, I observed significant differences in the way that duty solicitors defended their clients compared with privately instructed solicitors. With some exceptions, duty solicitors adopted a fairly passive role in criminal proceedings during which their clients pleaded "guilty"; they also limited their role to offering mitigation in an attempt to secure a reduced sentence.[10] Contrary to the findings of the Lammy Review (2017), I found that the majority of black and ethnic minority defendants whom I observed[11] were legally represented; however, legal representation appears to have made no difference to the outcome of the case since a majority of defendants still pleaded guilty and were convicted.

Tables C.2 and C.3 illustrate two important issues. First, the number of defendants from black and ethnic minority communities appearing in the courts is much higher than their proportion in the population of London (conversely, the number of white defendants is well below the total number of the white population of London). This disparity is presumably due to police reliance on their "stop and search" powers to arrest and charge individuals. Second, while individuals from all ethnicities have equal access to a lawyer, the problem is the apparent ineffectiveness of legal representation: a very high percentage of legally represented defendants still plead guilty. Since it was not possible for me to be present when lawyers interviewed their clients, it is not possible to know what advice a defendant was given, that is, about the merits of their case and how to plead. At the very least, my findings suggest that legal representatives funded by legal aid function primarily to process individuals into the CJS. The privately instructed solicitors who I observed in court were, on the other hand, better prepared than duty solicitors—even when their client pleaded guilty—and they took a far more active role in defending their clients. In this context, continued cuts in legal aid have resulted in growing numbers of experienced solicitors/barristers withdrawing their services from magistrates' courts leaving defendants to be represented by less experienced lawyers and duty solicitors.

---

[10] Following the work of Baldwin and McConville (1977) and given the poor quality of legal representation observable in court, it is not clear whether defendants who plead guilty were well advised to do so.

[11] In a significant number of the cases that I observed the defendant was "not produced" at their remand hearing because they had skipped bail, failed to attend, were sectioned in a mental hospital, or were not required to attend, for example, for a case management review, and so on. This is why the total number of defendants in tables C.2 and C.3 is less than the total number of cases I observed.

Finally, and as a direct result of privatisation, the probation service has been fragmented, resulting in a serious decline in their ability to assist the court and defendants (HMIP 2017b).[12] This situation has created lengthy waits for defendants to be assessed for mental health problems or for a report advising the court about its options for sentencing an offender (a period during which many defendants are remanded into custody). In relation to the cases I observed, magistrates/DJs asked for a probation report in only 15 per cent (36) of the 238 cases I observed; however, in only 16 (44 per cent of requests) of these cases was the recommendations of the probation officer fully accepted. It is worrying that the judiciary is not asking for pre-sentence reports, and one is entitled to ask whether this arises because they lack confidence in privatised probation companies, because they forget to ask for a report, or because magistrates fear that a pre-sentence report will limit their ability to sentence a defendant as they see fit (CJI 2018).

The second set of inter-related factors that potentially contributes to injustice arises from the impact of "legal language" in the CJS. Once arrested, most defendants are unable to understand the convoluted statutory language used by the police and CPS to arrest and charge them; their difficulties are compounded by the "legal discourse" used by judges and lawyers during court proceedings. As discussed in chapter 2, the lexical-grammatical structure of legal language with its many genres and registers is central to negotiating the "facts" of a case (Gibbons 1999) and it contributes to defendants misunderstanding or misapprehending the charges against them, which in turn silences defendants, witnesses, and complainants and probably contributes to guilty verdicts (Cammiss 2006).

While I have not examined legal discourse per se, my analysis has shown that the majority of defendants speak very briefly to their legal representative prior to their hearing, and that during proceedings they are locked in the dock. A defendant's dependence on their legal representative is reinforced by the requirement that a lawyer speaks for him/her: defendants who fail to observe this requirement are told to shut up and they may be sanctioned for interrupting proceedings. Perspex docks are virtually soundproof and communication—which is limited to confirming one's identity and making a plea—is through a microphone. It should be clear that a defendant's inability to hear and participate in their hearing/trial potentially

---

[12] Privatisation has resulted in the failure of probation services to deal with high rates of re-offending. See "Probation Service: we're poorly paid and the caseloads are unmanageable," *Guardian*, 13 March 2019), many privately-run CRCs are buckling "under the strain of commercial pressures." Also see "Increase in serious crimes by offenders on probation, figures show" (*Guardian*, 2 August 2017); and "Private parole companies 'lack resources for the job'" (*Observer*, 4 February 2018).

jeopardises their right to a fair trial under Art. 6(3) of the ECHR[13] (Owusu-Bempah 2018).

To be clear, it does not follow that even if the language of the court and the language spoken by a defendant is nominally the same, that is English or Welsh, that a defendant necessarily understands the case against them or the "discourse" of judges and lawyers. Their difficulty may be due to their "vulnerability," limited education, or lack of legal literacy, or because they do not speak/understand basic English or Welsh.[14] The problems facing a defendant are exacerbated at remand hearings and trials when the CPS fails to cite the specific statute/legislation that s/he is using to prosecute a defendant. As I have argued, there are multiple options available to the police/CPS to charge a defendant under the Public Order Act and sixty-four possible offences open to the authorities to charge a defendant with domestic violence. Without question, the specific charge made against a defendant has serious consequences in terms of a defendant's ability to establish a recognised legal defence for their alleged criminal behaviour.

It is important to remember that a large percentage of defendants are poor and illiterate members of the precariat. In this regard, Newburn (2016, 334) has argued that

> Whether we look at official statistics on arrest and incarceration, self-report studies of criminal offending, or surveys of crime victims, the same pattern

---

[13] Under Art. 6(3), "Everyone charged with a criminal offence has the following minimum rights: (a) to be informed promptly, in a language which he understands and in detail, of the nature and cause of the accusation against him; (b) to have adequate time and facilities for the preparation of his defence; (c) to defend himself in person or through legal assistance of his own choosing or, if he has not sufficient means to pay for legal assistance, to be given it free when the interests of justice so require; (d) to examine or have examined witnesses against him and to obtain the attendance and examination of witnesses on his behalf under the same conditions as witnesses against him; (e) to have the free assistance of an interpreter if he cannot understand or speak the language used in court." See https://www.echr.coe.int/Documents/Convention_ENG.pdf.

[14] During fieldwork I encountered two cases (*R 154* and *R 241*) where a defendant needed an interpreter, which the Legal Aid Board initially refused to authorise. My research did not examine whether defendants required the assistance of interpreters to allow them to participate in their hearing/trial. The problematic role of interpreting is discussed by Aliverti and Seoigh (2017, 150) who note that while defendants have a right to an interpreter, this right was fettered by austerity and a general "lack of concern for unpopular minorities" as well as by "the contractual arrangements in the provision of language services which have exacerbated longstanding problems to the detriment of non-English speakers."

> emerges: *lower socio-economic status is associated with greater involvement with the criminal justice system*, higher rates of criminal offending, and higher rates of various forms of victimization. *The relationship between socioeconomic deprivation and involvement in crime and the justice system holds not only for individuals . . . but also for neighbourhoods*. (my emphasis)

In 28 per cent (48) of the 173 remand hearings for which I have information, defendants were "poor" whether defined in terms of being homeless/sleeping rough, owing the court money, or having court fines deducted from their state benefits.[15] A defendant's ability to understand and participate in their hearing was also affected by the limited amount of time spent with, and information provided by, a solicitor prior to and during the hearing.

The third set of inter-related factors that affects the quality of justice in London's magistrates' courts arises from the nature of summary justice. Perhaps the most important issue is the brevity of remand hearings (most were concluded in less than twenty minutes, though hearings varied in length from four to forty-five minutes). In addition, legal procedure speeds up decision-making by skipping key stages as the court deals with a guilty plea or as it completes the PET form for a contested trial; this process constrains the ability of defendants to understand their hearing.

Additional factors that constrain the ability of individuals to defend themselves arise from a decision by the CPS to prosecute defendants who, for a variety of reasons including poor mental health or because they were sectioned or detained at a hospital under the *Mental Health Act (1983)*,[16] may not be competent to stand trial. In 11 per cent (20) of the 173 remand hearings for which I have data, the defendant was mentally ill; nevertheless, proceedings against them continued. This is a long-standing problem in the CJS, which the Ministry of Justice has consistently failed to address even though alternative proposals regarding "competence" have been available for some time (the most recent was produced by the Law Commission, 2016). Competence to stand trial is clearly linked to mental health, poverty, and illiteracy, which places defendants at a considerable disadvantage in their ability to understand the consequences of a "guilty" plea and the failure of the court to divert the case out of court and, following a conviction, the

---

[15] In a further 10-plus per cent of observed cases it was not clear what the defendants' financial status was because they were students, serving prisoners, and so on.

[16] In particular, see Section 37 and Part III of the Act: https://www.legislation.gov.uk/ukpga/1983/20/contents.

failure to offer drug treatment/rehabilitation[17] to prisoners (Lay Observers 2017; Gerry and Cooper 2017).[18]

As "The Lammy Review" (2017, 27) noted, "BAME defendants neither trust the advice they are given, nor believe they will receive a fair hearing." Lammy argued that there was a specific lack of trust in legally aided solicitors providing advice in police stations and at court. He argued that this situation could be addressed if lawyers fully explained to defendants their legal rights and their options. The extent of this problem can be glimpsed from my observational data: of the 238 hearings for which I have information, 48 per cent involved defendants from BAME communities.[19] In addition, at least 24 per cent of all defendants I observed were under the age of twenty-one. In short, and given high levels of guilty pleas and conviction rates, there must be some doubt about how well BAME and young people were legally defended.

The fourth factor that may give rise to injustice arises from the court's narrow focus on individual culpability. While magistrates/DJs are tasked with assessing wrongdoing, they fail to consider the history or the wider social or cultural context[20] in which an offence was committed. This defect in judicial vision is evident in the way domestic violence cases are decided, in certain types of fraud, and when vulnerable defendants are tried.

---

[17] In 22 (9 per cent) of the 238 hearings for which I have evidence, the defendant was given a rehabilitation order for drug or alcohol addiction. My impression was that many more defendants had addiction problems than the court recognised.

[18] Ministry of Justice (2017b, 40) statistics indicate that on average 20 per cent of offenders were found to suffer from alcohol misuse, 30 per cent showed signs of substance abuse, about 10 per cent showed signs of alcohol and substance abuse, 10 per cent exhibited signs of a "physical health need," approximately 65 per cent showed a "mental health need," 10 per cent were poor, and 10 per cent showed indications of "abuse." The level of vulnerability varied by race/ethnicity. These problems must be addressed by public policy and cannot be left to the CJS to deal with. According to *The Times*, illegal drug use in jails is "widespread" and drug tests indicate that illegal drug use is the highest in twelve years ("Drug laws 'keep police from bigger crimes,'" 4 April 2019).

[19] Official reports do not provide statistics on the racial identity of defendants appearing in magistrates' courts. The national figure on prosecutions for indictable offences indicates that defendants from black and mixed-ethnic groups are prosecuted at between two and four times higher than white defendants (MoJ 2017b, 42).

[20] The failure to "allow for cultural context" in investigating allegations of parental child abuse by immigrants was recently noted in the family courts, see "Police 'should allow for cultural context' in child abuse investigations" (*Telegraph*, 9 June 2016).

Judicial decisions based on incomplete information about a case are likely to be unsustainable and unfair. Injustice can also arise when similar offences are not decided in a similar manner, a situation that occurs when the CPS fails to consistently charge offenders (e.g., in drug cases) or when offenders receive different sentences for the same offence (Pina-Sanchez 2018). Finally, injustice can arise from the near impossibility of appealing against an unfair conviction (Sanders et al. 2010, 613–17; Jacobson 2013).

It goes without saying that austerity measures have undermined access to justice as well as the quality of justice in England and Wales. Thus, budget cuts have reduced police numbers, which translates into a reduction in the investigation of "low-level" crimes and a decline in the number of arrests. Budget cuts have undermined the ability of the CPS to fairly prosecute cases (as opposed to dropping prosecutions or failing to disclose evidence before a hearing). Cuts have also closed a large number of magistrates' courts, substantially reduced court staff, and contributed to the deterioration of court facilities and the collapse of ICT systems, which has meant that defence counsel and magistrates are often unable to access case files.[21] Finally, budget cuts affect the ability of forensic science[22] operations to obtain evidence that will secure a conviction. Even so, funding is not the principle problem affecting the quality of justice in magistrates' courts.

In addition, and as the House of Commons (2016b, ¶1) enquiry into the Criminal Justice System indicated and as my research also suggests, budget cuts have the effect of shunting problems from one area of the CJS to another area. The House of Commons found that,

> *The criminal justice system is bedevilled by long standing poor performance including delays and inefficiencies, and costs are being shunted from one part of the system to another.* Around two-thirds of trials in the Crown Court are delayed or do not go ahead at all. There was a backlog of 51,830 cases in the system awaiting a hearing at Crown Court as at September 2015. Victims and witnesses are having to wait longer for their day in court: 134 days between the case leaving the Magistrates' court and the start of the Crown Court hearing, compared to 99 days two years ago. Too much costly court time is wasted dealing with the consequences of parties simply not having done what they should have done, for example 38.4% of cases sampled in a 2015 inspection were not reviewed by the Crown Prosecution Service (CPS) before they reached court. The system is administered by

---

[21] See "UK's courts system 'on its knees' following major IT failure, lawyer's association says" (*Independent*, 24 January 2019).

[22] See "Top judge warns cuts in forensics could lead to fewer crimes solved" (*Evening Standard*, 4 February 2019); T. Wilson "Forensic science is in crisis—and this could have critical effects on UK legal system" (*Conversation*, 3 April 2019).

> different parts of government with different budgets and pressures and decisions taken by one part can create inefficiency and increase costs in other parts, for example if the police save money by not collecting expensive forensic evidence this can add to the work of the CPS in preparing their case. (emphasis in the original)

I began this book by asking how the courts are able to reach a guilty verdict without any apparent doubt, despite the elusiveness and complexity of truth and reality. The determination of guilt/innocence *is* a difficult task, but in magistrates' courts good decision-making is hindered by a number of factors: the discretionary and unfettered role of the police and the CPS, which creates difficult hurdles for defendants; the opacity of legal "language"; and brief hearings and poorly trained duty solicitors. My research supports the work of Danet (1980, 509) who argued that "[T]ruth is the outcome of dialogue, discussion, and the confrontation of opinions" between lawyers who construct the "facts" of a case using a discourse characterised by "different versions of reality" that are directly linked to taken-for-granted premises in the law. However, taking evidence and cross examination are characterised by the use of specific linguistic forms and language by the CPS, judges, and lawyers that is incomprehensible to the majority of defendants.

Furthermore, the "facts" in a case are constructed by lawyers to persuade a judge as to the guilt/culpability of their client in terms not only of their alleged actions but also of their utterances. However, and following Cammiss (2006), because the legal system is normatively closed but cognitively open, its engagement with litigant and defendant discourses transforms their testimony back into the language of law by "excluding and stigmatizing—defining out" their voices to reproduce the binary structure prevalent in legal language. This process allows the court to select "relevant" facts from different narratives to decide a case. Thus the question "how do courts determine guilt/innocence?" needs to be rephrased: the judicial process is not concerned with finding "the truth," it is about how judges deploy legal rules to referee and decide cases. Guilt and innocence is what a judge decides; their decisions may have no bearing at all on the truth in any particular case, which, in turn means that judicial decisions may not be just. Perhaps the best example of unjust and ineffective decisions can be found in the prosecution of domestic violence where three problems are readily apparent. First, the CPS fails to prosecute some defendants for "controlling behavior" (which would attract a heavier sentence) even though the evidence for this offence is clear (*B 153*). Second, the current prosecution strategy seems to be ineffective because convicted defendants repeatedly attack their victims (*BB 76*). Finally, we are experiencing rising levels of domestic violence regardless of police and judicial efforts, which means it is time to rethink the conventional approach to criminalising domestic violence.

With regard to the intersection between law and the precariat, the evidence from my research indicates that—even if we exclude "vulnerable" defendants with mental health problems from my calculations—at least 20 per cent of defendants are from the precariat, a class of individuals whose lives are defined by unstable labour, low and unstable incomes, and loss of basic citizenship rights. Almost without exception, this class of person is arrested and prosecuted for misdemeanours such as loitering, begging, sleeping rough, drug offences, assault, and fraud. And almost without exception the CJS fails to provide these defendants, many of whom have addiction problems, with an opportunity to access rehabilitation/treatment (the exceptions were *BB 46*, *R 194*, *S 155*, *R 139*, and *S 55*). Instead, convicted defendants are recycled through the CJS at great expense but without reducing the likelihood that they will stop offending (*B 49*, *R 194*, *R 81*, *R 42*, *BB 76*, *S 155*, *R 100*). Indeed, in addition to periods of imprisonment defendants are frequently fined, with the fine being deducted from their dwindling state benefits, which erodes their ability to survive without reoffending (*BB 49*, *R 42*, *B 49*, *R 100*, *S 55*).

Given the problems I have identified it should be evident that the quality of justice on offer in magistrates' courts is seriously flawed. However, I want to make it clear that the majority of defendants who appear before the court charged with a serious crime are guilty as charged: only serious crimes are investigated by the police with the facts put before a jury at a Crown court. These cases include prosecutions for terrorism,[23] homicide (*R 91*, *R 92*), rape, acid attacks/serious theft (*R 86*), knife crime (*R 224*, *R 223*), serious drug offences (*R 45*, *R 48*), sexual assault/possessing pornographic images (*R 111*, *R 107*), and serious fraud (*R 69*, *R 54*, *R 85*). Since the evidence for "either way" crimes was not presented at an individual's remand hearing, it is less evident to me whether they merited trial by jury at a Crown court (*R 24*, *R 63*). The question is, were defendants properly advised to ask for a jury trial? With regard to summary offences, it

---

[23] In 2019 the number of terrorists charged and brought to trial reached its highest level at 100 cases, a 20 per cent increase on the previous year. There are 650 active investigations at the moment. The level of arrests and prosecutions is straining the CJS's ability to investigate and fairly try these individuals (see "Terror convictions hit nine-year peak," *Ecns.cn*, 14 September 2019).

should be clear that the police do not investigate these offences.[24] This is especially clear with regard to domestic violence cases in which the victim provided evidence (*BB 76*, *T 1*) and in minor drug offences (where all the possession of cannabis cases hinged on a guilty plea). I note that significant police and judicial time is used to prosecute cases alleging possession of cannabis, which occur when the police use their "stop and search" powers (*R 121*, *R 133*, *R 135*, *R 61*). Given the discriminatory nature of stop and search arrests and the need to concentrate police resources on more "serious" crimes, the (discriminatory) use of stop and search practices to find drugs, as opposed to knives, should cease.[25]

Finally it is also clear that, on the one hand, the number of cases that the police fail to record and/or drop exceeds the number that are sent to be prosecuted and, on the other hand, that the CPS drop large numbers of cases prior to prosecution and fail to adequately review cases that they prosecute. The question is, why does this happen and what does it say about the quality of justice? It is also notable that some of the offences that individuals are charged with committing should be removed from the statutes due to the inherent unfairness in the way the offence is "proved" (i.e., Secs. 3, 4A, and 5 public order offences) and that some statutory offences should be substantially revised (i.e., by eliminating the ability of the police to arrest a person without independent, corroborative evidence as occurs under the *Public Order Act*). Secs. 3, 4, 4A and 5 of the *Public Order Act* should be revised to avoid criminalising speech acts/utterances, which may violate the right to freedom of expression as guaranteed by Art. 10 of the *European Convention on Human Rights* by devising a better way to distinguish between vernacular English and racial abuse. Furthermore, since it is clear that the police exercise wide discretion in the way they charge offenders,[26] the expectation should be that the police should be required to

---

[24] The police interview the claimant and the defendant and they may submit CCTV (if any) and evidence of 999 calls; this does not, in my view, constitute an adequate investigation of domestic violence.

[25] See "Drug laws 'keep police from bigger crimes'" (*Times*, 4 April 2019). *The Times* reports that arrests for possession of cannabis has halved since 2010; they support "the Portuguese model" where possession of more than a ten-day supply is illegal.

[26] I am concerned that the police appear to lower the charge against certain types of easy-to-prosecute cases, for example, for simple possession of a drug rather than supplying drugs, rather than carry out a more thorough investigation and charging a defendant with intent to supply drugs and so on.

charge individuals with committing a misdemeanour rather than a public order offence unless there are substantial reasons not to.

Recommendations

Somewhat reluctantly, I provide recommendations that could alleviate some of the problems identified in this book (suggestions specific to particular issues like decriminalising marijuana, etc., are indicated in the text). Given the extent of the problems experienced by the CJS, what is the way forward? While more money will help resolve some of the issues I have identified, it is time to think "outside the box" to identify solutions to longstanding problems.

Clearly the problems facing magistrates' courts are part and parcel of the problems faced by the police, the CPS, and the prison services. However, I limit my suggestions to first instance courts. A good starting point would be to provide better legal training to magistrates (while simultaneously appointing individuals who better represent the population served by the courts) enabling them to adequately evaluate police evidence and the case made by the CPS. This rebalancing of the role of magistrates would also require changing the legal advisor's role.

The Crown Prosecution Service is clearly experiencing difficulties in ensuring "equality of arms" between the prosecution and the defence. The power of the CPS needs to be enhanced vis-à-vis the police so that they can protect the innocent, protect individuals from arbitrary or oppressive treatment, and treat victims with care and respect by ensuring that prosecution decisions are less reliant on the police (Sanders 2016). It will also be important for the CPS to redress the current fragmented way in which they review cases to ensure that they prosecute cases "in the interest of justice."

I observed hearings in which vulnerable defendants were unable to give their evidence and hearings, which proceeded even though the defendant was sectioned and detained in a mental institution. This should not occur. The Government needs to fund a complete rollout of the Liaison and Diversion Services to all police stations and courts in England and Wales. It is the role of this service to identify individuals with mental health problems, learning disabilities, substance abuse, and other vulnerabilities and divert them away from the court to receive appropriate treatment or support[27] (Birmingham, Awonogun, and Ryland 2017; Dyer 2013; London

---

[27] Therapeutic courts have demonstrated their ability to change offender behaviour, reduce recidivism, and restore social relations within the family (see Bamborough, Shaw, and Kershaw 2014).

Assembly 2017). Where this service is not yet available, the decision to prosecute "vulnerable" defendants should be jointly exercised by the police, the CPS, and the judiciary to avoid potential unfairness.[28]

An important step to ensure justice would be to impose a statutory duty to assist vulnerable adult defendants in a similar fashion that is supposed to protect the rights of vulnerable witnesses, a right recognised in Part 3D of the Criminal Procedure Rules, which reads:[29]

> 3D.1 In respect of eligibility for special measures, "vulnerable" and "intimidated" witnesses are defined in sections 16 and 17 of the Youth Justice and Criminal Evidence Act 1999 (as amended by the Coroners and Justice Act 2009); *"vulnerable" includes those under 18 years of age and people with a mental disorder or learning disability; a physical disorder or disability; or who are likely to suffer fear or distress in giving evidence because of their own circumstances or those relating to the case.*
>
> 3D.2 *However, many other people giving evidence in a criminal case, whether as a witness or defendant, may require assistance*: the court is required to take "every reasonable step" to encourage and facilitate the attendance of witnesses and to facilitate the participation of any person, including the defendant (Crim PR 3.9(3) (a) and (b)). This includes enabling a witness or defendant to give their best evidence and enabling a defendant to comprehend the proceedings and engage fully with his or her defence. *The pre-trial and trial process should, so far as necessary, be adapted to meet those ends*. (my emphasis)

Vulnerable victims and witnesses are supposed to be identified by the police when a criminal file is created and before the file is passed to the CPS to prosecute; however, this does not happen (HMIC 2015). In contrast, vulnerable defendants are forced to rely on the discretion of the court and their common law rights. At the same time defence counsel, especially duty solicitors who spend little time with a defendant, are unlikely to be aware of their client's vulnerability and may fail to inform the court about their client or they may not insist on the use of special measures (Fairclough 2017; Gerry and Cooper 2017).[30] Vulnerable defendants do not have any statutory rights to ensure their ability to effectively participate in their trial, nor are advocates and judges provided with training to identify and manage a defendant's vulnerability. It is also the case that "intermediaries" who

---

[28] Justice (2017) recommended that cases involving mentally ill defendants should be handled by specially trained prosecutors and magistrates/judges.

[29] Source: https://www.justice.gov.uk/courts/procedure-rules/criminal.

[30] Special measures could help ensure that defendants understand the law and are capable of understanding questions, when to answer questions, whether to give evidence, and whether to plead guilty.

might assist vulnerable defendants to give their best evidence are not trained, registered, or routinely provided (unlike the situation with vulnerable victims or witnesses (Talbot 2012)).

To facilitate the above recommendations, the government must agree a workable definition of "vulnerability"[31] (Justice 2017) for defendants *and* victims. Government will also need to devise appropriate referral and sentencing guidelines for vulnerable defendants (Jacobson 2017, 2018) and it must finance support services that address the causes that underlie offending. In May 2019 the government finally realized that the problems arising from its privatization of the probation services were so severe that it was time to 'renationalize the supervision of criminals'. The government announced a new programme aimed at reducing reoffending by renationalizing the probation services.[32] The renationalization of probation services will hopefully be properly funded in order to provide timely, professional pre-sentence and psychiatric reports, and to oversee the rehabilitation of offenders. Preventing recidivism will, in the long-term, reduce the costs borne by the CJS.

The poor quality of legal representation, particularly by duty solicitors, needs to be addressed. The quality of representation needs to be improved via much better training (Hunter, Jacobson, and Kirby 2018) and legal aid fees should be increased to attract better qualified lawyers back into magistrates' courts and to allow adequate time for lawyers to advise clients about their rights, take instructions, and prepare a case for a hearing/trial.

The tired adage that "justice needs to be seen to be done" should be linked to the requirement that defendants should be assisted to understand the law in order to effectively participate in their case. Towards this end, legislation should be "translated" into ordinary English and "legal discourse" should be minimised to allow citizens to comprehend proceedings and understand their rights and responsibilities. A good first step towards

[31] As Peay (2011) has noted, the adoption of an appropriate definition of "vulnerability" is fraught with difficulties. If the definition adopted encompasses the full range of mental illnesses, the cost of implementing it will be immense. At the same time, it is clear that if there were better "mental condition defences" the human rights of mentally ill defendants could be protected and the issue of culpability for an offence could more readily be resolved. In the meantime, overturning wrongful convictions of mentally ill offenders is left to the appeals process, which leaves many mentally ill offenders detained under the *Mental Health Act (1983)* or wrongfully convicted and imprisoned.

[32] See: L. Dearden, 'Government renationalizes supervision of criminals in major U-turn after Chris Graylings probation failure' (*The Independent*, 17 May 2019).

this objective would be to remove the requirement that defendants are placed in the dock during their hearing by providing a "pleading bar."[33] A second step would be to insist that magistrates and DJs address defendants in a language that ordinary people understand (perhaps along the lines used in "therapeutic" courts).[34] A pragmatic approach would be to slowly roll out reforms along the lines I have suggested to ensure each is carefully implemented before the next phase is undertaken. Finally, the closure of courts must be followed by investment in the remaining courts to ensure facilities are repaired and that an effective ICT system can provide complete information on cases to all parties in advance of a hearing/trial.

---

[33] In Wimbledon and Highbury Magistrate's Courts, different types of "pleading bars" were used (though they were not present in every hearing room).
[34] I refer to the nature of judicial interaction with defendants in drug courts that engage and educate defendants in a language they understand.

BIBLIOGRAPHY

Albanese, Jay. "Deciphering the linkages between organized crime and transnational crime," *Journal of International Affairs* 66, 1 (Fall/Winter 2012): 1–16.

Aliverti, Ana and Rachel Seoigh. "Lost in translation: examining the role of court interpreters in cases involving foreign national defendants in England and Wales," *New Criminal Law Review* 20 (2017): 130–56.

All Party Parliamentary Group on Domestic & Sexual Violence. "Women's access to justice: from reporting to sentencing." London: Women's Aid. 2014.

Arnell, Paul. "The contrasting evolution of the right to a fair trial in UK extradition law," *International Journal of Human Rights* 22 (2018): 869–87.

Ashworth, Andrew. "Criminal justice and the criminal process," *British Journal of Criminology* 28, 2 (1988): 111–23.

Austin, John. *How to do things with words*. Oxford: Oxford University Press. 1962.

Baker, Scott, David Perry, and Anand Doobay. "A Review of the United Kingdom's Extradition Arrangements" (The Baker Review). London. 2011.
https://assets.publishing.service.gov.uk/government/uploads/system/uploads/attachment_data/file/117673/extradition-review.pdf.

Baldwin, John, and F. Feeney. "Defence disclosure in the magistrates' courts," *Modern Law Review* 9, 5 (1986): 593–607.

Baldwin, John, and Mike McConville. *Negotiated justice: pressures to plead guilty*. London: Martin Robertson. 1977.

Bamborough, Steve, Mike Shaw, and Sophie Kershaw. "The family drug and alcohol court service in London: a new way of doing care proceedings," *Journal of Social Work Practice* 28, 3 (2014): 357–70.

Batty, Elaine, Christine Beatty, Mike Foden, Paul Lawless, Sarah Pearson, and Ian Wilson. *The new deal for communities experience: a final assessment. The new deal for communities evaluation: final report, volume 7*. Centre for Regional Economic and Social Research, Sheffield Hallam University. 2010.

Beattie, J. "Sir John Fielding and public justice: the Bow Street Magistrate's Court, 1754–1780," *Law and History Review* 25, 1 (2007): 61–100.

Bedford, Sybille. *Would you let your wife read this book? The trial of Lady Chatterley's Lover*. London: Daunt Books. 2016 [1959].

Beeching Commission. *Report of Royal Commission on Assizes and Quarter Sessions 1966–1969*. HMSO. London. 1966–69.

Belina, Belinda. "Ending public space as we know it," *Social Justice* 38, 1/2 (2011): 13–27.

Benson, Michael. "Emotions and adjudication: status degradation among white-collar criminals," *Justice Quarterly* 7, 2 (1990): 515–28.

Bhardwa, Bina, and Tiggy May. "Chasing Ghosts: organized crime groups involved in fraud," *CIFAS Fraudscape* 2018: 17–19.

Birmingham, Luke, Olusola Awonogun, and Howard Ryland. "Diversion from custody—an update," *BJ Psych Advances* 23, 6 (2017): 375–84.

Bishop, Charlotte, and Vanessa Bettinson. "Evidencing domestic violence, including behaviour that falls under the new offence of 'controlling or coercive behaviour,'" *International Journal of Evidence & Proof* 22, 1 (2018): 3–29.

Bowen, Phil, Arsheen Qasim, and Lauren Tetenbaum. "Better courts: a snapshot of domestic violence courts in 2013." Centre for Justice Innovation. 2013.

Bradford, Ben, and Ian Loader. "Police, crime and order: the case of stop and search," in Ben Bradford, Beatrice Jauregui, Ian Loader, and Jonny Steinberg (eds.), *The SAGE handbook of global policing*, 241–66. London: SAGE. 2016.

Broadbent, Graeme. "Swearing and sec. 5 of the Public Order Act 1986," *Journal of Criminal Law* 77 (2013): 998–1013.

Butler, Judith. "Burning acts: injurious speech," *University of Chicago Law School Roundtable* 3 (2013): 199–221.

Button, Mark, and Graham Brooks. "From 'shallow' to 'deep' policing: 'crash-for-cash' insurance investigation in England and Wales and the need for greater regulation," *Policing & Society* 256, 2 (2016): 210–29.

Button, Mark, Dean Shepherd, and David Blackbourn. "The fraud 'justice systems': a scoping study on the civil, regulatory and private paths to 'justice' for fraudsters." Centre for Counter Fraud Studies, University of Plymouth. November. 2016.

Cammiss, Stephen. "Deciding upon mode of trial," *Howard Journal* 46, 4 (2007): 372–84.

Cammiss, Stephen. "'He goes off and I think he took the child': narrative (re)production in the courtroom," *Kings College Law Journal* 17 (2006): 71–95.

Campbell, John R. "'Guilt by association': contrasting views on the fairness of 'secret trials' of 'terrorists,'" in James Simeon (ed.), *Terrorism and Asylum*, Chapter 3. Njihoff, the Netherlands: Brill. 2020. Pp. 92-122.

Campbell, John R. "Can law achieve happiness? Critical reflections on criminal justice," *Journal of Comparative Law* 13, 2 (2018): 21-32.

Campbell, John R. *Bureaucracy, law and dystopia in the United Kingdom's asylum system*. Oxford: Routledge. 2017.

Campbell, John R. *Nationalism, law and statelessness. Grand Illusions in the Horn of Africa.* Oxford: Routledge. 2014.

Carlen, Pat. "The staging of magistrates justice," *British Journal of Criminology* 16, 1 (1976a): 48–55.

Carlen, Pat. *Magistrates' justice*. London: Martin Robertson. 1976b.

Centre for Justice Innovation (CJI). "The changing use of pre-sentence reports." 2018. http://justiceinnovation.org/portfolio/changing-use-pre-sentence-reports/.

Channing May. *Transnational crime and the developing world.* Washington, D.C: Global Financial Integrity. 2017.

CIFAS. Fraudscape 2018. London. 2018. https://www.cifas.org.uk/insight/reports-trends/fraudscape-report-2018.

College of Policing Operations. London. 2013. https://www.app.college.police.uk/app-content/operations/operational-planning/core-principles/.

Collier, Jane, Bill Maurer, and Liliana Suraez-Navez. "Sanctioned identities: legal constructions of modern personhood," *Identities* 2, 1–2 (1995): 1–27.

Conley, John, & William O'Barr. *Just words: law, language and power*. Chicago: University of Chicago. 1998. [2nd ed].

Conley, John, & William O'Barr. *Rules versus relationships: the ethnography of legal discourse*. Chicago: University of Chicago. 1990.

Cook, Dee, Mandy Burton, and Amanda Robinson. "Enhancing safety and justice: the role of Specialist Domestic Violence Courts in England and Wales." Paper given to the British Society of Criminology. England. 2006.

Crown Prosecution Office. "The prosecutors convention: legal guidance." London. 2009. https://www.cps.gov.uk/legal-guidance/prosecutors-conventions-2009.

Crown Prosecution Service. "CPS London borough performance assessments." West Minister Borough. London. January. 2010.

https://www.justiceinspectorates.gov.uk/crown-prosecution-service/wp-content/uploads/sites/3/2014/04/WEST_LBPA_Mar10_rpt.pdf.
Crown Prosecution Service. "Guidance on charging." 2013. https://www.cps.gov.uk/legal-guidance/charging-directors-guidance-2013-fifth-edition-may-2013-revised-arrangements.
Crown Prosecution Service. "Domestic abuse guidelines for prosecutors." CPS. London. 2015. http://www.cps.gov.uk/legal/d_to_g/domestic_abuse_guidelines_for_prosecutors/.
Crown Prosecution Service. "Violence against women and girls report." 10th ed. London. 2016–17. https://www.cps.gov.uk/sites/default/files/documents/publications/cps-vawg-report-2017_0.pdf.
Crown Prosecution Service. "The code for Crown prosecutors." October. 2018a. https://www.cps.gov.uk/publication/code-crown-prosecutors#section4.
Crown Prosecution Service. "Offensive weapons, knives, bladed and pointed articles." January. 2018b. https://www.cps.gov.uk/legal-guidance/offensive-weapons-knives-bladed-and-pointed-articles
Crown Prosecution Service. "Drafting the indictment." December. 2018c. https://www.cps.gov.uk/legal-guidance/drafting-indictment.
Crown Prosecution Service. "Stalking and harassment." May. 2018d. https://www.cps.gov.uk/legal-guidance/stalking-and-harassment.
Crown Prosecution Service. "Criminal Behaviour Orders." June. 2018e. https://www.cps.gov.uk/legal-guidance/criminal-behaviour-orders.
Crown Prosecution Service. "Violence against women and girls report." London. 2018/19. https://www.cps.gov.uk/publication/violence-against-women-and-girls.
Crown Prosecution Service. "Racist and religious hate crime: prosecution guidance." 2019a. https://www.cps.gov.uk/legal-guidance/racist-and-religious-hate-crime-prosecution-guidance.
Crown Prosecution Service. "Drug offences." London. March. 2019b. https://www.cps.gov.uk/legal-guidance/drug-offences.
Crown Prosecution Service. "Termination of proceedings (including discontinuance)." London. 2019c. https://www.cps.gov.uk/legal-guidance /termination-proceedings-including-discontinuance.
Crown Prosecution Service. "CPS data summary, quarter 2, 2019/2020." London. https://www.cps.gov.uk/publication/cps-data-summary-quarter-2-2019-2020.

Crown Prosecution Service. "Domestic abuse guidelines for prosecutors." London. N.d. a. https://www.cps.gov.uk/legal-guidance/domestic-abuse-guidelines-prosecutors.

Crown Prosecution Service. "Code for Crown prosecutors: the full code test." London. N.d. b. https://www.cps.gov.uk/publications/code_for_crown_prosecutors/codetest.html.

Crown Prosecution Service. "Public order offences incorporating the charging standard." London. N.d. c. https://www.cps.gov.uk/legal-guidance/public-order-offences-incoOrrporating-charging-standard.

Crown Prosecution Service. "Joint agency guide to the victim personal statement: a guide for all criminal justice practitioners." London. N.d. d. https://www.cps.gov.uk/sites/default/files/documents/legal_guidance/joint-agency-guide-victim-personal-statement_0.pdf.

Cuthbertson, Peter. "Who goes to prison? An overview of the prison population in England and Wales." Civitas. 2017.

Danet, Brenda. "Language in the legal process," *Law & Society Review* 14, 3 (1980): 445–564.

Darbyshire, Penny. 2002. "Magistrates," in M. McConville and G. Wilson (eds.), *The handbook of the criminal justice system*," chap. 16. Oxford: Oxford University Press. 2002.

Davidson, Rosemary, Ben Lloyd, and Adam Payter. "Recent developments in extradition law—some practical implications," *Criminal Law Review* 7 (2015): 505–21.

Dillon, Dennis, and Brian Fanning. 2013. "The Tottenham riots: the big society and the recurring neglect of community participation," *Community Development Journal* 48, 4 (2013): 571–86.

Doig, Alan, and Michael Levi. "A case of arrested development? Delivering the UK National Fraud Strategy within competing policing priorities" *Public Money & Management* 33, 2 (2013): 145–52.

Doig, Alan. *Fraud*. Portland, Oregon: Willan. 2006.

Donoghue, Jane. "Reforming the role of magistrates: implications for summary justice in England and Wales," *Modern Law Review* 77, 6 (2014): 928–63.

Drozdz, Martine. "Spatial inequalities, 'neoliberal' urban policy and the geography of injustice in London," *Justice spatiale—Spatial justice*, Université Paris Ouest Nanterre La Défense, UMR LAVUE 7218, Laboratoire Mosaïques, City, neoliberalisation and justice, 6. 2014. http://www.jssj.org/article/inegalites-spatiales-politiques-urbaines-neoliberales-et-geographies-de-linjustice-a-londres/.

Dyer, Wendy. "Criminal justice diversion and liaison services: a path to success?" *Social Policy and Society* 12, 1 (2012): 31–45.

Edelman, Murray. *The symbolic uses of politics*. Urbana Ill.: University of Illinois Press. 1964.

EMCDDA (European Monitoring Centre for Drugs and Drug Addiction). "Perspectives on drugs: synthetic cannabinoids in Europe." Lisbon. 2016a. http://www.emcdda.europa.eu/system/files/publications/2753/POD_Synthetic%20cannabinoids_0.pdf.

EMCDDA (European Monitoring Centre for Drugs and Drug Addiction). "Perspectives on drugs: cocaine trafficking into Europe." Lisbon. 2016b. http://www.emcdda.europa.eu/system/files/attachments/2641/Cocaine%20trafficking_POD2016.pdf.

European Union (EU). *EU Drug Markets Report*. "Amphetamine, methamphetamine and MDMA—trafficking and supply." 2016. http://www.emcdda.europa.eu/publications/eu-drug-markets/2016/online/amphetamines-ecstasy/consumer-market/trafficking-supply_en.

Extradition Judges. "Review of extradition. Westminster Magistrate's Court." 31 December 2010. https://assets.publishing.service.gov.uk/government/uploads/system/uploads/attachment_data/file/116950/written-reps-9.pdf.

Fairclough, Samantha. "'It doesn't happen here . . . and I have never thought it necessary for it to happen': barriers to vulnerable defendants give evidence by live-link in Crown court trials," *International Journal of Evidence & Proof* 2, 3 (2017): 209–29.

Falk-Moore, Sally. "Individual interests and organizational structures: dispute settlements as 'events' of articulation," in Ian Hammet (ed.), *Social anthropology and law*, 159–88. London: Academic Press. 1977.

Fassin, Didier. *Prison worlds: an ethnography of the carceral condition*. London: Polity Press. 2017.

Felsteiner, William, Richard Able, and Austen Sarat. "The emergence and transformation of disputes: naming, blaming, and claiming . . . ," *Law & Society Review* 15 (1980/81): 631–54.

Foyster, Elizabeth. *Marital violence: an English family history, 1660–1857*. Cambridge: Cambridge University Press. 2006.

Fraud Advisory Panel. "Intro. An Introduction to UK Legislation, 2015." *Criminal fraud in England and Wales*. N.d. https://www.fraudadvisorypanel.org/wp-content/uploads/2015/12/Criminal-fraud-in-England-and-Wales-December2015.pdf.

Garland, David. "The punitive society: penology, criminology and the history of the present," *Edinburgh Law Review* 1, 2 (1997): 180–99

Garland, David. *The culture of control: crime and social order in contemporary society*. Chicago: University of Chicago Press. 2002.

Garland, David. "Theoretical advances in the sociology of punishment," *Punishment & Society* 20, 1 (2018): 8–33.

Garner, Joel, and Christopher Maxwell. "The crime control effects of criminal sanctions for intimate partner violence." Award no. 2006-WG-BX-0004. US Department of Justice. 2011.

Garner, Sarah, Ruth Crocker, Michael Skidmore, John Graham, and Martin Gill. "*Reducing the impact of serious organized crime in local communities: organized fraud in local communities*." (Briefing 1). Perpetuity Research and the Police Foundation. 2016. http://www.police-foundation.org.uk/publication/organised-fraud-in-local-communities/.

Garriott, William, and Eugene Raikhel. "Addiction in the making," *Annual Review of Anthropology* 44 (2015): 477–91.

Gerry, Felicity, and Penny Cooper. "Effective participation of vulnerable accused persons: case management, court adaptation and rethinking criminal responsibility," *Journal of Judicial Administration* 26, 1 (2017): 265–75.

Gibbons, John. "Language and the law," *Annual Review of Applied Linguistics* 19 (1999): 156–73.

Gibbs, Penelope. "The role of the magistrates." Transform Justice. January. 2016.

Gibson, Bryan, and Winstone Gordon. *Introduction to the magistrates' court*. London: Waterside Press. 2008.

Gilmore, Joanna, William Jackson and Helen Monk. "'That is not facilitating peaceful protest. That is dismantling the protest': anti-fracking protesters' experiences of dialogue policing and mass arrest," *Policing and Society* 29, 4 (2017): 1–16.

Good, Anthony. "'Undoubtedly an expert'? Anthropologists in British asylum courts," *Journal of the Royal Anthropological Institute* 10 (2004): 113–33.

Goodall, Kay. "Incitement to racial hatred: all talk and no substance?" *Modern Law Review* 70, 1 (2007): 89–113.

Goodwin, Charles. "Professional vision," *American Anthropologist* 96, 3 (1994): 606–33.

Grant, Thomas. *Jeremy Hutchinson's case histories*. John Murray: London. 2016 [2006].

Grenier, Amanda, Chris Phillipson, Debbie Rudman, Stephanie Hatzifilalithis, Karen Kobayashi, and Patrik Marier. "Precarity in late life: understanding new forms of risk and insecurity," *Journal of Aging Studies* 43 (2017): 9–14.

Griffiths, Cerian Charlotte. "Prosecuting fraud in the metropolis, 1760–1820." PhD dissertation, University of Liverpool. 2017.

Habermas, Jurgen. *The structural transformation of the public sphere.* Cambridge: MIT Press. 1991.

Harne, Lynne, and Jill Radford. *Tackling domestic violence: theories, policies and practice.* Maidenhead: McGraw Hill: Open University Press. 2008.

Harris, B. "Trial by jury or by magistrates?" *British Journal of Criminology* 16 (1976): 184–86.

Heard, Catherine, and Alex Tinsley. "The power of the Interpol Red Notice," *International Enforcement Law Reporter* 28, 8 (2012): 297–302.

Helms, Rebecca. "Constrained waiver of trial rights? Incentives to plead guilty and the right to a fair trial," *Journal of Law & Society* 46, 3 (2019): 423–47.

Her Majesty's Inspectorate of Constabulary. "Report on an inspection visit to police custody suites in the Metropolitan Police Service Borough of Hammersmith and Fulham." July. 2011. https://www.justiceinspectorates.gov.uk/prisons/wp-content/uploads/sites/4/2014/03/hammersmith fulham-2011.pdf.

Her Majesty's Inspectorate of Constabulary, Criminal Justice Joint Inspection, and H.M. Crown Prosecution Service Inspectorate. "Witness for the prosecution: identifying victim and witness vulnerability in criminal case files." November. London. 2015. https://www.justiceinspectorates.gov.uk/hmicfrs/wp-content/uploads/vulnerability-in-criminal-case-files.pdf.

Her Majesty's Inspectorate of Constabulary and Fire and Rescue Services. "A progress report on the police response to domestic abuse." London. 2017a. https://www.justiceinspectorates.gov.uk/hmicfrs/wp-content/uploads/progress-report-on-the-police-response-to-domestic-abuse.pdf.

Her Majesty's Inspectorate of Probation. "The work of probation services in courts." Manchester. 2017b.

Home Affairs Committee. "Policing in the 21st century," vol. 1. HC 364-I. London. 2007/8.

Home Affairs Committee. "Policing of the G20 protests: eighth report of session 2008–09." HC 418. June. London. 2009a.

Home Affairs Committee. “Policing of the G20 protests.” June. London. 2009b.

Home Office. “Statistical bulletin on the public disorder of 6th to 9th August 2011–September 2012 update.” Home Office. London. 2012a. https://www.gov.uk/government/uploads/system/uploads/attachment_data/file/219665/august-public-disorder-stats-bulletin-130912.pdf.

Home Office. “Public disorder of 6th–9th August 2011 statistical tables—September 2012.” London. 2012b. https://www.gov.uk/government/statistics/statistical-bulletin-on-the-public-disorder-of-6th-9th-august-2011--2.

Home Office. “2016–20 strategy to end violence against women and girls.” Home Office. London. 2016. https://www.gov.uk/government/publications/strategy-to-end-violence-against-women-and-girls-2016-to-2020.

Home Office. “Crime outcomes in England and Wales: year ending 2017.” 2nd ed. Statistical Bulletin HOSB 09/17. London. July. 2017a. https://assets.publishing.service.gov.uk/government/uploads/system/uploads/attachment_data/file/633048/crime-outcomes-hosb0917.pdf.

Home Office. “How domestic abuse-related offences were dealt with by the police,” in *Crime outcomes in England and Wales, year ending March 2019*. London. March. 2018a.

Home Office. “Drug misuse: findings from the 2017/18 Crime Survey for England and Wales.” Statistical Bulletin 14/18. July. 2018b. https://assets.publishing.service.gov.uk/government/uploads/system/uploads/attachment_data/file/729249/drug-misuse-2018-hosb1418.pdf.

Home Office. “The scale and nature of fraud: a review of the evidence.” London. 2018c.

Home Office. “The Cross-Government Fraud Landscape Report 2018.” Cabinet Office. London. 2018d.

Home Office. “Hate crime, England and Wales, 2018.” London. 2018/2019.

Home Office. “Anti-social Behaviour, Crime and Policing Act 2014: Anti-social behaviour powers. Statutory guidance for frontline professionals.” London. 2019. https://assets.publishing.service.gov.uk/government/uploads/system/uploads/attachment_data/file/823316/2019-08-05_ASB_Revised_Statutory_Guidance_V2.2.pdf.

House of Commons. “Policing in the 21st century. Home Affairs Committee—seventh report.” 30 October. London. 2007/8.

House of Commons. *Policing of marches and demonstrations*. SN/HA/05013. Library. 2009a.

House of Commons. "Justice Committee—Ninth Report. The Crown Prosecution Service: gatekeeper of the criminal justice system." London. 2009b.

House of Commons. "The August 2011 riots: a statistical summary." House of Commons Library. 2014. http://researchbriefings.parliament.uk/ResearchBriefing/Summary/SN06099#fullreport.

House of Commons. "The role of the magistracy." House of Commons Justice Committee. London. 2016a. https://publications.parliament.uk/pa/cm201617/cmselect/cmjust/165/165.pdf.

House of Commons. "Efficiency in the criminal justice system." The Committee of Public Accounts. London. 2016b.

House of Commons. "Acid attacks." Briefing Paper No. CBP 8041. Library. London. 2017.

House of Commons. "Transforming rehabilitation—ninth report of session 2017/18." Justice Committee. London. Report HC 482. 2018. https://publications.parliament.uk/pa/cm201719/cmselect/cmjust/482/482.pdf.

House of Commons. "Court statistics for England and Wales." Briefing Paper Number CBP 8372. London. 2019a.

House of Commons. "The Offensive Weapons Bill 2017–2019." Library. Briefing Paper no. 08349. London. 2019b.

House of Commons. "Knife crime in England and Wales." Briefing Paper SN4304. London. June. 2019c. file:///C:/Users/Admin/Downloads/SN04304%20(1).pdf.

House of Lords. "Facilitating peaceful protest—tenth report." Joint Committee on Human Rights. HL paper 123. 2010/11.

House of Lords. "Communications Committee—first report. Social media and criminal offences. London. 2014. At: https://publications.parliament.uk/pa/ld201415/ldselect/ldcomuni/37/3702.htm.

House of Lords. "Extradition law and practice." Select Committee on Extradition. Parliament. 2nd Report. London. 2014–15. https://publications.parliament.uk/pa/ld201415/ldselect/ldextradition/126/126.pdf.

Hoyle, Carolyn, and Andrew Sanders. "Police response to domestic violence: from victim choice to victim empowerment?" *British Journal of Criminology* 40 (2000): 14–36.

Human Rights Watch. "Precarious justice arbitrary detention and unfair trials in the deficient criminal justice system of Saudi Arabia." *Human Rights Watch* 20, 3(E). New York. 2008.

Hunter, Gillian, Jessica Jacobson, and Amy Kirby. "Judicial perceptions of the quality of criminal advocacy." Institute for Criminal Policy Research. London. 2018. https://www.barstandardsboard.org.uk/media/1939251/judicial_perceptions_of_criminal_advocacy__final_report__june_2018.pdf.

Institute for Fiscal Studies. "Police work force and funding in England and Wales." Nuffield Foundation. IFS Briefing Note BN 208. London. 2017.

Institute of Economic Affairs (IEA). Joint Venture. "Estimating the size and potential of the UK cannabis market." IEA Discussion Paper No. 90. London. 2018.

Jackson, John. "Justice, security and the right to a fair trial: is the use of secret evidence ever fair?" *Public Law* (2013): 720–36.

Jackson, Nicki. "Domestic violence courts," in *Encyclopaedia of Domestic Violence*, 262–67. New York: Routledge. 2007.

Jacobson, Jessica. "By mistakes we learn?—A review of criminal appeals against sentence." Transform Justice. London. 2013. http://transformjustice.org.uk/main/wp-content/uploads/2013/12/Transform-Justice_Appeals-report.pdf.

Jacobson, Jessica. Introduction to P. Cooper and H. Norton (eds.), *Vulnerable people in the criminal justice system: a guide to law and practice*, 1–20. Oxford: Oxford University Press. 2017.

Jacobson, Jessica. "Balancing accessibility and authority: towards an integrated approach to vulnerability in the criminal courts," in P. Cooper and L. Hunting (eds.), *Access to justice for vulnerable people*, 219–33. London: Wiley. 2018.

Jacobson, Jessica, and Jenny Talbot. "Vulnerable defendants in the criminal courts: a review of provision for adults and children." Prison Reform Trust: London. 2009.

Jacobson, Jessica, and Mike Hough. "Missed opportunities and new risks: penal policy in England and Wales in the past twenty-five years," *Political Quarterly* 89, 2 (2018): 177–86.

Jacobson, Jessica, Gillian Hunter, and Amy Kirby. *Inside Crown court: personal experience and questions of legitimacy*. Bristol: Policy Press. 2016.

Jeffrey, Bob, Tufail Waqas, and Will Jackson. "Policing and the reproduction of local social order: a case study of Greater Manchester," *Journal on European History of Law* 6, 1 (2015): 118–28.

Jivraj, Stephen. "Are self-reported health inequalities widening by income? An analysis of British pseudo birth cohorts born, 1920–1970," *Journal of Epidemiological Community Health*. 2020. doi:10.1136/jech-2019-213186.

Joshi, Raj, and Brian Gibbins. "Reform of the United Kingdom extradition law," *International Organized Crime* 51, 5 (2003): 51–55.

Judicial College. *Adult court book bench.* 2016. London.

Judiciary of England and Wales. *Magistrates' courts disclosure review.* London. May. 2014.

Justice. *In the dock: reassessing the use of the dock in criminal trials*. London. 2015.

Justice. *Mental health and fair trial*. London. 2017.

King, Michael. "A status passage analysis of the defendant's progress through the magistrates' court," *Law and Human Behaviour* 2, 3 (1978): 183–221.

Kirby, Amy, Jessica Jacobson, and Gillian Hunter. "Effective participation or passive acceptance: how can defendants participate more effectively in the court process?" Institute for Criminal Policy Research, Birkbeck, University of London and Howard League What is Justice? Working Papers 9. 2014.

Lammy Review. "An independent review into the treatment of, and outcomes for, black, Asian and minority ethnic individuals in the criminal justice system." London. 2017. https://www.gov.uk/government/publications/lammy-review-final-report.

Law Commission. *Criminal law offences relating to public order*. HMSO. London. 1983. https://s3-eu-west-2.amazonaws.com/lawcom-prod-storage-11jsxou24uy7q/uploads/2016/07/LC.-123-CRIMINAL-LAW-OFFENCES-RELATING-TO-PUBLIC-ORDER.pdf.

Law Commission. *Unfitness to plead*. London. London. 2016. https://www.lawcom.gov.uk/project/unfitness-to-plead/.

Lay Observers for England and Wales. "Fragmented approach to duty of care for detained persons." London. 2017. https://layobservers.org/fragmented-approach-duty-care-puts-people-held-court-custody-transported-escort-contractors-risk/.

Lesser, Rachel. *English indices of deprivation 2015*. Briefing 2016-01. GLA Intelligence, Mayor of London. 2016.

Leveson, Sir Brian. *Review of efficiency in criminal proceedings*. Judiciary of England & Wales. London. 2015.

Lightowlers, Carley, and Hannah Quirk. "The 2011 English 'riots': prosecutorial zeal and judicial abandon," *British Journal of Criminology* 55, 1 (2015): 65–85.

London Assembly. "Offender mental health." Health Committee. London. 2017. https://www.london.gov.uk/sites/default/files/omhfinal.pdf.

Lord Chief Justice. "Judicial diversity statistics 2017." London. 2017. July. https://www.judiciary.gov.uk/wp-content/uploads/2017/07/judicial-diversity-statistics-2017-1.pdf.

Magistrates Association. 2019. "Effective community sentences and the role treatment requirements can play in preventing deaths in custody." Independent Advisory Panel on Deaths in Custody. July. London.

Mather, Lynn, and Barbara Yngvesson. "Language, audience, and the transformation of disputes," *Law & Society Review* 15, 3/4 (1980/81): 775–821.

May, Tiggy, and Bina Bhardwa. *Organized crime groups involved in fraud*. London: Palgrave MacMillan. 2018.

McBarnet, Doreen. *Conviction: the law, the state and the construction of justice*. London: Palgrave Macmillan. 1981.

McBarnet, Doreen. "Magistrates' court and the ideology of justice," *British Journal of Law & Society* 8, 2 (1982): 181–97.

McConville, Mike, and John Baldwin. *Courts, prosecution and conviction*. Oxford: Clarendon Press. 1981.

McConville, Mike, Jacqeline Hodgson, Lee Bridges, and Anita Pavlovic. *Standing accused: the organization and practices of criminal defence lawyers in the UK*. Oxford: Clarendon Press. 1994.

McKeever, Grainne, Mark Simpson, and Ciara Fitzpatrick. "Destitution and paths to justice." J. Rowntree Foundation & Legal Education Project. London. 2018. https://www.jrf.org.uk/report/destitution-and-paths-justice.

Mertz, Elizabeth. "Language, law, and social meanings: linguistic/anthropological contributions to the study of law," *Law & Society Review* 26 (1992): 413–33.

Mertz, Elizabeth. "Legal language: pragmatics, poetics, and social power," *Ann. Review of Anthropology* 23 (1994): 435–55.

Methvin, Elyse. "Offensive language crimes in law, media and popular culture," in *Oxford Research Encyclopaedia of Criminology*. 2017. doi:10.1093.acrefore/9780190264079.013.281. July.

Metropolitan Police Service. "Four days in August: strategic review into the disorder of August 2011." Final Report. March. London. 2012.

Mews, Aidan, Joseph Hillier, Michael McHugh, and Cris Coxon. "The impact of short custodial sentences, community orders and suspended sentences on re-offending." Ministry of Justice, London. 2015.

Ministry of Justice. "Criminal Procedure and Investigations Act 1996 (section 23(1)) code of practice revised in accordance with section 25(4) of the Criminal Procedure and Investigations Act 1996." London. 1996. https://assets.publishing.service.gov.uk/government/uploads/system/uploads/attachment_data/file/447967/code-of-practice-approved.pdf.

Ministry of Justice. "Statistical bulletin on the public disorder of 6th to 9th August 2011–June 2012." Statistics Bulletin. 2012a. (Accessed on 2 February 2019). https://www.gov.uk/government/uploads/system/uploads/attachment_data/file/219665/august-public-disorder-stats-bulletin-130912.pdf.

Ministry of Justice. "Statistical bulletin on the public disorder of 6th to 9th August 2011–September 2012 update." September. 2012b. https://www.statewatch.org/news/2011/oct/uk-moj-stats-aug-riots-11.pdf.

Ministry of Justice. "Senior presiding judge for England and Wales: better case management information." October. London. 2015a. Accessed 19 October 201. https://www.judiciary.gov.uk/wp-content/uploads/2015/09/better-case-management-information-pack-1.pdf.

Ministry of Justice. "Criminal procedure rules." 2015b. (Accessed 2 July 2017). https://www.justice.gov.uk/courts/procedure-rules/criminal/docs/2015/crim-proc-rules-2015-part-01.pdf.

Ministry of Justice. "Criminal justice system statistics publication. Magistrates: pivot table analytical tool for England and Wales. 2015c. Time period: 12 months ending December 2005 to 12 months ending December 2015." https://assets.publishing.service.gov.uk/government/uploads/system/uploads/attachment_data/file/524338/magistrates_-court-data-tool.xlsx.

Ministry of Justice. "Criminal justice statistics. Quarterly update to March 2016." Ministry of Justice. August. 2016a. https://www.gov.uk/government/uploads/system/uploads/attachment_data/file/614414/criminal-justice-statistics-quarterly-december-2016.pdf.

Ministry of Justice. "Criminal court statistics quarterly, England and Wales, April to June 2017." 2017a.

Ministry of Justice. "Statistics on race and the Criminal Justice System 2016, London." November. 2017b.

https://assets.publishing.service.gov.uk/government/uploads/system/uploads/attachment_data/file/669094/statistics_on_race_and_the_criminal_justice_system_2016_v2.pdf.

Ministry of Justice. "Judicial diversity statistics 2018." London. 2018a.

Ministry of Justice. "Criminal justice statistics quarterly, England and Wales, September 2016 to September 2017." Main Points. London. 2018b. https://www.judiciary.uk/about-the-judiciary/who-are-the-judiciary/diversity/judicial-diversity-statistics-2018/.

Ministry of Justice. "Criminal court statistics quarterly, England and Wales, January to March 2018 (annual 2017)." June. London. 2018c. https://assets.publishing.service.gov.uk/government/uploads/system/uploads/attachment_data/file/720026/ccsq-bulletin-jan-mar-2018.pdf.

Ministry of Justice. "Remand Hearings Pivot Tool 2019." https://www.gov.uk/government/statistics/criminal-justice-system-statistics-quarterly-december-2016.

Morgan, Rod. "Magistrates: the future according to Auld," *Journal of Law & Society* 29, 2 (2002): 308–23.

Morgan, Rod. "Summary justice: fast but fair?" Centre for Crime and Justice Studies, Kings College London. 2008.

Morgan, Rod. *The judiciary in the magistrates' courts*. Home Office & Lord Chancellors Office. London. 2000.

Mulcahy, Linda. *Legal architecture: justice, due process and the place of law*. Oxford: Routledge. 2011.

Murphy. Thomas. "The admissibility of CCTV evidence in criminal proceedings," *International Review of Law, Computers & Technology* 13, 3 (1999): 383–404.

National Audit Office. Crown Prosecution Service. HC 400 Session 1997–98. London. 1997.

National Audit Office. "Crown Prosecution Service: effective use of magistrates' courts." London. February. 2006.

National Audit Office. "Probation: landscape review." HC 1100. March. 2013/14.

National Audit Office. "Efficiency in the criminal justice system." HC 852. London. 2016.

National Crime Agency. "European arrest warrants, wanted from the UK, Part. 1, 2009–2017." London. 2018.

National Offender Management Services. "Supporting community order treatment requirements." February. 2014. https://assets.publishing.service.gov.uk/government/uploads/system/uploads/attachment_data/file/426676/Supporting_CO_Treatment_Reqs.pdf.

Newburn, Tim. "The 2011 England riots in recent historical perspective," *British Journal of Criminology* 55, 1 (2015): 39–64.

Newburn, Tim. "Social disadvantage, crime and punishment," in Dean Hartley and Lucinda Platt (eds.), *Social advantage and disadvantage*, 322–40. Oxford: Oxford University Press. 2016.

Nobles, Richard, and David Schiff. "Criminal justice: autopoietic insights," in Jiri Priban and David Nelkan (eds.), *Laws new boundaries: the consequences of autopoiesis*. Chap. 9. Ashgate. 2001.

Nordstrom, Carolyn. "Global fractures," *Social Analysis* 52, 2 (2008): 71–86.

O'Barr, William. "The language of the law," in C. Ferguson and S. Heath (eds.), *Language in the USA*, 386–406. Cambridge: Cambridge University Press. 1981.

Office for National Statistics. "Domestic abuse in England and Wales—data tool." London. 2016. https://www.ons.gov.uk/peoplepopulationandcommunity/crimeandjustice/datasets/domesticabuseinenglandandwalesdatatool.

Office of National Statistics. "Domestic abuse in England and Wales, year ending March 2017." November. 2017. https://www.ons.gov.uk/peoplepopulationandcommunity/crimeandjustice/bulletins/domesticabuseinenglandandwales/yearendingmarch2017#police-referrals-to-the-crown-prosecution-service.

Office of National Statistics. "Domestic abuse in England and Wales, year ending March 2018." November. 2018a. https://www.ons.gov.uk/peoplepopulationandcommunity/crimeandjustice/bulletins/domesticabuseinenglandandwales/yearendingmarch2018#domestic-abuse-recorded-by-the-police.

Office of National Statistics. "Overview of fraud and computer misuse statistics for England and Wales." January. London. 2018b. https://www.ons.gov.uk/peoplepopulationandcommunity/crimeandjustice/articles/overviewoffraudandcomputermisusestatisticsforenglandandwales/2018-01-25.

Owusu-Bempah, Abenaa. "The interpretation and application of the right to effective participation," *International Journal of Evidence & Proof*, 22, 4 (2018): 321–41.

Peay, Jill. *Mental health and crime*. Routledge: New York. 2011.

Peck, Jamie. "Zombie neoliberalism and the ambidextrous state," *Theoretical Criminology* 14, 1 (2010): 104–10.

Pina-Sanchez, Jose. "Location and sentencing: to what extent do contextual factors explain between court disparities," *British Journal of Criminology* 58, 3 (2018): 529–49.

Player, Elaine, Julian Roberts, Jessica Jacobson, Mike Hough, and James Rowbottom. "Remanded in custody: an analysis of recent trends in England and Wales," *Howard Journal* 49, 3 (2010): 231–51.

Plotnikoff, Joyce, and Richard Woolfson. "A fair balance? Evaluation of the operation of disclosure law."

Research, Development and Statistics Directorate. RDS occasional paper no 76. Home Office, London. 2001.

Police Federation and Policy Studies Institute. "The role and responsibilities of the police." London. 1996.
http://www.psi.org.uk/publications/archivepdfs/Role%20pol/INDPOL-0.P.pdf.

Police Foundation. "The briefing—policing domestic abuse." Police Foundation. London. 2014.

Pratt, John, and Michelle Miao. "Risk, populism, and criminal law," *New Criminal Law Review* 22, 4 (2019): 391–433.

Pudney, Stephen. "Home Office Research Study 253. The road to ruin? Sequences of initiation into drug use and offending by young people in Britain" (London, England: Home Office Research, Development, and Statistics Directorate, December). 2002.
https://www.ukcia.org/research/TheRoadToRuin.pdf.

Rawls, John. *A theory of justice*. Cambridge: Cambridge University Press. 1971 [1999].

Reichert, Irving. "The magistrates' courts: lay cornerstone of English Justice," 57 *Judicature* (1973) 138–44.

Reiner, Robert. *The politics of the police*. 4th ed. Oxford: Oxford University Press. 2010.

Release. "Drugs, the law and human rights. The numbers in black and white: ethnic disparities in the policing and prosecution of drug offences in England and Wales." London. 2011.
https://www.release.org.uk/publications/numbers-black-and-white-ethnic-disparities-policing-and-prosecution-drug-offences.

Release. 2018. "The colour of injustice: 'race,' drugs and law enforcement in England and Wales." London.
https://www.release.org.uk/sites/default/files/pdf/publications/The%20Colour%20of%20Injustice.pdf.

Riots Communities and Victims Panel. "Four days in August: an interim report on the 2011 English Riots." London. 2012.

Rock, Paul. *The social world of an English crown court: witnesses and professionals in the Crown Court Centre at Wood Green*. Oxford: Clarendon Press. 1993.

Rumbold, John. "Diabetes and criminal responsibility," in *Criminal Law & Justice Weekly* 174 (2010): 21–24.
Ryder, Nicholas. "'Too scared to prosecute and too scared to jail?' A critical and comparative analysis of enforcement of financial crime legislation against corporations in the USA and the UK," *Journal of Criminal Law* 82, 3 (2018): 245–63.
Sainsbury Centre for Mental Health. "Mental health care and the criminal justice system." No. 38. 2009. https://www.centreformentalhealth.org.uk/briefing-39-criminal-justice.
Sanders, Andrew. "Constructing the case for the prosecution," in N. Lacey (ed.), *A reader in criminal justice*, chap 4. Oxford: Oxford University Press. 1994.
Sanders, Andrew. "Core values, the magistracy, and the Auld Report," *Journal of Law and Society* 29, 2 (2002): 324–34.
Sanders, Andrew. "The CPS—30 years on," *Criminal Law Review* 2 (2016): 82–98.
Sanders, Andrew, Richard Young, and Mandy Burton. *Criminal justice.* Oxford: Oxford University Press. 2010.
Schneider, Freidich. "The financial flows of transnational crime and tax fraud in OECD countries: what do we (not) know?" *Public Finance Review* 41, 5 (2013): 677–707.
Schneider, Jane, and Peter Schneider. "The anthropology of crime and criminalization," *Annual Review of Anthropology* 37 (2008): 351–73.
Scraton, Phillip. "'If you want a riot, change the law': the implications of the 1985 White Paper on Public Order," *Journal of Law & Society* 12, 3 (1985): 385–93.
Searle, John. "What is a speech act?" in Max Black (ed.), *Philosophy in America*, 221–39. Allen & Unwin. 1965.
Searle, John. "Indirect speech acts," *Syntax and Semantics*, 3 (1975): 59–82.
Sentencing Council. "Supplying or offering to supply a controlled drug/Possession of a controlled drug with intent to supply it to another." Misuse of Drugs Act 1971 s.4(3), Misuse of Drugs Act 1971, s.5(3). London. 2012. https://www.sentencingcouncil.org.uk/offences/item/supplying-or-offering-to-supply-a-controlled-drug-possession-of-a-controlled-drug-with-intent-to-supply-it-to-another/.
Sentencing Council. "Theft offences—definitive guide. London. 2016a. At: https://www.sentencingcouncil.org.uk/wp-content/uploads/SC-Theft-Offences-Definitive-Guideline-content_FINAL-web_.pdf.

Sentencing Council. "Sexual offences—definitive guide." London. 2016b. https://www.sentencingcouncil.org.uk/wp-content/uploads/Sexual-Offences-Definitive-Guideline-web5.pdf.

Sentencing Council. "Assault guidelines (including for the use of corrosive substances)." London. 2017. https://www.sentencingcouncil.org.uk/news/item/sentencing-guidelines-and-offences-involving-corrosive-substances/.

Sharp, Douglas. "Who needs theories in policing? An introduction to a special issue on policing," *Howard Journal* 44, 5 (2005): 449–59.

Sharpling, D. 2006. 'The Developing Role of the Crown Prosecution Service', *Interlia* 40-43.

Shorter Oxford English Dictionary. Oxford: Oxford University Press. 1933.

Sidnell, Jack, and N. J. Enfield. "How to distinguish a wink from a twitch," *HAU* 7, 2 (2017): 457–65.

Silverleaf, Nicola. "The magistracy and the 'uniformed' judiciary: double standards?" in Mathew Rogers and Penelope Gibbs (eds.), *Rethinking judicial independence*, 6–10. Transform Justice. London. 2017.

Sklansky, David. "The problems with prosecutors," *Annual Review of Criminology* 2018: 451–69.

Small, Jamie. "Classing sex offenders: how prosecutors and defence attorneys differentiate men accused of sexual assault," *Law & Society Review* 49, 1 (2015): 109–41.

Soubise, Laurene. "Prosecuting in the magistrates' courts in times of austerity," *Criminal Law Review* 11 (2017): 847–59.

Spaulding, Norman. "The enclosure of justice: courthouse architecture, due process and the dead metaphor of trial," *Yale Journal of Law and the Humanities* 24 (2012): 311–43.

Standing, Guy. *The precariat: the new dangerous class*. Bloomsbury Academic: London. 2011.

Standing, Guy. "The precariat: today's transformative class?" *Great Transition Initiative*. October. 2018. https://greattransition.org/publication/precariat-transformative-class.

Stark, Evan. *Coercive control: the entrapment of women in personal life*. Oxford: Oxford University Press. 2007.

Tait, David. "Glass cages in the dock? Presenting the defendant to the jury," *Chicago-Kent Law Review* 86 (2011): 467–95.

Talbot, Jenny. "Fair access to justice: support for vulnerable defendants in the criminal courts." Prison Reform Trust. 2012.

Taylor, James. "White-collar crime and the law in nineteenth-century Britain," *Business History* 60, 3(2018): 343–60.

Tiratelli, Matteo, Paul Quinton, and Ben Bradford. "Does stop and search deter crime? Evidence from 10 years of London-wide data," *British Journal of Criminology* 58, 5 (2018): 1212–31.

Towers, Jude, and Sylvia Walby. "Measuring the impact of cuts in public expenditure on the provision of services to prevent violence against women and girls." Report for Northern Rock Foundation and Trust for London. Lancaster University. January. 2012

Transparency International. "London property: a top destination for money launderers." London. N.d. https://issuu.com/transparencyuk/docs/final_s041329_v8_hrnc__1_.

Trust for London. *London's Poverty Profile 2011*. New Policy Institute. London. 2011.

Trust for London. "Inner city pressure: the voices of low income working families in inner London on the complex challenges they fact." London. 2017.

UK. "Public Order Bill: second reading." Hansard. London. 1986. http://hansard.millbanksystems.com/commons/1986/jan/13/public-order-bill.

UK. *Policing low-level disorder: police use of section 5 of the Public Order Act 1986.* Home Office Research Study 135. London. 1994.

UK. *Entry into the criminal justice system: a survey of police arrests and their outcomes.* Research & Statistics Directorate Report. Home Office. London. 1998.

UK. *User guide to Home Office immigration statistics*. London. 2012.

UK. "'Insulting words or behaviour': Sec. 5 of the Public Order Act 1986." House of Commons. SN/HA/5760. January. London. 2013.

UK. *Race disparity audit*. Cabinet Office: London. 2017a. https://assets.publishing.service.gov.uk/government/uploads/system/uploads/attachment_data/file/686071/Revised_RDA_report_March_2018.pdf.

UK. "Key measures. Q3. 2016–17." Crown Prosecution Service. London. 2017b. https://www.cps.gov.uk/publications/performance/key_ measures/key_measures_Q3_2016_17.pdf.

UK. *Domestic violence in England and Wales*. Briefing Paper no. 6337. June. House of Commons Library. 2017c.

UK. UN drug situation report. Public Health England, London. 2017d.

UK. Serious violence strategy. Home Office. London. 2018a.

UK. Women's budget group: violence against women and girls briefing. October. 2018b. https://wbg.org.uk/wp-content/uploads/2018/10/VAWG-October-2018-w-cover-2.pdf.

UK. "UK drug situation report." Public Health England, London. 2018c.

UK. "Ending violence against women and girls 2016–2020 strategy refresh." March. 2019.

Umphry, Martha. "Law in drag: trials and legal performativity," *Columbia Journal of Gender and Law* 21 (2012): 114–28.

Wacquant, Loic. "The global firestorm of law and order: on punishment and neoliberalism," *Thesis Eleven* 122, 1 (2014): 72–88.

Waddington, David. "Coercion and accommodation: policing public order after the Public Order Act," *British Journal of Sociology* 45, 3 (1994): 367–85.

Welsh, Lucy. "Are magistrates' courts really a 'law free zone,'" *British Society of Criminology* 13, 3 (2013): 3–16.

Welch. Lucy. "The effects of changes to legal aid on lawyers; professional identity and behaviour in summary criminal cases: a case study," *Journal of Law & Society* 44, 4 (2017): 559–95.

Westmarland, Nicole, Kelly Johnson, and Clare MacGlynn. "Under the radar: the widespread use of 'out of court resolutions' in policing domestic violence and abuse in the United Kingdom," *British Journal of Criminology* 58, 1 (2018): 1–16.

Wintersteiger, Lisa. "Legal needs, legal capability and the role of public legal education; a report by Law for Life: The Foundation for Public Legal Education." The Legal Education Foundation. 2015. http://www.lawforlife.org.uk/wp-content/uploads/Legal-needs-Legal-capability-and-the-role-of-Public-Legal-Education.pdf.

Wright, J. "Editorial comment: proceeding without caution," *Law Society Gazette* 34, 8 September, 12 (2011): 2.

Yngvesson, Barbara. "Contextualizing the court: comments on the cultural study of litigation," *Law & Society Review* 24, 2 (1990): 467–75.

INDEX